COOKING TECHNIQUES

© 1981 by Tree Communications, Inc.

Little, Brown and Company Publishers
34 Beacon Street
Boston, Massachusetts 02106

Library of Congress Cataloguing Number 81-52235

Printed in the United States of America

ISBN 0-316-93753-3

Sara Bowman, designer
Yaron Fidler, production

A

Published simultaneously in Canada by Little,
Brown and Company (Canada), Limited

COOKING TECHNIQUES

How to do anything a recipe tells you to do

By Beverly Cox, with Joan Whitman
Photographed by Steven Mays

Little, Brown and Company, Boston/Toronto

ACKNOWLEDGMENTS

We would like to thank the following companies for generously providing the equipment and accessories used throughout this book.

B. & P. Stone and Marble Supply Corporation, Jamaica, N.Y., for the pastry marble

J. and D. Brauner, Inc., New York, for the chopping boards

The Caloric Corporation, Topton, Penn., for the gas range

Commercial Aluminum Cookware Company, Perrysburg, Ohio, for pots and pans

Corning Glass Works, Corning, N.Y., for glass cookware

Farberware, New York, for the food processor and numerous pots and pans

Richard Ginori Corporation of America, New York, for china

F. Gorevic & Son, Inc., New York, for silver platters

J. A. Henckels Zwillingswerk, Inc., Elmsford, N.Y., for cutlery

The Hobart Corporation, KitchenAid Division, Troy, Ohio, for the KitchenAid mixer

James II Gallery, New York, for the Regency coalport porcelain platter

Mouli Manufacturing Company, Belleville, N.J., for assorted kitchen tools

D. Porthault, Inc., New York, for several fine tablecloths

Quaker Maid Kitchens, Leesport, Penn., for a kitchen cabinet

Rowoco, Inc., Mamaroneck, N.Y., for many kitchen tools, molds, and baking pans

Terrafirma Ceramics, New York, for handmade serving platters

Wear-Ever Aluminum, Inc., Chillicothe, Ohio, for bakeware

The following persons were generous in sharing their knowledge about food and equipment:

Dr. Franz Aliquo, general manager, Jack McDermott, and Raphaella Ramirez of *Richard Ginori*

George Bente of *J. A. Henckels*

Michael DeMartino's of *DeMartino's Fish and Oyster Market*

Edward Jobbagy of *Pacific Seh Hotel Supply Company*

Bob Mayers of *University Place Market*

Judy McBee of *Farberware*

Joan Wolf of *Rowoco*

We are grateful to the following consultants who helped us in demonstrating the techniques:

Fabrizio Bottero

Lynn Kutner

Harriet Reilly

Frances Tang

Dale Whitsell

We are also indebted to Ruth Michel and Gene Young for their careful scrutiny of the text and photographs.

CONTENTS

1 Vegetables and Herbs   7

2 Meat   79

3 Poultry   159

4 Fish and Shellfish   209

5 Stock   271

6 Pâtés   277

7 Pasta and Rice   291

8 Eggs   321

9 Butter   353

10 Pancakes and Crêpes   359

11 Breads   373

12 Pastry   423

13 Cakes and Cookies   473

14 Fruits   507

   Index   539

INTRODUCTION

In a perfect world, we could grow up in homes with people who love to cook and who share their knowledge with us. I was lucky because my mother was such a person.

But if you missed that experience because you were doing something else while meals were being prepared (or because meals were only perfunctory), this book will serve as a surrogate. It shows you in easy-to-follow step photographs how to do everything a recipe tells you to do but doesn't describe clearly enough. You can look over my shoulder to see how I seed a tomato, measure flour, scale a fish, fit a pie crust into the pan without stretching it, chop an onion, and roll pasta.

I'll also share some of the more intricate cooking techniques that I learned at the Cordon Bleu and those that I acquired since from watching professional cooks and then doing them myself. These may inspire you to broaden your skills and attempt something you never dared to do before. Because in the end you have to do them yourself to gain experience and confidence.

Many chapters in this book, which is organized like a cookbook, open with photographs of techniques that apply generally to most foods in the particular category. Chapter 1, for example, shows how to peel, slice, julienne, steam, stir-fry, and purée vegetables. Techniques peculiar to specific vegetables follow, with the vegetables in alphabetical order.

Throughout the book I have emphasized the attention to detail that contributes to the final presentation of a dish. This was always stressed in my mother's kitchen, and I think appearance is essential to our enjoyment of good food.

BEVERLY COX, MAY, 1981

1
VEGETABLES
AND HERBS

GENERAL

Peel

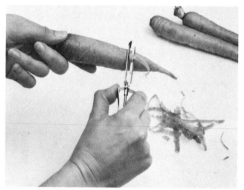

1 When using a stationary curved peeler, pull it toward you.

2 If you use the swivel-bladed kind, peel away from you. In either case, follow the contour of the vegetable and take off as little peel as possible.

Core

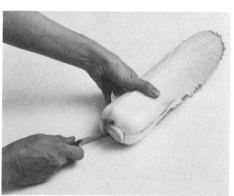

1 Leaf vegetables such as cabbage, endive, and fennel should have about one inch of core removed. It tends to be tough and sometimes bitter. Cut around it at an angle using a sharp knife.

2 Pull out the cone-shaped core and discard.

Chop

Chop and mince are often used interchangeably, depending on the recipe writer. Chop is the more general term and can mean a coarse or fine texture. Mince means very finely chopped.

1 Hold the knife in one hand and press the point lightly with the other. The point always stays on the chopping surface. Bring the knife up and down rapidly, moving it to cover the whole pile of vegetable.

2 Gather the vegetable together with your knife.

3 Continue to chop to the desired degree of fineness.

Slice

This is an easily mastered technique that produces even rounds of vegetables in a few seconds. The fingers that hold the vegetable are curved under so you don't cut yourself and the knife slides up and down the knuckles.

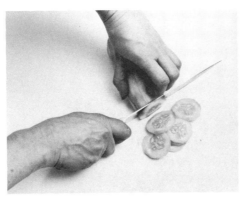

1 Hold a long vegetable firmly with one hand, fingers curved under. Slice, moving the fingers back as a guide for the knife to determine the thickness of the slice.

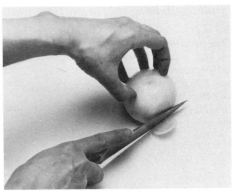

2 For a round or oval vegetable, cut a thin slice from one side so the vegetable will sit steadily and not roll around.

Slice, continued

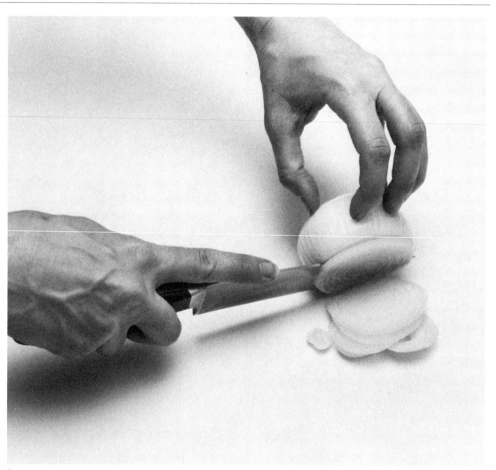

3 Position the vegetable cut side down and hold it with one hand, fingers curved under. Cut down into rounds of even thickness.

Julienne a long vegetable

Julienne is a technique that is used in both classic French cooking and in the nouvelle cuisine. It means to cut into fine strips and produces a vegetable that is decorative and quickly cooked.

1 Peel the vegetable and cut into two-inch lengths.

2 Stand each length on end and hold it firmly with your fingertips. Slice as thin as possible.

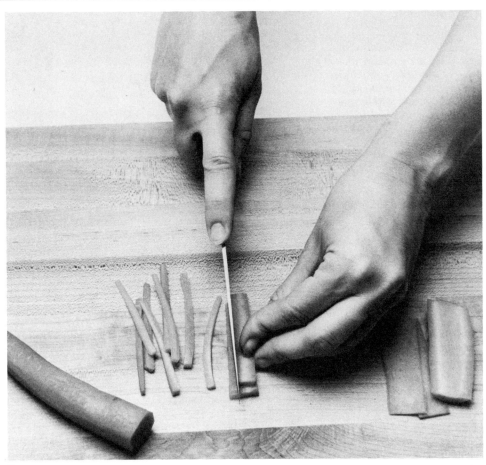

3 Stack two or three slices and cut into very fine strips.

Julienne a round vegetable

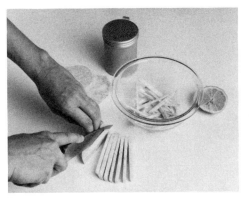

1 Thinly slice the vegetable and peel each slice. This is particularly good to do with vegetables that discolor quickly, such as potatoes and celery root. Cut each slice into strips.

2 Stack two or three strips and cut into halves lengthwise.

Cut into ovals

Vegetables cut into ovals cook evenly and are attractive around a roast or served by themselves. However, it is wasteful unless you use the scraps in stock or soup.

1 Peel and cut round vegetables such as turnips and potatoes into quarters, or eighths if they are very large.

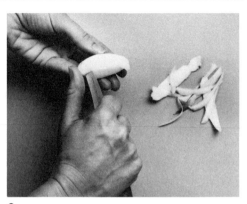

2 Round off all the corners and edges with a sharp knife.

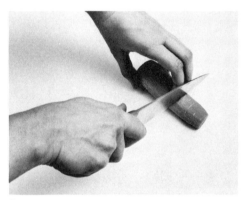

3 Cut long vegetables such as carrots and zucchini into one-and-one-half-inch lengths.

4 Round off the edges with a sharp knife.

Cut on the bias

Vegetables to be stir-fried are often cut on the bias so that a larger surface is exposed to the heat and the vegetables cook more quickly.

1 Hold the knife almost parallel to the length of the vegetable and slice down. The knife can be held straight up and down.

2 Or it can be held at an angle to the cutting board.

Snip

Some herbs, such as dill and chives, bruise easily and will release too much liquid if chopped. They should be snipped with sharp kitchen shears.

Shred

Leaf vegetables and herbs are frequently cut into shreds, or a chiffonade. It is easy to do with a knife and looks nicer than when done with a grater. The closer the slices, the finer the shred.

1 For a round cabbage, cut into halves and cut out the hard core. Place it cut side down and cut vertical slices close together all the way through.

2 For a long cabbage, slice crosswise down the length of the vegetable.

Shred, continued

3 For lettuce leaves, roll the leaf lengthwise around the stalk.

4 Then cut crosswise into thin slices.

Steam

This is the way I prefer to cook many vegetables because I like them undercooked. The nutrients are not lost in the water, as with boiling, and the color of green vegetables is preserved. (I use a metal steamer, which is a double boiler with a perforated bottom. It holds more than the collapsible "daisy" steamer and you can poach in the bottom pan while you steam in the top.) I sometimes flavor the vegetable by sautéeing it briefly in butter after I steam it.

Bring a small amount of water to a full boil below a pan with a perforated bottom. Add the vegetable, cover, and cook until just crisp-tender.

Stir-fry

This is also a good way to cook vegetables quickly and retain the nutrients. I use it mostly for Oriental dishes using finely cut vegetables. A wok is the best utensil for stir-frying because its rounded shape and sloping sides make for easy tossing and quick cooking. Heat is distributed evenly over a large area and you need very little oil. But you can use a heavy skillet.

1 Heat a wok by rolling it back and forth over medium-high heat.

2 You can tell if the pan is hot enough by putting in a drop of cold water. It should bounce and sputter.

3 Pour a small amount of oil around the upper rim and let it run down the sides.

Stir-fry, continued

4 Add a few slices of garlic and ginger to season the oil if you wish. Cook slices for a few seconds and discard them.

5 Add the finely cut vegetables and scoop and toss them so that they cook evenly and quickly—less than a minute. Scoop from the center out to the sides so that the vegetables fall back to the bottom.

Sauté

Sautéed vegetables are cooked quickly in a small amount of hot oil and butter, oil alone, or clarified butter (plain butter will burn) until lightly browned and tender. Use a pan with sloping sides so the vegetables are constantly in motion, moving up the sides and falling back. They should actually jump (sauter, in French) so that they turn over and cook evenly on all sides. Vegetables must be dry and not crowded in the pan. Otherwise they will steam and give off their juices.

This is a frequently used technique that is well worth the practice. Grasp the handle with both hands and move the pan back and forth. Lift up slightly on the backward pull to make the vegetable jump and redistribute itself.

Braise

Vegetables cooked by this method—principally leaf vegetables such as endive, celery, cabbage, and lettuce—are simmered in butter and a small amount of liquid in a covered pan. If the vegetable is very juicy you don't need extra liquid. Braising produces a lightly browned and moist result.

1 Put the trimmed vegetable in a pan with butter and add a small amount of water or broth. Cover the pan tightly.

2 Simmer on top of the stove until just tender, not mushy. Uncover and cook briefly until vegetable is lightly browned.

Parboil

This is always a preliminary step to further cooking. Insert prepared vegetable into boiling water for a few minutes just to soften it. In this case, the eggplant will be stuffed and baked.

Blanch and refresh

Vegetables are blanched, or par-boiled, to soften them. The two terms are interchangeable. Blanching is also used to lessen the taste of strong-flavored vegetables. Refresh means to plunge the hot food into cold water to stop the cooking and retain the color. I use this method for fresh herbs and thinly sliced vegetables that will be used for garnish. Put them into a sieve before blanching. It is easier to lift them out.

1 Lower the vegetables into boiling water and cook briefly just to soften them.

2 Plunge them into cold water to refresh them. I'm using thinly sliced cutouts to decorate a pâté.

Purée

I like the taste and appearance of puréed vegetables, and I also use them frequently as a base for sauces and soups. A food processor does a marvelous job of puréeing (everything but potatoes, which come out like glue). But a conical, finely meshed sieve (called a chinois) and a food mill do an equally good job.

1 Push the vegetables through the *chinois* by running the wooden pestle around the edges.

2 A food mill comes with disks of varying sizes, from coarse to very fine. Turn the handle, and the vegetable is forced through by the metal blade.

Tie a bouquet garni

A bouquet garni is a mixture of herbs and seasonings that flavors a stock or stew and then is removed and discarded. When using fresh herbs, it's nice to tie them in pieces of celery, which add their own flavor. Dried herbs should be enclosed in cheesecloth so they don't fall out.

1 Trim a stalk of celery and cut it into two pieces about three inches long.

2 Fit the herbs into the hollow of one piece of celery and cover with the second piece.

3 Tie together securely with kitchen twine.

4 Put dried herbs, or a mixture of fresh and dried, in a double thickness of cheesecloth.

5 Gather the edges of the cheesecloth and tie in a neat bundle.

ACORN SQUASH

Split and scoop out seeds

1 With a long, heavy knife, cut the squash into halves lengthwise. Push down first with one hand and then the other using a seesaw motion to cut through the hard shell.

2 Scoop out the seeds with a metal spoon and scrape out any stringy fibers.

3 Shave off a very thin slice from the bottom of each half so the squash will sit straight. Then bake according to recipe.

ARTICHOKES

Trim for cooking whole

1 If the stem is long enough to grasp, break it off rather than cutting it, so that you pull off some of the tough fibers attached to the stem.

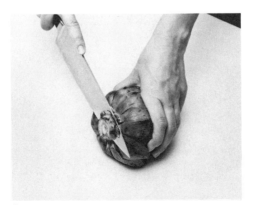

2 Trim off the rest of the stem with a knife, cutting neatly and as close to the base as possible.

3 Rub the cut portion with lemon to keep it from discoloring.

Trim for cooking whole, continued

4 Lay the artichoke on its side and hold it firmly by the base. Cut about one inch off the top cone of leaves.

5 Pull off the tough outer leaves from the bottom.

6 Trim off about one-half inch of each leaf using kitchen shears. This makes the artichoke look attractive and removes the tough, often sharp, tips. Rinse thoroughly under cold running water.

7 Rub all cut portions with lemon. The artichokes can now be steamed, boiled, or stuffed (see following instructions).

Stuff

1 Trim the artichoke as for cooking whole (see previous instructions). Grasp it firmly in both hands and pull back the leaves from the top.

2 Move your hands around the artichoke, spreading the leaves evenly to expose the small cone of inner leaves.

3 With a sharp knife, cut out the soft cone.

4 Scoop out the fuzzy choke using a grapefruit spoon, or melon-ball cutter, good instruments because they are sharp.

5 Put the stuffing into the hollowed-out cavity and the spaces between the leaves, pushing down firmly with your fingers. Stuffed artichokes are baked or cooked in a Dutch oven on top of the stove.

Cut out bottom and cook au blanc

Artichoke bottoms (also called hearts) are very special and well worth the effort needed to prepare them. They are cooked in a mixture of flour, water, lemon juice, and salt, called a blanc, which you use for foods that discolor quickly. They can then be sautéed and filled with baby carrots, peas, or any vegetable of your choice.

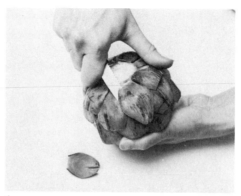

1 Break off the stem and trim sharp tips of leaves so that the artichoke will be easier to handle. Starting at the bottom and using a sharp knife, cut off leaves in a semicircular motion.

2 Continue cutting leaves, moving up from the base and all around the artichoke. Discard the leaves.

3 When you get to the soft inner cone of leaves, slice it off. Trim the bottom just to neaten it. Drop into cold water and lemon juice so it won't discolor.

4 In a nonaluminum pan, dissolve about one-quarter cup of flour in a little water to make a paste and stir well. Add about a quart of water, two tablespoons lemon juice, and salt.

5 When the mixture comes to a simmer, add the artichoke bottoms and cook until tender.

6 Scoop out the choke with a melon-ball cutter or a grapefruit spoon. The bottoms can then be sautéed and stuffed.

ASPARAGUS

Peel and trim

1 Cut off the woody ends, leaving some of the white stalk.

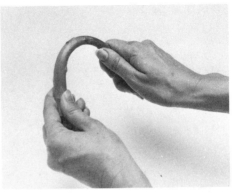

2 If you want to serve just the tips, bend a spear to feel where the tender tip ends, and break it at that point. The lower part of the spears can be used for purées or in soup.

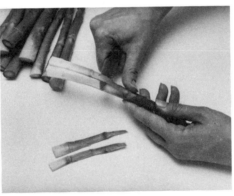

3 If asparagus is young, you don't need to peel it. But thick spears will cook more evenly if peeled to within two inches of the tip. A sharp knife gets below the fibers better than a vegetable peeler.

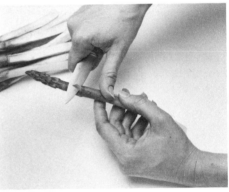

4 Trim off any scales near the tip, and wash asparagus in cold running water.

BEETS

Trim

1 Cut off tops, leaving about two inches attached to beets so they won't bleed when cooked. Leave the root on for the same reason.

2 If the beets are young and tender, use the greens for salads or cook like spinach. Pull the tough stems out of the leaves.

Cook and peel

Always cook beets before peeling; otherwise they will lose their bright color. I prefer to bake them because it is less messy, but boiling or steaming them is also fine.

1 Wrap each beet in aluminum foil and bake in a moderate oven for about three hours.

2 When cool, cut off tops and root. The peel pulls off easily with your fingers.

BROCCOLI

Trim and cut into flowerets

1 Select tightly clustered broccoli with no yellow buds. Trim off the woody bottom of the stem.

2 Pull off the leaves.

3 If the broccoli stalks are thick, peel off the tough skin with a sharp paring knife.

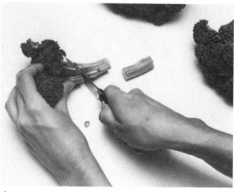

4 Cut the stalks into bite-size pieces.

5 Insert your knife behind the short stems and slice down, cutting off the flowerets. The stalks and the flowerets can be cooked and served together, or the stalks can be used separately for salads or purées.

BRUSSELS SPROUTS

Trim and cut cross in base

1 The smaller and more compact the sprout the better the flavor. Trim off any yellowing leaves and cut off the stem.

2 Make two slashes crosswise in the stem end so the leaves and the tougher core will cook evenly.

CABBAGE

Core

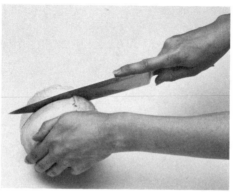

1 Cut the cabbage in half through the core end.

2 Cut down at an angle on either side of the V-shaped core and remove it.

Stuff leaves

The rib from each leaf is removed because it is tough and will not cook as quickly. I like to tie stuffed cabbage leaves with scallion greens because they are both pretty and edible.

1 Core a whole cabbage and pull off the leaves. Parboil the leaves for a minute or two and slice off the rib that runs up the middle of each leaf.

2 Put a small amount of stuffing at the stem end and fold the leaf over.

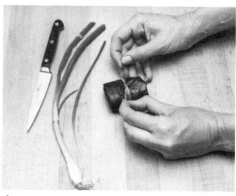

3 Roll, folding in the sides as you go.

4 Tie with long thin strips of scallion green, or with kitchen twine.

Stuff whole

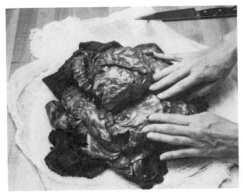

1 Trim the bottom and parboil the whole cabbage just until outer leaves are tender. Place on a double thickness of dampened cheesecloth and spread the leaves out and down with your hands.

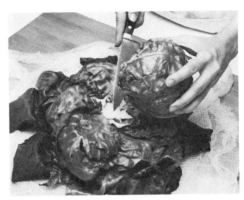

2 When you can't open any more leaves, cut out the center piece, chop it, and add to the stuffing.

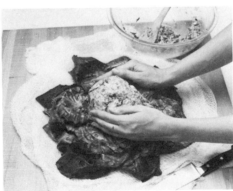

3 Put a mound of stuffing in the center of the cabbage.

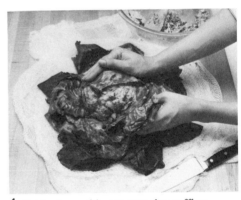

4 Fold a layer of leaves over the stuffing.

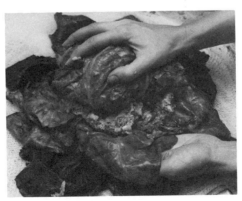

5 Put a small amount of stuffing in the outer leaves and fold them up toward the center.

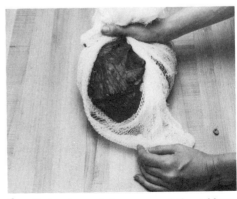

6 Pull the cheesecloth up around the cabbage and gather it at the top. Twist the top and tie it with kitchen twine. The cabbage can then be cooked in boiling water or stock.

CARROTS

Assemble a flower

Carrot flowers make an attractive garnish for pâté or fish. They can also be used in the bouquet of crudités at the end of the chapter.

1 Slice a carrot into very thin rounds and put them into ice water so they will bend slightly. Thread three slices off center on a toothpick or bamboo skewer.

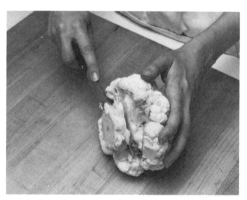

2 Top with a piece of black olive.

CAULIFLOWER

Trim and cut into flowerets

Cut a cauliflower into pieces before you cook it so the tender flowerets and the tougher core will be done at the same time.

1 Pull off leaves.

2 Cut off the stem close to the head.

3 Slice off the flowerets all around the inner core.

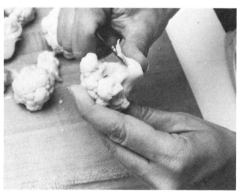

4 Peel the stems of the flowerets quite deep.

5 If the stems are more than a quarter inch in diameter, split them to facilitate cooking.

6 Slice the inner core. Wash the flowerets and core pieces in a colander and drain well. Cook together by steaming or boiling.

Re-form in bowl after cooking

This is a nice way to present cauliflower at the table

1 Heat a bowl that is slightly smaller than the original cauliflower head and brush with butter. Starting with the longest flowerets, place them in the bowl with the stems pointing up toward the center.

2 Add the flowerets with the shorter stems around the sides of the bowl and place the cut slices in the center.

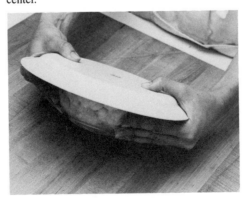

3 Hold a serving plate over the bowl and invert the bowl onto it.

4 The cauliflower will be re-formed and can be served in its seemingly normal shape.

CELERY

Peel and trim

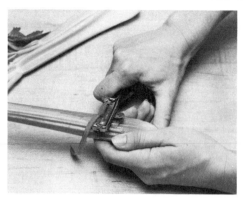

1 If celery is rough looking, the coarse outer strings should be pulled off with a vegetable peeler.

2 Cut off leaves and tips of stalks and use in stock or soup.

CELERY ROOT

Trim and peel

Celery root makes a wonderful salad when cut into julienne. Or the slices can be cubed and cooked like potatoes. It is easier to peel individual slices rather than the whole root because it is so knobby.

1 Scrub this knobby root, also known as celeriac or knob celery, with a vegetable brush to remove dirt, then trim off both ends.

2 Because peeled celery root discolors quickly, slice only as much as you want to use at one time. Keep the rest in a plastic bag in the refrigerator.

3 Rub all cut sides with lemon to prevent discoloring.

4 Peel each slice with a sharp knife.

CHERRY TOMATOES

Stuff

1 Cut a thin slice from the stem end.

2 Scoop out the seeds and pulp with a small metal measuring spoon.

3 Using a pastry bag outfitted with a star tube, pipe a small amount of filling into the cavity. I've used seasoned cream cheese.

Cut into flower garnish

1 Select large, firm tomatoes, and cut out the stem. Using only the tip of the knife, divide the top into petals by cutting the skin into halves, then quarters and eighths. Don't cut into the flesh.

2 With your knife pull the skin back gently to form pointed petals.

CHILI PEPPERS

Core and seed

For a very spicy dish, just break off the stem, rinse the pepper under cold running water, and chop. But for a milder flavor, you should remove the seeds, which are the hottest part. Wear rubber gloves so the oils won't burn your skin, and wash them before removing.

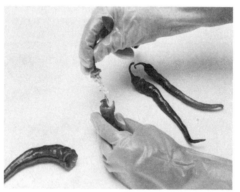

1 Cut around the top with a sharp knife. Pull out the core and seeds by the stem, and discard.

2 Split the pepper lengthwise. Remove any remaining seeds and scrape out the fine ribs.

CORN

Cut off kernels or pulp

There are special scrapers for removing kernels from the cob, but a sharp knife does a satisfactory job. Just be careful not to cut too deeply; you want only the milky kernels, or niblets.

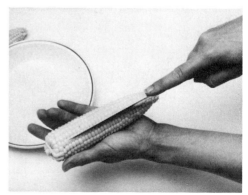

1 Hold the corn upright and scrape off the kernels with a sharp knife.

2 For cream-style corn without the skins of the kernels, cut through the middle of each row of kernels with a sharp knife.

3 Lightly scrape off the milky pulp with your knife, leaving the skin on the ear.

CUCUMBERS

Decorate and slice whole

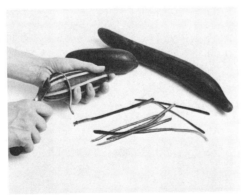

1 If the cucumber is waxed, scrub it well with a vegetable brush. Using a citrus stripper, pull off peel at even intervals.

2 You can also pull the tines of a fork down the length of the skin. If you are using the long, thin cucumbers, this is easier to do neatly if you cut them into halves.

Decorate and slice whole, continued

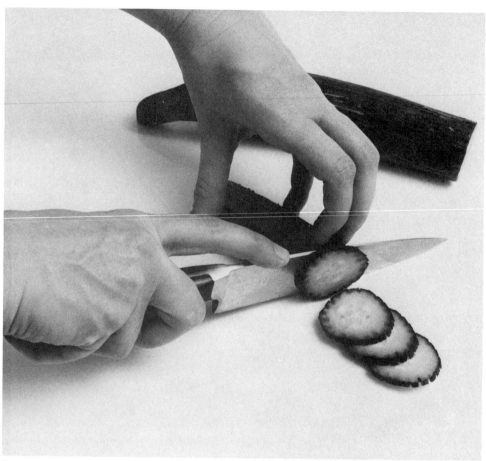

3 Slice into thin rounds.

Peel, seed, and slice

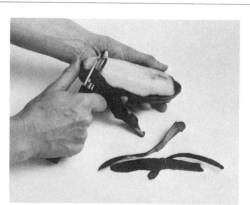

1 Peel the skin with a vegetable peeler, exerting light but even pressure so you don't lose valuable flesh.

2 Cut the cucumber in two lengthwise, and scoop out the seeds using a melon-ball cutter or small metal measuring spoon.

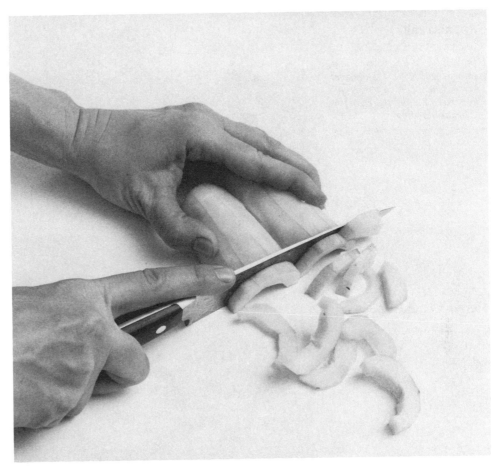

3 Place halves side by side and slice into crescents.

DANDELION GREENS

Clean and trim

1 Leave the greens attached to the stem and swish them in a bowl of cold water to remove sand. Keep changing the water until it is clear.

2 Cut off the stems and use the greens in salad or cook like spinach.

EGGPLANT

Slice and salt

Eggplant has a lot of liquid that, if retained, will make a dish watery or cause the slices to absorb oil when fried. Salting the eggplant draws out this liquid.

1 Trim off the ends of the eggplant and slice it.

2 Place the slices on a rack and salt them lightly on both sides. Let drain for about thirty minutes, then wipe off salt with a paper towel.

Remove cooked pulp

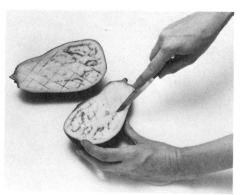

1 Cut the eggplant into halves lengthwise and score the flesh by making diagonal cuts about one-quarter inch deep. This will make it cook more evenly. Rub the cut surfaces with lemon.

2 After baking in a 375-degree oven for thirty minutes, the soft pulp is easily scooped out with a metal spoon.

Stuff

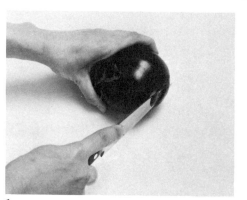

1 If necessary, cut a thin slice from the bottom of the eggplant so it will sit firmly.

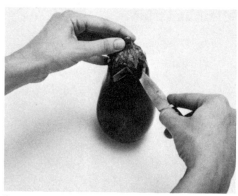

2 Cut off the top carefully by following the outline of the leafy stem. Push your knife all the way into the center in a zigzag pattern.

3 Hollow out the eggplant with a melon-ball cutter, leaving a shell about one-half inch thick. Sprinkle the scooped-out flesh with lemon juice. Then blanch, drain, and sauté it. Add to your cooked stuffing.

4 Parboil the shell for a minute or two. Fill with the stuffing and replace the top. Bake until the stuffing is warmed. If the eggplant is small, serve one to each guest. Otherwise, scoop out the stuffing at the table.

FENNEL

Trim

1 Trim the tops of the fennel. The leafy green part can be chopped and used as a garnish, like parsley. The fennel bulb is usually quartered and braised.

2 It can also be sliced raw and used in salads. Fennel has an anise flavor.

GARLIC

Peel and chop

1 Tap the garlic clove lightly with the blade of a chopping knife, just to break the skin.

2 Pull off the skin and trim both ends.

Peel and chop, continued

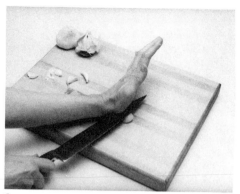

3 Crush the garlic with the tip of your knife, pressing down with the heel of your hand. This technique facilitates chopping.

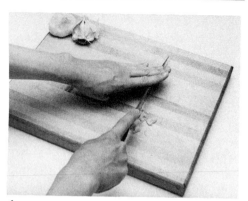

4 Chop to the desired degree of fineness.

GINGER

Slice and peel

Unpeeled whole ginger root will keep for at least a week in a plastic bag in the refrigerator. Sliced ginger will keep indefinitely if stored in sherry in an airtight container and refrigerated.

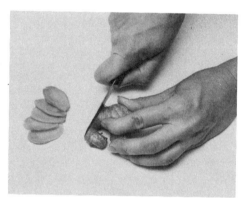

1 Thinly slice as much ginger as you will use at one time. It is easier to peel the individual slices rather than the whole knobby root.

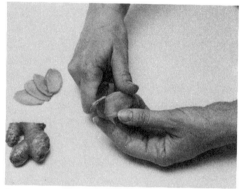

2 Peel each slice. Chinese cooks leave the peel on if they are using the ginger to flavor oil because the ginger is then discarded.

HORSERADISH

Peel and grate

If fresh horseradish is available, its flavor is definitely superior to the commercial variety. Peel only as much as you need because the remainder will keep better if left unpeeled and stored in a plastic bag in the refrigerator.

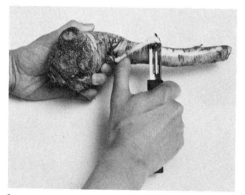

1 Hold the root firmly with one hand and peel with a vegetable peeler. Grate coarsely on a metal grater.

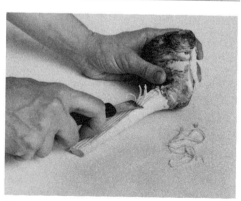

2 You may also pull a citrus zester over the firm flesh to produce thin curls, which make an attractive garnish for cold beef.

JERUSALEM ARTICHOKES

Slice

This is a misnamed vegetable because it is actually a member of the sunflower family and is sometimes called a sunchoke. It can be served raw or cooked like a potato.

1 Scrub the knobby skin with a vegetable brush and slice the Jerusalem artichoke raw for salads. It does not need to be peeled.

2 Put the slices into water with a little salt and lemon juice to keep them from discoloring.

KALE

Trim

Cut off and discard the stems. Trim off the tough center rib that runs up the leaf. Kale is cooked like spinach, but it does not shrink as much.

LEEKS

Trim and clean

Leeks have a lot of sand and dirt embedded at the base of their leaves. You have to open them up to be able to remove this.

1 Trim off the roots at the base and cut off the tops of the leaves, leaving the tender green part.

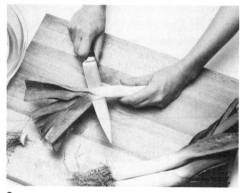

2 Insert your knife about two inches from the base and pull it up through the leaves. Turn the leek and repeat. If the leek is large, cut the leaves again.

3 The leaves can then be opened up, which makes it easier to clean them.

4 Swish the leek in a bowl of cold water until all sand and dirt are removed. Pour out the dirty water and repeat until water is clear.

LETTUCE

Dry

Salad greens must be completely dry after they are washed. If there is water on them an oil-based dressing will not coat them.

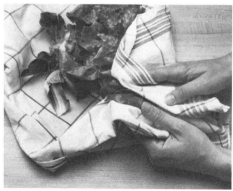

1 Pat the lettuce dry in a kitchen towel.

2 Or place in a spin dryer, which is a handy and efficient piece of equipment to own.

Tear

Salad is easier to eat if it is served in bite-size pieces. Tear the lettuce by hand; cutting with a knife bruises the leaves.

MUSHROOMS

Clean

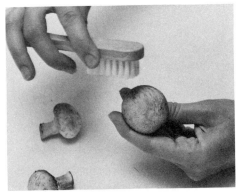

1 Wipe mushrooms with a damp paper towel. Don't wash them because they are porous and will absorb too much moisture.

2 If you are very fastidious, you can use a soft mushroom brush to remove any dirt.

Slice

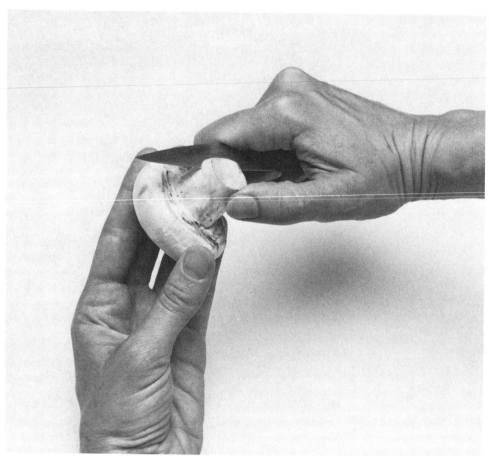

1 Trim the woody bottom off the stem.

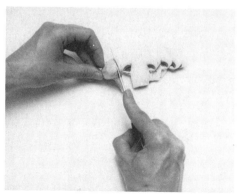

2 Steadying the cap with one hand, slice through cap and stem into umbrella shapes. This is the best shape for sautéeing, or cooking quickly.

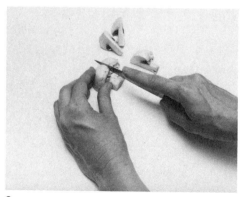

3 For stews and fricassees where you need a sturdier mushroom that will hold its shape, or for chopping, slice the whole mushroom into quarters or eighths, depending on size.

Twist in towel

1 To extract moisture from mushrooms, as for duxelles, spoon very finely chopped mushrooms into a kitchen towel.

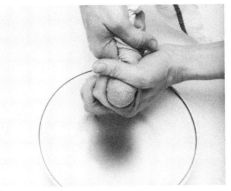

2 Twist into a ball and squeeze until liquid comes out. Discard the liquid.

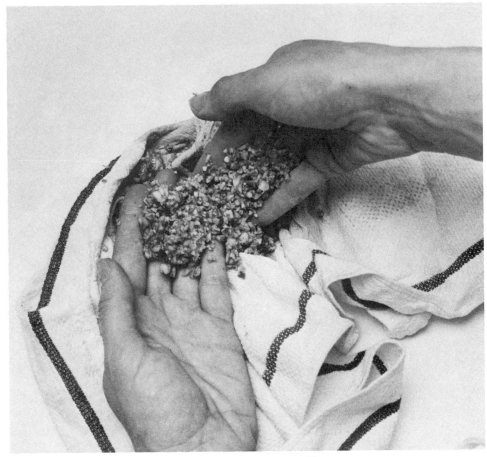

3 The dry mixture is then ready to be sautéed and used in stuffings.

Stuff

1 Remove stem by breaking it off. Save the stems for stock or stuffings.

2 Pour two or three drops of oil into each cap.

3 With your fingers, stuff the caps (I'm using seasoned bread crumbs) until nicely mounded. They are then ready to be baked on an oiled baking sheet.

Cut decoratively

Aztec and fluted mushrooms are an impressive garnish on fish, meat, or poultry dishes and are quite easy to do. The Aztec is my favorite because it is unusual and not seen as often as fluted. Because these mushrooms are primarily decorative, you may want to peel them if there are any brown spots on the caps. After they are decorated, the mushrooms should be poached in a little water, butter, and lemon juice.

Cut Aztec mushrooms

1 Using a small paring knife with a sharp point, make two shallow cuts across the cap, marking it into quarters as a guide for the design.

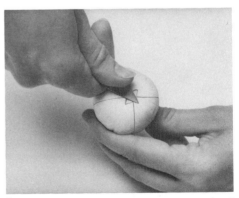

2 Hold the blade of the knife loosely in one hand and press down gently on the flat side of the tip with your thumb, making four indentations on the top of the cap.

Cut Aztec mushrooms, continued

3 Move the knife to the side of the cap and start making indentations with the tip all around the mushroom in even rows. You will have two or three indentations in each quadrant, depending on the size of the mushroom.

4 Continue making indentations in rows around the cap until you reach the edge. Use only very gentle pressure near the edge because the cap is more likely to break.

Flute I

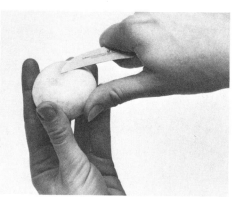

1 A knife with a curved blade makes the task of fluting less difficult. Hold the blade loosely and make a shallow slit starting at the center of the crown.

2 Continue the slit almost to the edge of the cap. Your knife will turn toward you; your thumb acts as a pivot.

3 Make a parallel slit, going in at a slight angle toward the previous one.

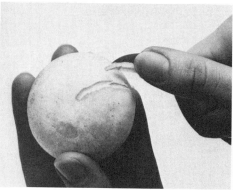

4 Pull out the thin crescent of mushroom.

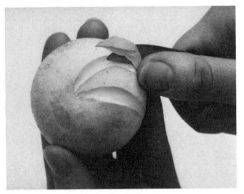

5 Continue to cut out shallow crescents around the cap in a symmetrical pattern.

6 Pressing gently with the tip of your knife, make a star-shaped pattern in the center crown.

Flute II

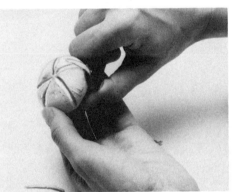

1 An easier way to flute a mushroom is with a citrus stripper, but the result will not be as professional looking. Start at the crown and, with only slight pressure, pull down to cut out shallow wedges.

2 The center of the mushroom can be decorated with a star pattern by making indentations with the tip of the knife.

OKRA

Trim and slice

1 If the okra is to be quickly sautéed or steamed alone as a vegetable, trim the ends very slightly so the juices don't run out.

2 For a stew or gumbo, where you want the sticky juices for flavor and thickening, trim the ends a little deeper and slice.

ONIONS

Chop

Chopping onions in this manner happens so quickly you don't have time to cry.

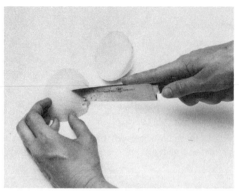

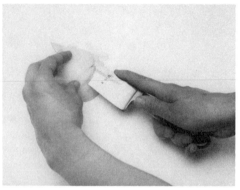

1 Slice a peeled onion into halves through the root end. Place the cut side of the onion on a chopping board and make vertical slices close together up to but not through the root.

2 Hold the top of the onion half firmly with one hand and make slices parallel to the cutting board, starting at the bottom and moving up. Again, leave the root intact.

3 Then slice through from the top and onion dice will fall off. If you want a more finely minced onion, chop the dice.

Cut into petals

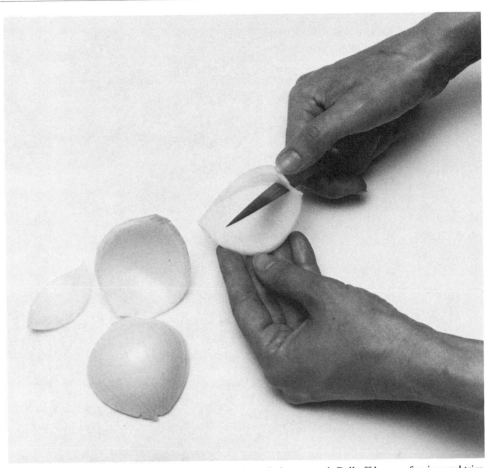

Peel and trim off the ends of the onion. Cut in two through the root end. Pull off layers of onion and trim with a knife to form petals, which are frequently used in Oriental dishes.

Scoop out for stuffing

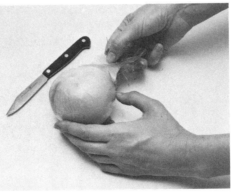

1 Boil the onions in their skins for five minutes, no longer. Peel and cut a small slice from the top.

2 With a melon-ball cutter, scoop out the onion, leaving a shell about one-half inch thick. Fill with stuffing.

Peel small white onions

1 Boil the onions in their skins for less than a minute. Drain and trim off the ends.

2 The skin will slip off easily.

3 Cut a cross in the root end, which keeps the onion from falling apart.

PARSLEY

Trim for chopping

1 Hold parsley tightly bunched and, with a sharp knife, cut off stems.

2 Keep the bunch together and, using your fingers as a guide, cut through. Continue to move your fingers back and make successive cuts. Then chop to desired degree of fineness.

Dry chopped parsley

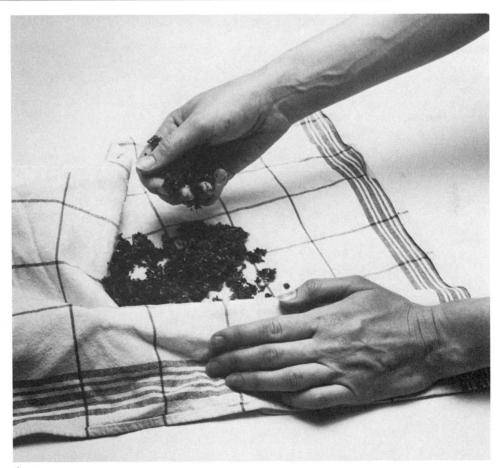

1 If the parsley is damp, put it in a kitchen towel.

Dry chopped parsley, continued

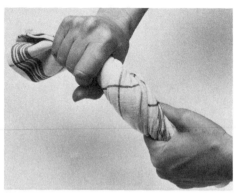

2 Twist both ends until water comes out.

3 The chopped parsley is then fluffy and is easier to sprinkle on dishes as a garnish.

PARSNIPS

Peel and core

Parsnips should be steamed or boiled before peeling because they discolor quickly. You also get a thinner peel after cooking, which can take from fifteen minutes to one-half hour, depending on the size and age of the parsnips.

1 With the point of your knife, slit the skin down one side. Pull the peel around with your knife.

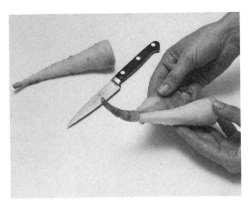

2 Then pull off with your fingers.

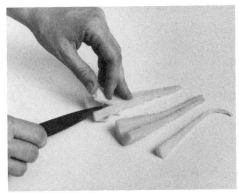

3 Cut the parsnip into halves lengthwise. Pry out the core, which tends to be tough, with the tip of your knife.

PEPPERS

Peel

Peeling peppers is a matter of personal taste and culture. Mexicans always peel their hot peppers, the Chinese never do. Italians usually roast sweet peppers and then remove the charred, papery skin.

1 Hold the pepper over a gas flame using a long-handled fork until skin chars. Or put the pepper under the broiler and turn frequently.

2 Pull off the skin with your knife. You can also wrap the charred pepper in a damp towel and rub the skin off.

Remove seeds and fibers

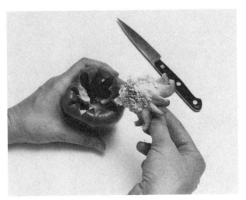

1 Cut around the stem end with a sharp knife, and pull out the inner core and seeds.

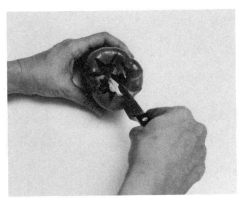

2 Scrape out the white fibers. The pepper can then be stuffed, sliced into rounds, or chopped.

Cut into flowers

1 Make these just before using. Cut in a zigzag pattern around the top third of the pepper, pushing the knife through to the center.

2 Pull apart into two flowers. It usually makes a prettier garnish to leave the seeds in.

POTATOES

Cut into various shapes

Although mashed potatoes are my favorite, I like potatoes in all forms. Try cubing them for frying rather than slicing them—more will fit in the pan and it is easier to brown them on all sides.

1 Slice the potato lengthwise and cut each slice into quarter-inch strips for french fries.

2 Slice the potato lengthwise and cut each slice in two, then into one-inch cubes for frying.

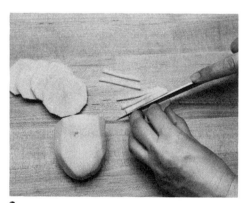

3 Slice the potato into rounds and cut each round into thin strips for shoestring potatoes. Cut the strips again for the finer matchstick potatoes.

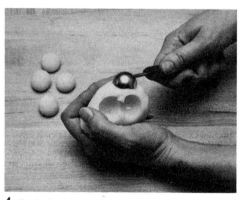

4 Push down into the potato with a melon-ball cutter, twist, and pull up for potato balls.

Scoop out and refill baked shells

1 Cut off the top third of a baked potato.

2 Scoop out the cooked pulp with a melon-ball cutter or a spoon, and purée through a food mill or fine sieve. Beat in butter and milk.

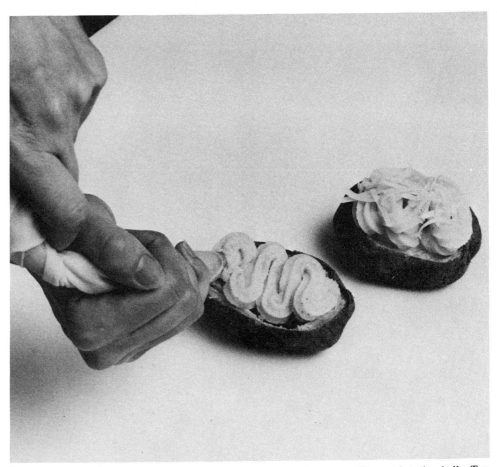

3 Outfit a pastry bag with a star tube and fill with the seasoned potatoes. Pipe out into the shells. Top with cheese, if desired, and bake until lightly browned.

PUMPKIN

Prepare for baking

1 Pull off the stem and wash the pumpkin. Use a large heavy knife to cut the pumpkin in two through the stem end, pushing down with the heel of one hand and then with other hand in a seesaw motion.

2 Scoop out the seeds and stringy fibers, and divide the pumpkin halves into quarters for baking. The cooked pumpkin meat can then be easily scraped out for soup or pie.

Peel

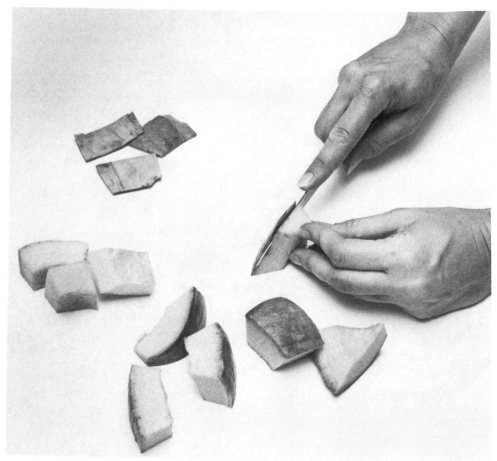

For most pumpkin dishes, you can cube the quarters and peel after cooking, which is easier because the pulp is soft. For a sauté or gratin, where there is no preliminary cooking, peel the cubes of pumpkin before cooking.

RADISHES

Cut into flowers

Radishes make colorful garnishes for an hors d'oeuvre platter or individual servings of antipasto. Choose the roundest ones you can find to carve into roses. Use longer ones for sliced flowers. For either one, cut off the stem and the root. Put into ice water when finished so that petals open. They will last for several days in the refrigerator.

Cut into flower I

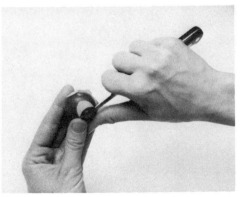

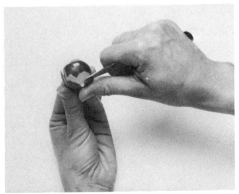

1 With a small sharp knife, outline an oval-shaped petal on the round radish and slice down behind it, using your thumb as a guide so you don't slice through.

2 Continue to cut adjoining petals all around the radish. A knife with a curved blade makes it easier.

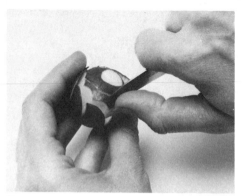

3 Cut down at an angle in a neat circle behind the row of petals.

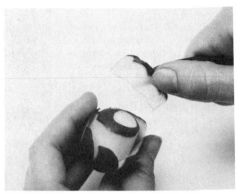

4 Pull out this section, which will make the petals stand out.

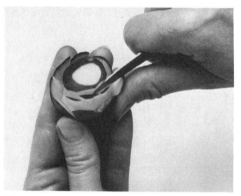

5 Cut another row of oval-shaped petals.

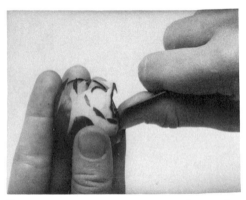

6 Cut down and in to remove another section behind the second petals.

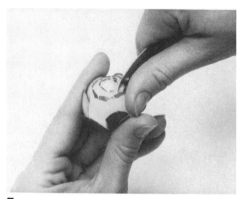

7 Make crisscross slices in the top.

8 Drop into ice water.

Cut into flower II

With a long radish, make parallel vertical slices down almost to the bottom but not through. It is easier if you start in the middle and work out toward each end. Drop into ice water.

RUTABAGA

Peel and cube

1 Rutabaga, which is also called yellow turnip, is covered with wax unless it is locally grown. Peel this off completely.

2 Slice and cube it, and treat like turnip or potato.

SCALLIONS

Trim

Use both the white and the green part for seasoning and in salads. Cut off the wilted ends of the leaves and trim off the root. Then slice or chop according to need.

Cut into flower

Scallions are wonderful vegetables for garnishing. I save the green leaves for aspic decorations, such as on a pâté, and for the bouquet of crudités at the end of the chapter. The flowers are easy to do and will keep for several days in the refrigerator.

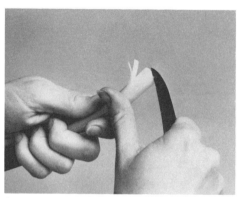

1 When trimming the scallion, leave two or three inches of fresh green. With the tip of your knife, make thin, petal-like slices down about an inch and all the way around the outside of the bulb.

2 Continue to make inch-deep cuts on the inside of the bulb.

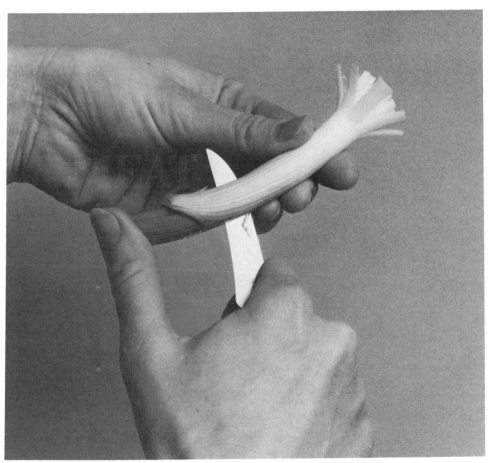

3 Holding the bulb away from you, insert the knife midway into the green leaves and pull toward you.

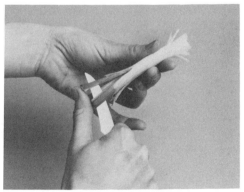

4 Turn the scallion and repeat.

5 Drop into ice water and the petals and leaves will curl.

SHALLOTS

Peel and chop

1 This mild-flavored member of the onion family is chopped like an onion. Peel the shallot with a sharp paring knife, leaving root end intact.

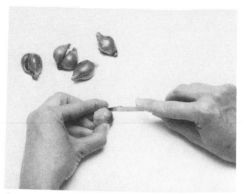

2 Make vertical slices close together up to but not through the root end.

3 Holding your knife parallel to the cutting board, make several slices up to the root end.

4 Hold the root end with one hand and slice down from the top into a fine dice.

SNOW PEAS AND SUGAR SNAPS

String

Both of these varieties of peas can be eaten raw or quickly stir-fried, pods and all.

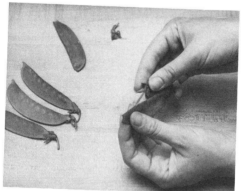

1 Unless snow peas are very young, pull off the string by breaking the tip and pulling it down the straight side of the pod, with the string attached.

2 Sugar snaps have a slightly fuller pod—more like regular peas—and are strung in the same way as snow peas.

SPAGHETTI SQUASH

Prepare and scoop out cooked pulp

Ignore the printed instructions that sometimes come with spaghetti squash telling you to cut it lengthwise. If you cut through the middle you will get longer strands.

1 Cut the raw squash in two through the middle and scoop out seeds and fibers.

2 After it is steamed or baked, the long strands of flesh pull out easily with a fork. Serve with butter and seasoning or with a pasta sauce.

SPINACH

Trim

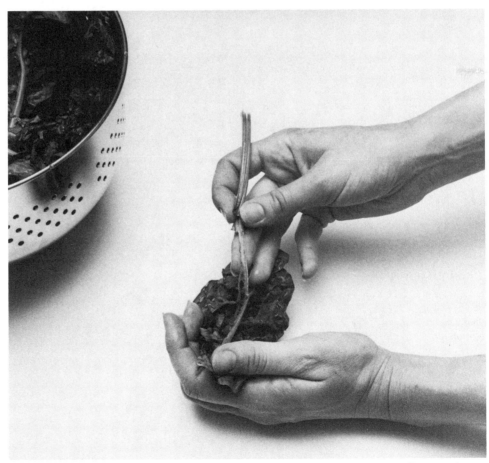

Wash the spinach well in a colander. With your fingers, pull off stems and any tough fibers running up into the leaves.

Drain

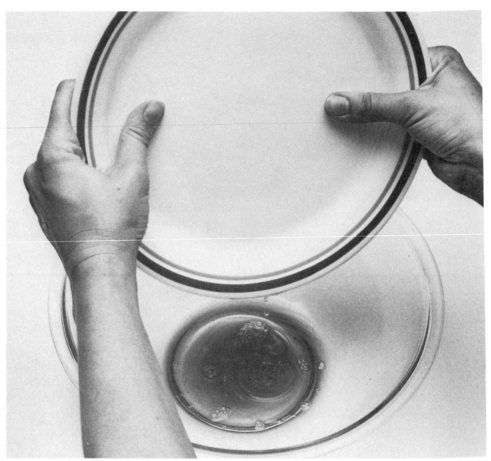

Put cooked spinach on a plate. Put another plate on top and squeeze the moisture out by pressing the plates together.

SQUASH

Cut into flowers

Summer squash is quite pliable and easy to work with. The flowers are an attractive garnish for a roast, or can be part of the bouquet of crudités at the end of the chapter.

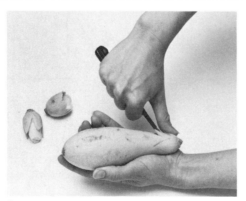

1 About one inch from the stem end, make a very thin zigzag cut with the point of your knife.

2 Cut off the end of the squash about three inches up.

3 Using the point of your knife, slice down behind the petals and remove a thin strip so that petals will stand out.

4 Cut shallow, oval-shaped petals in a circle around the squash and remove a thin strip behind them. Continue to cut rows of petals to the top.

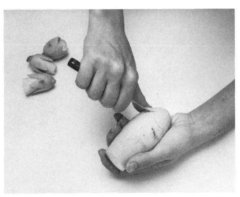

5 Using the large end of the squash, cut thin oval petals all around the bottom. Cut another row of slightly thicker petals, going in at an angle toward the core.

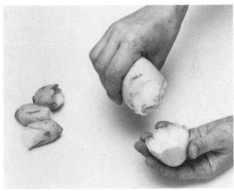

6 Twist the flower slightly and pull away from the rest of the squash. Use the center section for purées.

SWISS CHARD

Trim

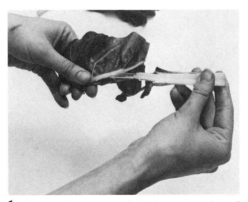

1 Break off the stems of this hearty member of the beet family.

2 Pull out the tough center rib from each leaf. Use the stems for purées; cook the leaves like spinach.

TOMATOES

Peel

I never peel tomatoes if I'm serving them raw. But you will end up with pieces of peel throughout a cooked dish or sauce unless you peel the tomatoes first.

1 Put the tomato into boiling water for exactly ten seconds, then drain.

2 Cut around the core with a sharp knife and discard.

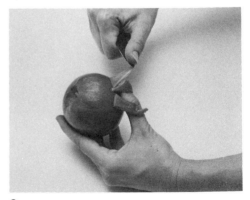

3 Peel back the skin.

Seed

1 Cut the peeled tomato in two through the middle.

2 Gently squeeze the tomato half to remove seeds and some juice.

3 If necessary, pull out any remaining seeds with your fingers. The tomato is then ready to be sliced, chopped, baked, or broiled.

Form a rose I

Both of these tomato roses are pretty and decorative as garnishes. The first one is easy to do with a sharp knife and is good for salads or hors d'oeuvre platters. The second is more difficult, but I prefer it because it's more realistic and unusual. I make several at a time and freeze them, then use to garnish a ham or other cold meat.

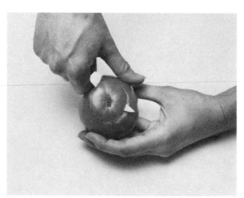

1 Cut a slice from the bottom without severing it from the tomato.

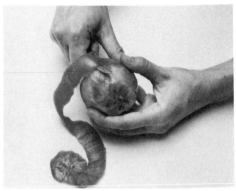

2 Continuing from the base, cut a thin strip in one piece all around the tomato. The strip should be about three-quarters of an inch wide.

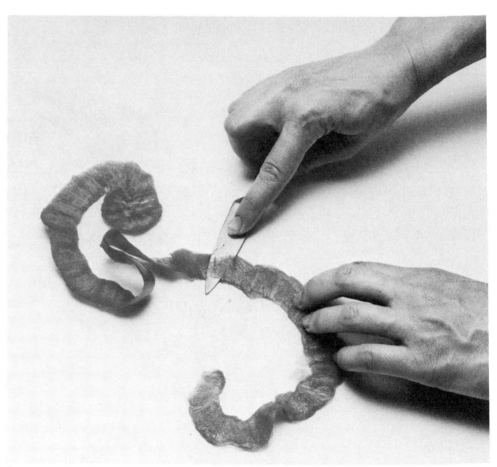

3 Carefully scrape off any excess flesh from the long strip.

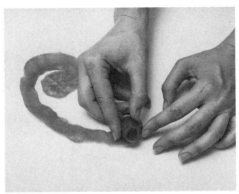

4 Start rolling the strip from the top, skin side down. Use your fingers to keep the center from popping out.

5 Place the rolled strip on the bottom slice, and it will open naturally into a flower.

Form a rose II

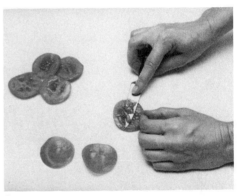

1 Cut six thin slices from the outer sides of a ripe tomato. You may need three tomatoes for two flowers.

2 Carefully shave off any flesh from the slices. Save the three prettiest slices for the outside of the rose.

3 Prepare softened butter and put into a pastry bag. Squeeze out a mound about two inches in diameter onto a square of wax paper.

4 Roll the thinnest slice, skin side in, into a tight cylinder. Press it upright into the center of the butter.

Form a rose II, continued

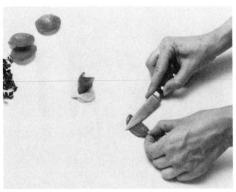 

5 Bend one slice in half, skin side in, and crease it with your knife.

6 Push it into the butter, slightly opened, around one side of the center cylinder. Repeat with another slice and place it on the other side.

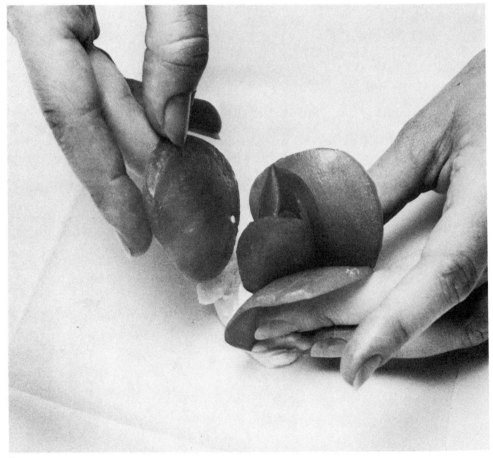

7 Press the three outside petals into the butter, skin side out. Bend them down slightly.

8 Hide the butter by surrounding the rose with parsley sprigs.

9 The finished rose can be frozen on the wax paper and used when needed. Put a toothpick through the center to anchor it to the ham or other cold meat. Brush lightly with aspic to make it shine.

Hollow out for stuffing

1 Cut off a slice from the stem end for a lid. If necessary, cut a thin slice from the bottom so the tomato will sit firmly.

2 With a sharp paring knife, carefully cut around the inside of the tomato without piercing the bottom. Leave one-half inch of shell.

3 Scoop out the pulp and seeds with a spoon.

4 Sprinkle the inside with salt, which will draw out some of the water, and invert the tomato on a rack to drain.

TURNIPS

Cut into flower

Turnips are my favorite vegetable for carving because they are pliable and easy to work with. The flowers will keep for at least two days in the refrigerator. Use them to garnish roasts, an hors d'oeuvre platter, or in the bouquet of crudités at the end of the chapter.

1 Select small, evenly shaped purple turnips. Rinse off loose dirt and cut off root. At the bottom, make zigzag cuts with the tip of a sharp knife, going about a third of the way up.

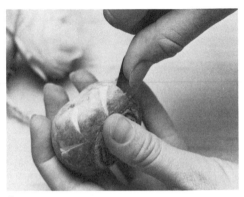

2 Put your knife behind each point and pull it out to form the bottom petals.

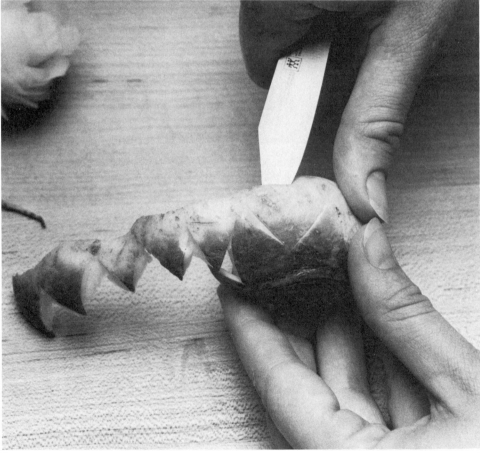

3 Remove a thin strip from behind the petals by cutting down at a slight angle almost to the base and moving your knife around the turnip. This will make the petals stand out.

4 Slice off the top to within one inch of the petals.

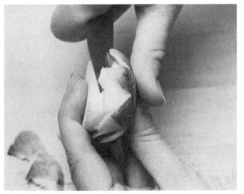

5 Cut another row of petals, this time very thin ovals, with just the tip of your knife.

6 Take out another strip of turnip from behind the petals.

Cut into flower, continued

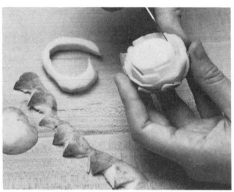 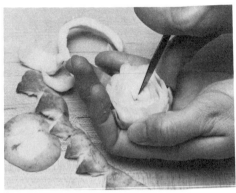

7 Continue to cut petals and remove strips until you reach the top.

8 Make crisscross cuts in the center.

9 Drop into ice water and the feathery petals will open.

ZUCCHINI

Scoop out and stuff

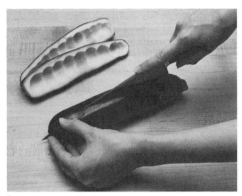

1 Scrub the zucchini with a vegetable brush, and cut it into halves lengthwise.

2 Scoop out the flesh with a melon-ball cutter, which leaves a scalloped shell. Sauté the flesh and mix with bread crumbs and herbs for stuffing. Pour a few drops of oil into the shell.

3 Fill the shell, pushing the stuffing into the scallops, which gives it a finished look.

ASSEMBLE BOUQUET OF CRUDITÉS

Assemble a bouquet of crudités

This is a dramatic and unusual centerpiece for a buffet table. Many of the flowers, such as turnips, radishes, and scallions, can be cut a couple of days ahead and refrigerated in ice water. But the bouquet should be assembled just before the party. I use whatever is seasonal and fill in with vegetables that are always available, including those with naturally formed flowers such as cauliflower and broccoli. The bouquet is also pretty with just two colors.

1 Wedge a red cabbage into a bowl so that it sits firmly. Insert bamboo skewers of varying lengths into the cabbage. The skewers can be dyed with food coloring like Easter eggs.

2 Or cover the skewers with long, hollow strips of scallion greens.

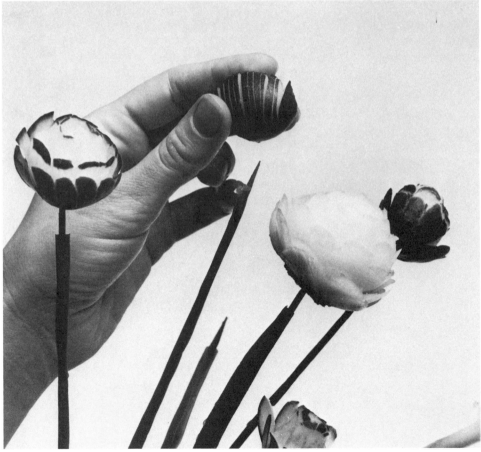

3 Press vegetable flowers onto the tops of the skewers.

2
MEAT

GENERAL

Cube

Meat should be cut into uniform one- or two-inch cubes for stews and skewer cooking so the cubes cook evenly.

1 Slice a small cut of meat into the desired width.

2 Cut into uniform cubes and trim off any fat and membranes.

Skewer

Alternate cubed meat and vegetables on a metal skewer. (I'm using lamb, onions, green and red peppers.) Don't crowd the pieces because you want all sides exposed to the heat.

Grind or chop

It is best to grind or chop your own meat because you know what you are getting. You can also incorporate seasonings while you are grinding so they are well blended with the meat. A food processor is the easiest tool to use, but a meat grinder or a chopping knife will produce satisfactory results.

1 If using a food processor, fit the metal blade in place and add uniform cubes of meat to the container. Add them in small batches so that the container is not crowded.

2 Turn the machine on and off every few seconds until the meat is the desired consistency. Don't overprocess or the meat will be mushy.

3 If using a meat grinder, outfit it with the proper disk for the desired thickness and press cubes of meat through with a wooden pestle.

4 If chopping by hand, cut the meat into cubes using a large chef's knife.

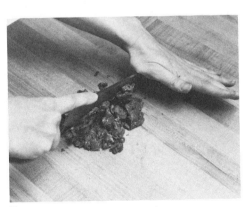

5 Then chop the cubes coarsely.

6 Continue to chop to the desired consistency.

Shape into meatballs

1 Dip your fingers into water to moisten them.

2 Break off a small amount of chopped meat.

3 Roll the meat between the palms of your hands just until a smooth ball is formed.

Slice and pound

Lean boneless cuts of meat—leg of veal for scaloppine; shell or top round steak for carpaccio and rouladen; loin of pork for braciòla— are thinly sliced and then pounded to an even thickness. Plastic wrap laid over the meat will prevent the flesh from tearing.

1 Put the meat in the freezer just until it is firm. Lay it on a flat surface and hold it flat with the palm of one hand. Slice the meat with the blade of your knife parallel to the board.

2 Pull up on the top slice and cut off at the end.

3 Put each slice between pieces of plastic wrap and pound from the center out to the edges so that the meat is of an even thickness. It will be about double its original size.

Dredge

Foods to be sautéed or browned before further cooking are frequently given a coating of flour to protect them from the hot fat if they are delicate, like variety meats, or to seal in their juices. You can also dredge foods in corn starch, cracker crumbs or sugar. The food to be dredged in flour should be dry, and should be cooked immediately. Otherwise, the natural moisture in the food will seep into the flour and make it gummy.

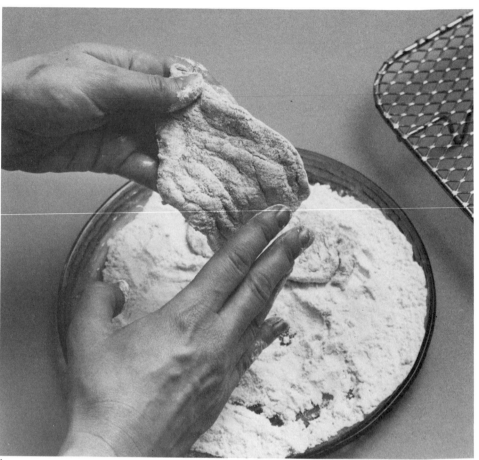

1 For large or delicate pieces of food, put a large amount of seasoned flour in a flat pan and dip the pieces in the flour to coat them evenly on all sides.

2 Pat and shake the pieces of food to remove excess flour and place them on a rack until all are coated.

3 For small pieces of food, put the seasoned flour in a paper bag and add the food, a few pieces at a time. Twist the top shut and shake the bag vigorously.

Bread

Many foods are breaded before they are fried to give them a crisp coating that keeps the food moist and tender. The food is first lightly coated with flour and then egg. The egg makes the crumbs adhere and keeps the natural moisture of the food from seeping out. Crumbs can be fine fresh bread crumbs, cracker crumbs, or corn meal. Don't use the commercially available dry bread crumbs because they are too fine and the coating will be gummy. Refrigerate the breaded food for at least an hour before cooking so the coating becomes firm and set.

1 Have plates of flour, beaten egg, and crumbs laid out. Dip or roll the food in flour so that it is lightly coated on all sides. Shake it as you lift it out to get rid of excess flour.

2 Lay each piece of food in lightly beaten egg, turning to coat it on all sides.

3 Then dip in crumbs. Place the breaded food on a wire rack so the air can circulate around it.

Slice across the grain

When a lean cut of meat is to be used for stir-frying or quickly cooked dishes such as stroganoff, cut it across (or against) the grain. This breaks the fibers and tenderizes the slices.

Shred

1 For stir-fry Oriental dishes, stack thin slices of meat that is slightly frozen and hold them with one hand, fingertips curved under.

2 Slice down into fine shreds.

Butterfly a chop

An opened-out veal or pork chop looks attractive and will cook more quickly. The chop should be at least one and one-half inches thick to butterfly it.

1 Put the chop bone side down. With a sharp knife, cut through the meaty back almost through the chop.

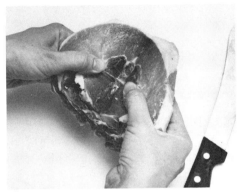

2 Pull the chop apart with your hands so that it will lie flat.

Cut incisions in fat

Trim fat off steaks and chops, but leave about one-half inch to keep the juices in. Cut parallel incisions around the edges so fat won't curl in cooking.

Lard

Narrow strips of fatback, called lardoons, are sometimes inserted into very lean cuts of meat that need long cooking in liquid. The fatback melts in the cooking and adds moisture and flavor. You need special larding needles for this procedure.

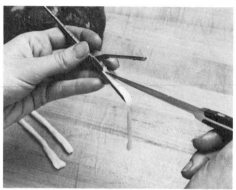

1 For small cuts of meat, push fresh strip of fatback into a small larding needle using the tip of your knife.

2 Close the needle over the fatback.

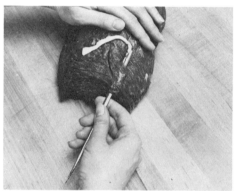

3 Push the needle in at an angle slanted against the grain of the meat.

4 Repeat several times about an inch apart. Trim off the fatback even with the roast.

5 For large roasts, use a long needle. Push the empty needle through the roast along the grain, turning it clockwise to create a hole.

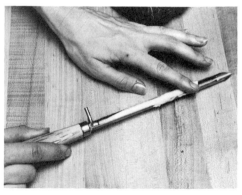

6 Remove the needle and discard any meat that is in it. Fill the needle with fatback.

7 Push the needle into the hole. Rotate it clockwise until it comes out the other end.

8 With the point of a knife, lift up the fatback from the end of the needle.

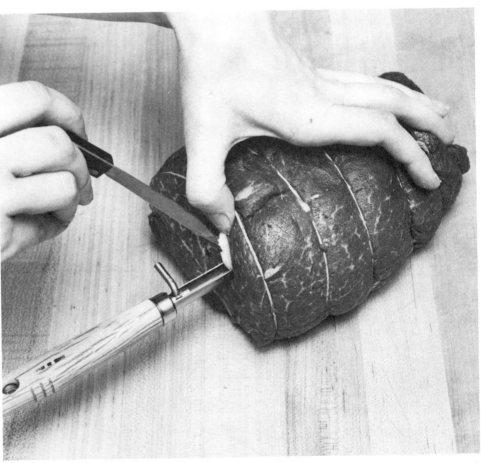

9 Holding this end of the fatback with the tips of your fingers, pry up the other end with your knife and secure it with your thumb.

Lard, continued

10 Hold both ends of the fatback and pull out the needle with a gentle rocking motion.

11 Repeat until the roast is well larded—about one strip for each inch of diameter. Trim off the ends of the fatback.

Bard

Lean cuts of meat to be roasted are often covered with thin sheets of fatback, called bardes *in French, to add moisture and flavor.*

1 Place thin sheets of fatback over the top of the roast—in this case, a fillet of beef.

2 Tie the roast lengthwise and in several places crosswise, depending on the size of the roast.

3 Place narrow strips of fatback along the sides of the roast.

4 Tie the roast along its length at two-inch intervals.

Wrap in caul fat

This is another way to add moisture and flavor to lean cuts of meat. Caul fat is the lacy membrane of the pig's stomach and usually has to be ordered from the butcher.

1 Lay the roast (I'm using a stuffed loin of pork) on a large sheet of caul fat and season the roast.

2 Pull up the caul fat to enclose the roast.

3 Tie the roast in several places to secure the caul fat.

Form a crown roast

This is a dramatic way to serve lamb, pork, or veal chops. Have the butcher saw off the chine bone, which is part of the backbone, from two racks of meat. It will make carving easier.

1 Score the ribs on either side of the racks in a straight line about two inches from the ends. The rack at the left has already been trimmed.

2 Remove the meat from between the ends of the ribs by cutting them down to the guidelines. Save the scraps for stuffing.

3 Scrape any remaining meat off the bones.

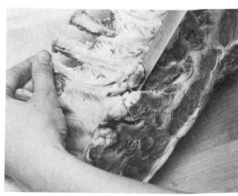

4 Cut around the base of each rib to loosen it from surrounding meat and any fragments of the sawed-off chine bone.

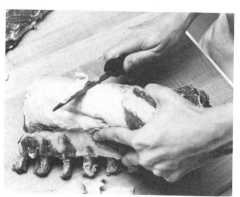

5 Turn the rack over and trim off excess fat. This meaty side of the rack will be on the inside of the crown.

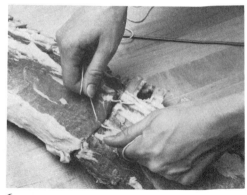

6 With a long trussing needle and string, sew one end of one rack to the other in two or three places, depending on size. Tie securely.

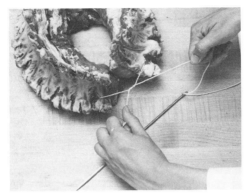 

7 Bend the racks, meaty side in, and sew together.

8 Tie string around the outside of the crown.

9 Stuff the center and score the stuffing. Put a cap of aluminum foil on each rib and bake according to recipe directions. To serve, carve between each rib.

Brown a whole roast

Meats should be browned before they are braised to seal in the juices. The meat must be dry and the fat quite hot. Use oil or a combination of oil and butter (butter alone will burn).

1 Wipe the meat with paper towels.

2 Heat the oil or butter and oil in a deep braising pan. When the foam from the butter subsides, add the meat.

3 Turn the meat using wooden spatulas so you do not pierce the skin. Brown it evenly on all sides.

4 Turn and brown the meat on each end.

Brown cubed meat

1 Dredge cubes of meat in flour to dry them and give them a nice crust when browned.

2 Brown only a few cubes at a time over medium-high heat. If they are crowded in the pan they will steam in their own juices rather than brown. Turn them with tongs so that they brown evenly on all sides.

7 The finished frill opens out like a flower.

BEEF

Score and skewer porterhouse steak

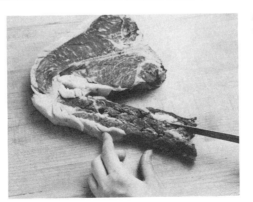

1 Make crisscross incisions to tenderize the tail, which is tougher than the rest of the porterhouse.

2 Attach the tail to the steak with a wooden skewer. The whole steak will then cook evenly.

Score and skewer porterhouse steak, continued

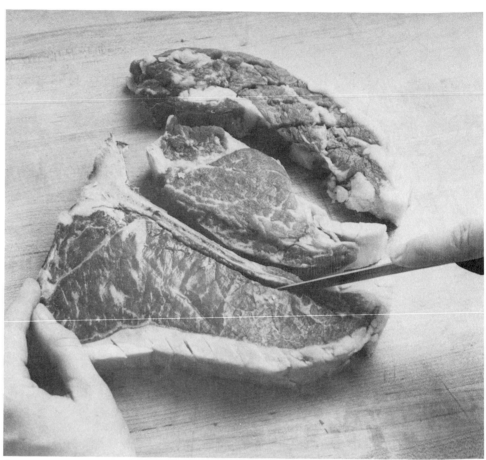

3 The porterhouse can also be divided into the long shell, a rounder fillet, and the tail. They can all be cooked separately.

Pound peppercorns into steak

Peppercorns are a delicious way to season any steak that you are going to panfry. (I'm using fillets cut from the tenderloin.) The cooked steaks will have a charred and crunchy exterior.

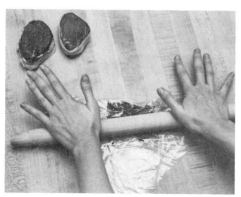

1 Put whole black peppercorns between pieces of plastic wrap. Press down with a rolling pin just to crack them.

2 Pound the peppercorns with the end of your rolling pin to crack any that didn't break open.

3 Press the coarsely cracked pepper into both sides of the steak. Let rest at room temperature for about fifteen minutes before panfrying.

Trim tenderloin

The tenderloin is a lean and luxurious cut of beef that can be cooked whole as a roast or cut into steaks. A trimmed tenderloin will weigh about one-third its original weight because of the large amount of fat that is removed.

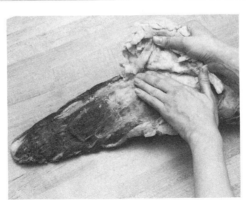

1 With your fingers, pull up the thick outer layer of fat.

2 Use a boning knife to cut off as much fat as possible.

**Trim tenderloin,
continued**

3 Keep lifting and cutting off all fat.

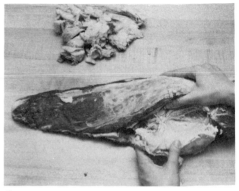

4 There is a large lump of fat running along inside the tenderloin. Pull this out with your fingers.

5 After removing all the fat, pull up the large membrane that covers the tenderloin. Scrape and cut it off with your knife.

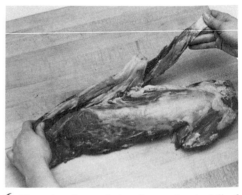

6 There is a large chain of meat that is full of gristle that runs the length of the tenderloin. Pull this off with your fingers.

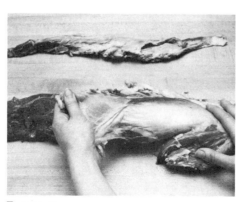

7 Pull off another layer of transparent membrane that covers the tenderloin.

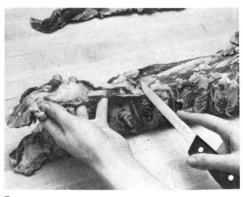

8 Turn the tenderloin over and pull up on the chain of gristle that runs halfway down the length of the tenderloin.

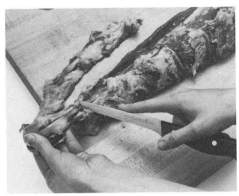

9 Pull and release the gristle with your knife.

10 Turn the tenderloin back to its smooth side. Pull up and start to cut off what is called the silver skin, a tough membrane.

11 Remove the silver skin in small pieces. Don't try to get it all off at once because you will pierce the meat.

12 Trim off any remaining fat and sinews.

Shape tenderloin for roast

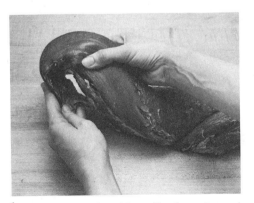

1 Turn under the thin tail of a trimmed tenderloin.

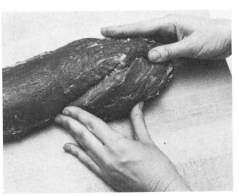

2 Press the two wings of meat into the head of the tenderloin to make it more compact.

Shape tenderloin for roast, continued

3 Tie the tail end.

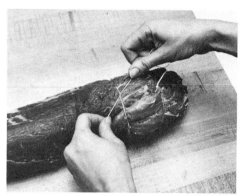

4 Tie the head end.

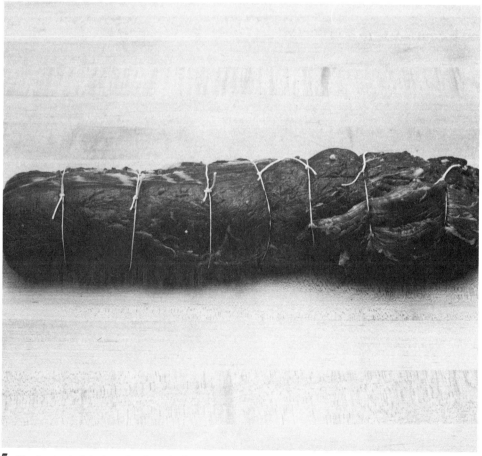

5 Tie the tenderloin loosely along its length at two-inch intervals. It is then ready to be roasted.

Cut tenderloin into steaks

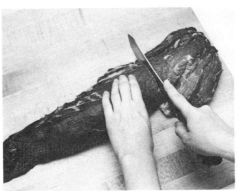

1 With a sharp knife cut a trimmed tenderloin just below the head, which is the sirloin section.

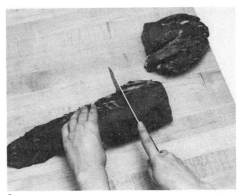

2 Cut the next section into a four-inch-thick chateaubriand.

3 Next comes a three-inch-thick fillet.

4 Cut off three one-inch-thick tournedos, leaving the tail.

5 Tie the first sirloin section at two-inch intervals into a compact roast.

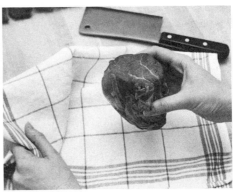

6 Place the chateaubriand on end on a kitchen towel.

Cut tenderloin into steaks, continued

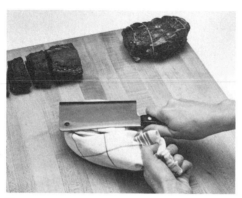

7 Cover the meat with the towel and pound it with the side of a cleaver or a heavy skillet to make it into a compact steak.

8 Divide the fillet into two steaks, known as filets mignons.

9 Fasten a slice of bacon around each filet mignon and each tournedos. This gives them flavor and keeps them moist.

10 Slice the tail piece.

11 Cube the tail slices for sautéeing or chop for steak tartare.

12 Scrape the meat off the two chains that were removed from the side and back of the tenderloin. The meat can be ground and used in clarifying stock.

13 The choice cuts from the tenderloin, starting at upper left, are: the chateaubriand, the sirloin roast, filets mignons and tournedos, cubed tail meat.

Carve rib roast

You can carve the roast into thick slices including one rib, which is known as the Diamond Jim Brady style. But for more modest appetites, I prefer what is called the English style, which is to cut it into one-quarter inch slices. Always let a roast rest for fifteen minutes to settle the juices after you take it out of the oven.

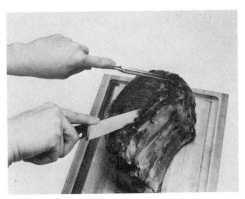

1 Place the roast on its side and make a cut two inches deep along the length of the rib.

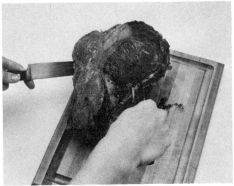

2 Using your fork and the flat of your knife so as not to pierce the meat, turn the roast rib side down.

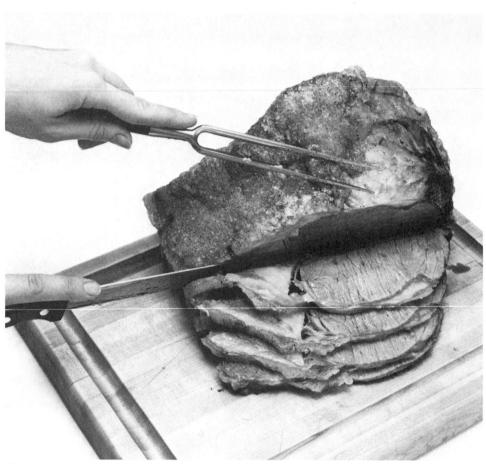

3 Cut a number of quarter-inch slices until you reach the end of your two-inch cut, which is about the width of one rib. Lift the slices off and put them on a serving platter.

4 Turn the roast back on its side and make another two-inch cut next to the rib.

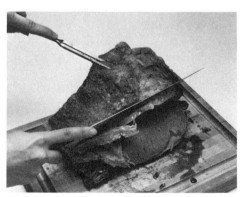

5 Continue slicing the desired number of pieces. The ribs are good to nibble on or they can be made into deviled ribs.

Butterfly, stuff, and roll a flank steak

A lean and economical cut of meat, flank steak can be filled with a variety of stuffings, braised, and served with a sauce. You can also cut a pocket in the flank steak, stuff it, and sew the opening.

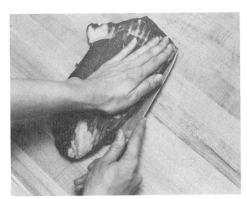

1 Hold the meat flat with one hand and cut part way through with a sharp knife. Keep the blade parallel to the board.

2 Lift up the top layer of meat and continue carefully to cut the two pieces further apart.

3 Open out the meat and cut just far enough so it will lie flat—about one-half inch from the edge.

4 Season the meat and put a layer of stuffing (I'm using chopped spinach, cheese, garlic, and raisins) to within one inch of the edge.

5 You can put peeled hard-cooked eggs on top of the stuffing, which will be attractive when the meat is sliced.

6 Fold in the sides of the flank steak.

7 Starting at the thickest side, roll the meat tightly to enclose the stuffing.

8 Tie kitchen twine lengthwise around the rolled meat.

9 Make crosswise ties at two-inch intervals down the length of the roll. Then braise according to recipe directions.

LAMB

Prepare and carve rack

A rack of lamb is an elegant cut of meat and makes an impressive presentation when you interlace the bones. Have the butcher cut off the chine bone from the ribs. Trim the ends of the ribs so that both sides of the rack are of equal length.

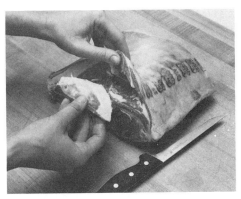

1 With a boning knife, cut under the slab of fat and follow the flat bone that runs parallel to the ribs.

2 Remove the bone, which will make carving easier.

3 With a cleaver, cut down about an inch between each rib at the base.

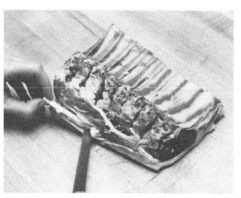

4 Cut out the strip of yellow fat that runs under the sawed-off chine bone.

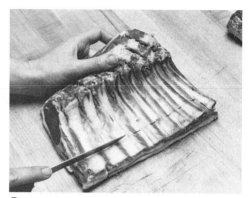

5 Score the bones on both sides about one and one-half inches from the ends to fix a guideline.

6 Cut and scrape off the meat from the ends of the ribs down to the guideline, which is called frenching.

7 Cut off all but one-quarter inch of fat from the back of each rack.

8 Stand the racks up in a roasting pan, fat side out. Interlace the ribs.

9 Cover the ends of the ribs with a length of aluminum foil, which will keep them from becoming charred. Season and roast according to recipe directions.

10 To carve, cut between the first two ribs on one side.

11 Then cut off the rib on the other side. Continue to cut on alternate sides, which will keep the rack standing until all the ribs are carved.

Bone and butterfly leg

A butterflied, or flattened, leg of lamb is excellent grilled, or it can be rolled into a roast that is easy to carve. Boning the lamb is not difficult because there are only four bones to remove—hip, tail, leg, and shank. Look ahead to steps 11 and 17 to see the shapes of these bones.

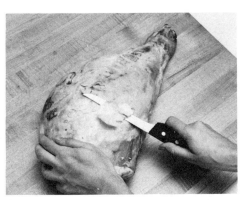

1 Cut off excess fat from the leg.

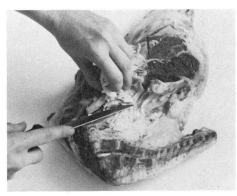

2 Turn the lamb fat side down. Pull up and cut off the glob of fat above the tailbone, which runs along the bottom of the photograph.

3 Cut behind the length of the hipbone, following the contour of the bone with your knife.

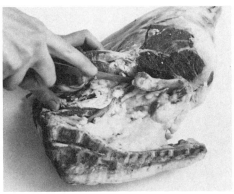

4 Cut around the knobby joint that connects the hipbone to the tailbone.

Bone and butterfly leg, continued

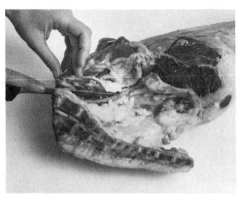

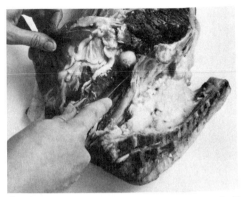

5 Work along the upper part of the tailbone, which curves up to connect to the hipbone. Loosen the flesh all along this bone by keeping the blade of your knife next to the bone.

6 When the flesh is loosened, you will see a ball joint that connects the leg to the hipbone. Release the ball from the socket by cutting the ligament around the ball with the tip of your knife.

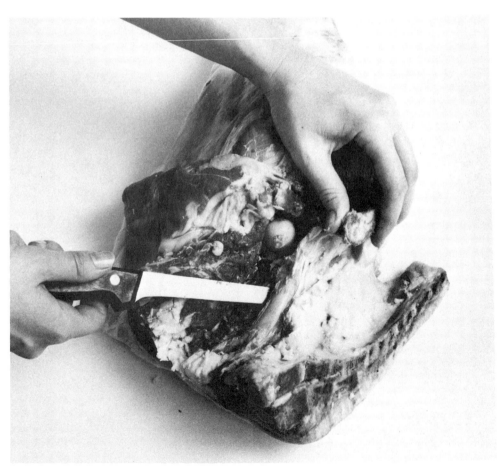

7 Lift up the released part of the hipbone and cut along the upper part of the tailbone.

8 Lift up on the upper part of the tailbone and cut under and around the large section of the tailbone.

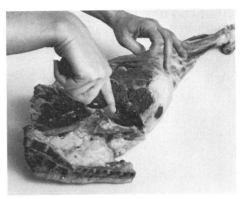

9 Go back up to the hipbone and feel behind it with your finger; then cut along the contour of the bone to free it.

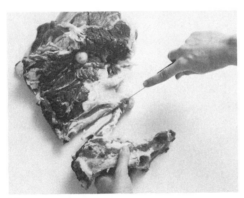

10 Pull the hipbone toward you and free the tailbone completely.

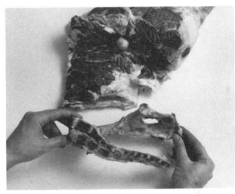

11 The hipbone and tailbone are freed in one piece. All meat and sinew have been cleaned off so you can see the shape of the bones.

12 The ball joint that is exposed is the hip end of the leg bone.

13 Cut along the leg bone, freeing the flesh on either side, to the next ball joint, which is the knee.

14 Cut on either side of the knee joint and then along the long shank bone.

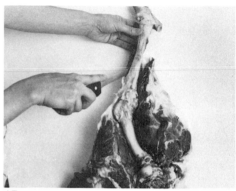

15 Lift up the shank bone and free the flesh behind it and the leg bone by scraping close to the bone with your knife.

16 Pull on the leg bone and carefully free the ball joint from the flesh.

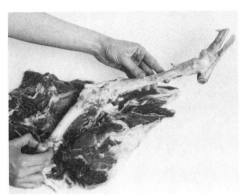

17 The leg and shank bones are removed in one piece.

18 Turn the lamb around, shank end facing you, and feel the thickest section of the leg. Fold it out as you cut through, following the membrane.

19 Flatten and open up the lamb still further by making incisions in the thickest section.

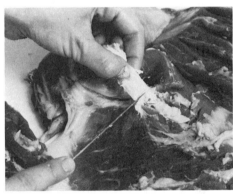

20 Pull up and cut off any remaining gristle and membranes.

21 Turn the lamb over and cut off the large pieces of fat remaining on the skin side.

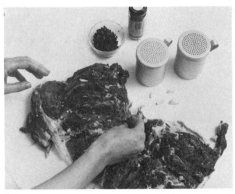

22 Season the butterflied lamb and grill, broil, or roll for a roast.

Prepare leg for roasting

It is easier to carve a leg of lamb that has been completely boned and rolled. But if you want to keep the look of the leg, remove the hipbone and tailbone, leaving the leg and shank in.

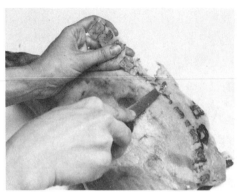

1 With your boning knife trim off excess fat and shave off the meat stamps (which are harmless vegetable dyes but not very attractive). French the end of the shank bone to give you a handle when you carve.

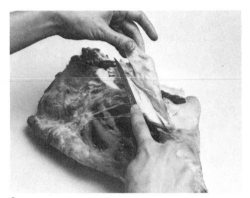

2 Turn the lamb over and remove the hipbone and tailbone (steps 2 through 11 in the preceding instructions). Remove any gristle and the fat on top of the leg bone.

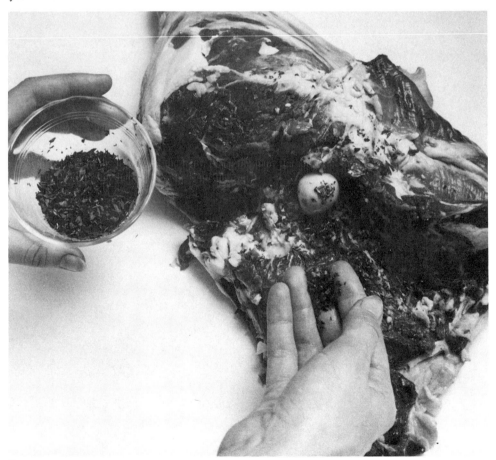

3 Season the flesh of the lamb.

4 Push up the bottom flap of meat.

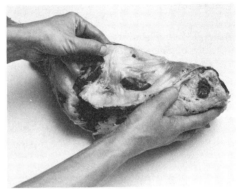

5 Fold the top flap of meat over to meet the bottom flap, covering as much exposed flesh as possible.

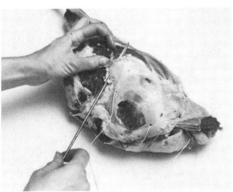

6 Sew the flaps closed with a trussing needle and string.

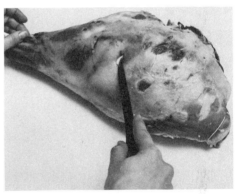

7 Turn the lamb over. Make several incisions with the tip of your knife and insert slivers of garlic to season the roast.

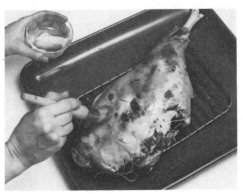

8 Put the meat on a rack in a roasting pan and brush with oil.

9 Pat herbs into the oil, which makes them adhere to the meat. Roast according to recipe directions.

Carve leg

There are only two tricks to carving a leg of lamb: Remove the hipbone and tailbone before cooking and use a sharp slicing knife.

1 With a towel, hold the lamb by the frenched shank bone. If you have removed the hipbone and tailbone, the end is boneless and easy to slice.

2 Carve off thin slices vertically until you reach the ball joint, which is the hip end of the leg bone.

3 Turn the lamb over and cut several slices on a slant down to the leg bone.

4 When you have cut three or four slices, cut along the leg bone toward you and release the slices.

5 Lift off the slices and put them on a serving platter. Continue to slice and cut toward you along the leg bone until you have enough to serve your guests.

Form lamb duck

This is something to amuse and amaze your friends. It is an elegant way to prepare a boneless leg of lamb, which is shaped into the form of a duck and covered with pastry. You can have the butcher butterfly the lamb if you want to save time, but be sure he saws the shank bone properly so the head of the duck will be nicely shaped.

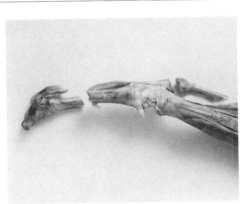

1 Have the butcher saw off the end of the shank bone. Have him also cut off the small bone that protrudes from the next knobby joint. The remaining shank will form the head of the duck.

2 Bone and butterfly the leg of lamb, but leave the piece of gristle at the shank end. Season the opened-up lamb with salt, pepper, and herbs.

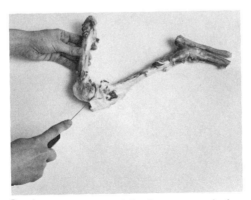

3 Cut through the ball joint that connects the leg to the shank bone. Discard the leg.

4 Roll the piece of gristle at the shank end around your finger and turn it under the lamb so that it is on the outside. It will form the duck's tail.

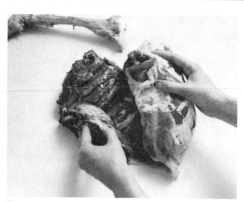

5 Roll the less meaty side of the lamb under and toward the center.

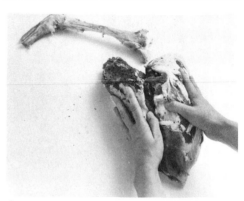

6 Roll the meaty side to the center.

7 Fit the shank bone in for the head and mold the meat into a pleasing shape.

8 Tie a length of trussing string around the circumference of the meat. With a trussing needle and string, take a few stitches in the meat around the neck to hold it securely.

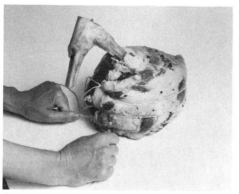

9 Tie two more strings around the body of the duck.

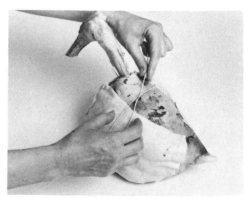

10 Tie fatback on the sides of the body.

11 Put the lamb in a roasting pan and cover the shank bone with aluminum foil. Roast the lamb at 425 degrees for fifteen minutes. Lower temperature to 375 degrees and cook until very rare, about fifteen minutes a pound, boned. Remove string.

12 Remove the barding and let the lamb cool for several hours. Place on a flat baking sheet and brush the lamb with beaten egg.

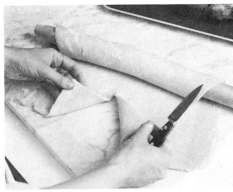

13 Roll out a sturdy pastry, like pâte à pâté, to one-quarter inch. Trim the oval edges and cut straight across one end.

14 Roll the oval end of the pastry onto a rolling pin and cut a slit in the other end for the neck.

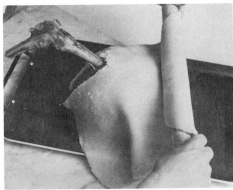

15 Roll all the pastry around the rolling pin.

16 Lift the pastry over the lamb, fitting the slit over the head like a cape.

Form lamb duck, continued

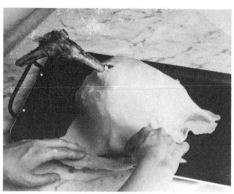

17 Trim off any excess pastry.

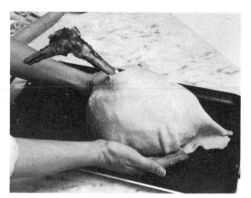

18 Tuck the pastry under the meat.

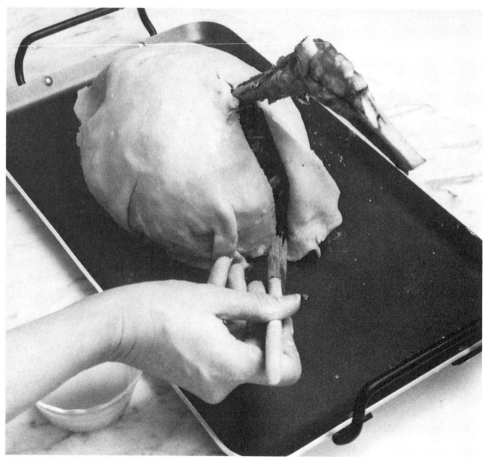

19 Brush one side of the neck flap with beaten egg and pull the other side over so it adheres.

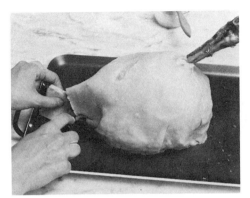

20 Trim excess pastry from around the tail.

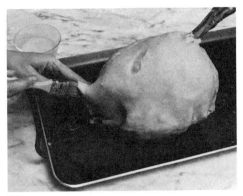

21 Brush the tail pastry with beaten egg and press to shape it.

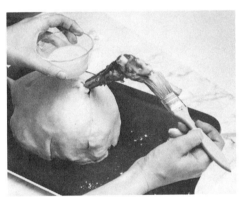

22 Brush the beak and neck with beaten egg.

23 Drape another piece of pastry over the head and press to make it adhere.

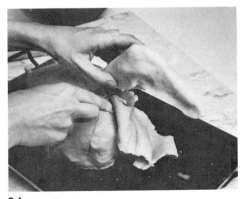

24 Cut off excess pastry.

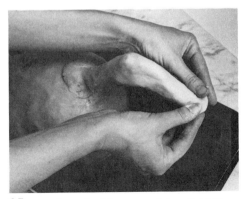

25 Press the end of the pastry into a flat bill.

Form lamb duck, continued

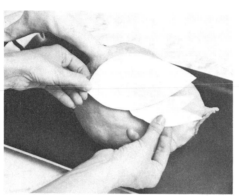

26 Cut cardboard wings and hold them against the duck to determine the size you want.

27 Roll out scraps of pastry, place the cardboard wings on it, and cut around the cardboard.

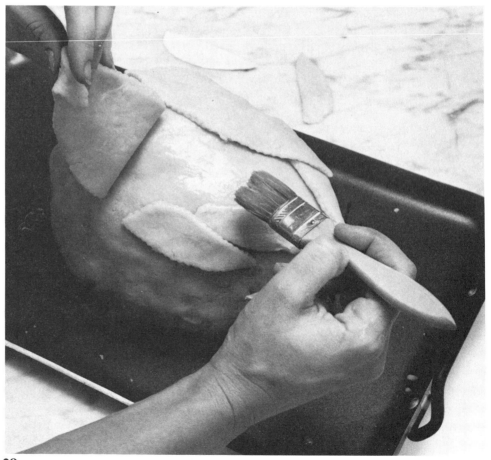

28 Brush the pastry with beaten egg and press on the wings.

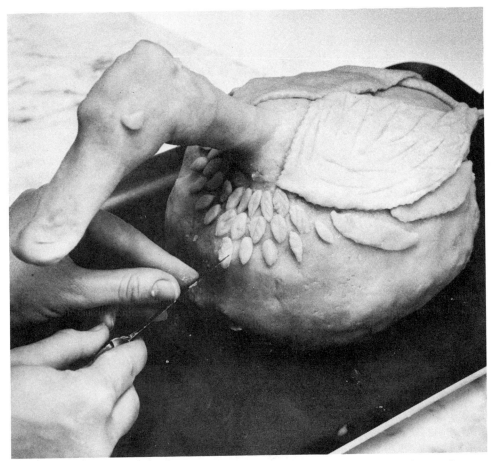

29 Decorate the duck with smaller pieces of pastry. Bake in a 375-degree oven for about an hour, or until pastry is brown.

PORK

Cut a pocket in chop and stuff

Cutting a pocket this way between the ribs of the chop creates only a small opening that is easily closed. The stuffing and juices will therefore not escape. The trick is to move your knife inside in a sawing motion without widening the opening.

1 Select double loin chops and make an inch-long incision between the two ribs near the bone. Move the end of the blade of the knife back and forth to widen the pocket inside.

2 Without enlarging the opening, widen the pocket inside with your finger.

Cut a pocket in chop and stuff, continued

3 Fill the pocket with stuffing, pushing it in with your fingers.

4 Cross two toothpicks over the opening, inserting them through the fat, and tie with kitchen twine.

Slice fatback for larding

Fatback comes from the layer of fat over the back of the pig and is used for larding, barding, or to line terrines. It should be fresh, not salted. It is best to have the butcher cut the fatback used for barding and lining terrines because it is difficult to cut the necessary large thin slices. Fatback for larding is a simpler procedure.

1 Place fatback with rind side up and pound with a meat pounder or heavy skillet to flatten it.

2 Holding the blade parallel to the board, slice off the rind, easing it up with your other hand as you cut.

3 Cut the fatback into wide strips.

4 Slice into narrow strips, called lardoons, and put in ice water. They will keep refrigerated for a week if wrapped in wax paper.

Cook bacon

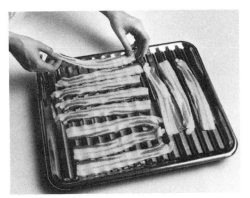

1 If you are cooking a large amount, place the bacon on a broiler rack in a pan and cook it in a 400-degree oven. This prevents shrinkage and the fat can drip into the pan.

2 For a few slices, place the bacon on a griddle over low heat.

3 Hold the bacon with a spatula and pour off the fat as it accumulates, which produces crisper slices.

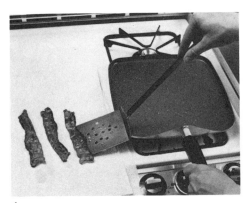

4 Drain on paper towels.

HAM

Prepare for baking

All smoked hams—even those marked "fully cooked"—benefit from further cooking. If the ham comes with a cloth cover and/or a heavy rind, it should be poached before baking. An ordinary supermarket ham can be baked and glazed without poaching. Ham is the hind leg of a pig and, like leg of lamb, should have the hipbone (or aitch bone) removed to facilitate carving. The hipbone will look slightly different depending on whether the ham comes from the right or left leg, but the procedure is the same.

1 If the ham has a cloth covering and/or a heavy rind, place it in a pan with water to cover. Simmer for thirty minutes if fully cooked, otherwise for fifteen minutes a pound.

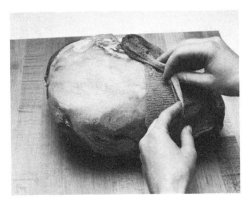

2 When cool enough to handle, pull off the cloth covering.

Prepare for baking, continued

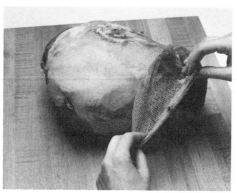

3 If the ham has a rind slit it and pull it off with your fingers, leaving about one-half inch of fat.

4 Turn the shank end away from you. Look ahead to step 8 to see the shape of the hipbone when removed. With a boning knife, start to cut around one side of the hipbone.

5 Follow the contour of the bone, keeping your knife blade against the bone.

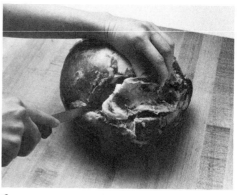

6 After cutting completely around the bone, cut behind it to loosen it.

7 Cut around the ball joint that connects the hip to the thigh. This takes patience because it is connected by tough cartilage.

8 The hipbone is totally removed and the ham is ready to be baked.

Score fat and glaze

Scoring makes the fat open up in baking so the glaze can seep down in when it is added.

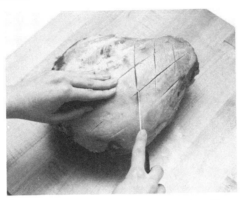

1 Score the fat side of the ham by cutting diagonally into the fat, thus making diamond patterns all over.

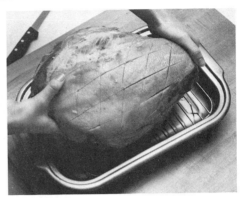

2 Put the ham on a rack and bake it in a moderate oven for about an hour.

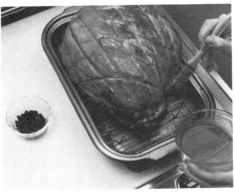

3 Remove the ham from the oven and brush with a glaze—I'm using mustard, brown sugar, Worcestershire sauce, and fruit juice. Brush into the scored fat, which will have opened up.

4 Stud each diamond with a whole clove and return the ham to a hot oven for about fifteen minutes.

Carve

You can french the shank bone of a ham the same way as for a leg of lamb. Or you can leave about three inches of meat around the shank bone to use as an anchor for your knife.

1 To get neat, large slices of ham, cut off a base, and then carve the rounder, meaty side of the leg first, which is on the left in this photograph. The shank is pointed away from you. The cloves have been removed.

2 Slice off three or four thin slices from the less meaty side to form a base.

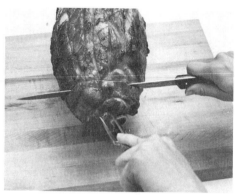

3 Turn the ham over on the base, meaty side up, and anchor your fork in the meat just above the shank bone. Slice down to the bone, about three inches from the end of the shank bone.

4 Slice down to the bone about one-half inch from the first cut, going in at an angle to the base of the first slice.

5 Using your fork and knife, remove this wedge of meat, which will facilitate removing the later slices.

6 Starting where the wedge of ham was removed, make thin, parallel slices down to the bone—as many as you want to serve at one time. Use your fork to steady the ham.

7 Cut under the slices of ham by holding your knife parallel to the shank bone and running it along the bone.

8 Lift out the slices with your knife and fork.

9 Continue cutting slices in the same manner as needed. Then turn the ham and cut from the less meaty side.

Re-form a boneless ham

Serve ham this way for a buffet, because guests don't need plates and fork. The ham is eaten with toothpicks.

1 Slice a boneless cooked ham in uniform one-half-inch-thick slices.

2 Stack them in the order they are sliced and match the sides so it looks like the original ham.

Re-form a boneless ham, continued

3 When you get to the bottom of the ham, place the ham flat and slice parallel to the board. Keep a slice about one and one-half inches thick for the top.

4 Take the bottom piece and spread it with a mixture of butter and Dijon mustard. This will be the base of the re-formed ham.

5 Cut the next slice into bite-size cubes.

6 With a spatula, lift the cubes and place them on the base.

7 Spread the mustard butter over the cubed slice. Continue until all the slices are cut into bite-size pieces and spread with the mustard butter.

8 Put the top piece on the reconstituted ham and brush the ham with several layers of aspic. Let each layer harden before brushing with another layer.

Re-form a boneless ham, continued

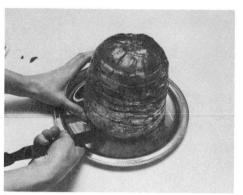

9 With a spatula, transfer the ham to a serving platter.

10 Decorate with a tomato rose or kumquats with their leaves. To serve, lift off the top and let guests remove pieces of seasoned ham with toothpicks.

SAUSAGES

Prepare casings

Sausage casings are the intestines or bladder of hogs, cattle, and sheep and are available in pork stores and from good butcher shops. The casings are usually preserved in salt and should be soaked in cold water and drained before using. Cut them into manageable lengths—about a yard long—and test them to see if there are any holes in the casings. I prefer to let water run through them, but you can blow into them like a balloon to see if they leak.

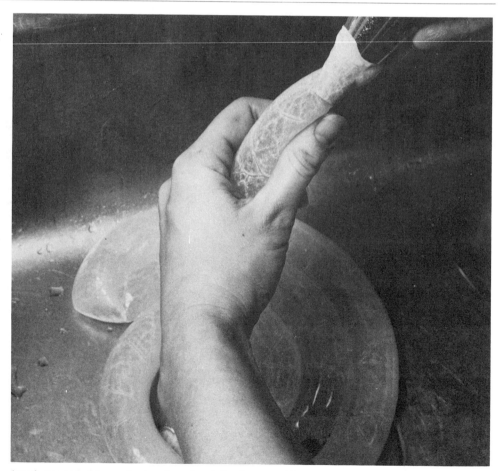

Attach one end of the casing to a funnel and slowly run tepid water into it, supporting the casing with one hand. Cut off any section that leaks.

Stuff by machine

Always fry a small piece of sausage filling before stuffing the casings and taste it for seasonings. The filling and the equipment should be chilled to facilitate stuffing. Be careful to support the casing so that it is straight and no air bubbles are allowed to form.

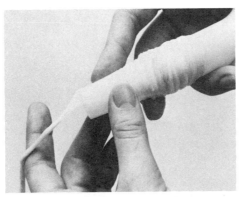

1 Gently push the sausage casing onto the funnel.

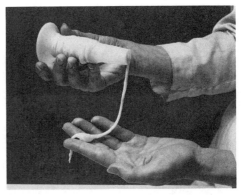

2 Leave a six to eight inch piece of casing loose at the end so that air can escape.

3 Attach funnel to the machine and support the sausage casing with one hand while pushing filling down with the other. As each sausage is the desired length, twist it, forming a link. Twist the next one the other way.

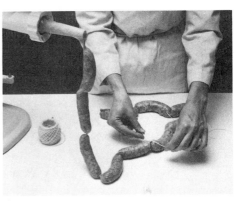

4 When you have five or six sausages, stop and tie them with kitchen twine.

Form in cheesecloth

If you don't have a sausage-stuffing machine, this is a good way to form sausage that will be sliced and fried. It also makes a good sausage for cooking in pastry.

1 Brush an 8-by-12-inch double thickness of cheesecloth with melted shortening or lard. Then moisten your hands and form sausage mixture into a cylinder.

2 Roll the cylinder in the cheesecloth.

**Form in cheesecloth,
continued**

3 Twist and tie the ends of the cheesecloth. Chill the sausage until firm. Remove cheesecloth before cooking.

SUCKLING PIG

Stuff, roast, and carve

For this dramatic presentation, plan to serve no more than six persons because there is very little meat on a true suckling pig. Order the pig from a butcher and have him remove the eyeballs (which explode in cooking).

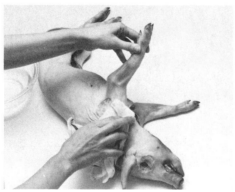

1 Wipe the outside of the pig with a damp cloth, including behind and in the ears.

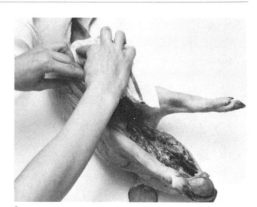

2 Wipe the cavity with a damp cloth.

 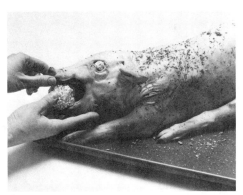

3 Rub the cavity and the outside with coarse salt and a mixture of herbs.

4 Stuff the mouth and eyeballs with foil, which will keep the cavities open while the pig cooks.

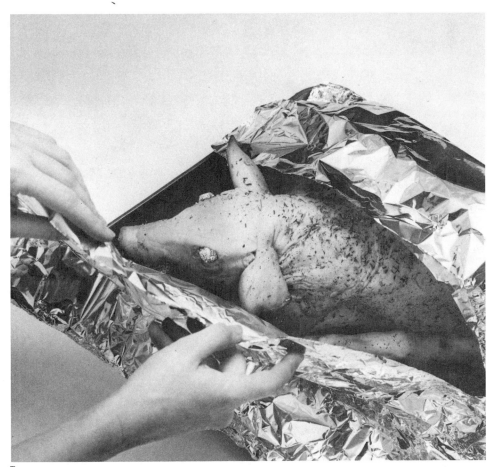

5 Put the pig in a roasting pan lined with foil and cover the pig loosely with foil. Refrigerate for about twelve hours or overnight.

6 Remove the pig from the refrigerator and wipe off the salt and herbs.

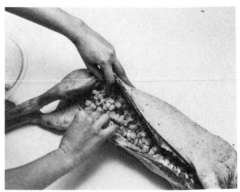

7 Stuff the cavity loosely with any poultry or other stuffing.

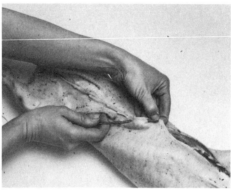

8 With a trussing needle and a long soft string, sew up the cavity from tail to chin. Leave a long end of string at the tail so you can pull it out in one piece.

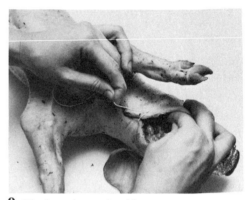

9 Tie the string at the chin.

10 With another length of string, run the trussing needle through the chin.

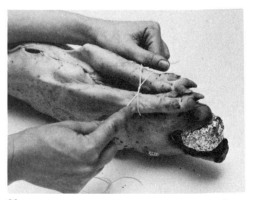

11 Tie the two ends of string up over the forelegs to keep them compact.

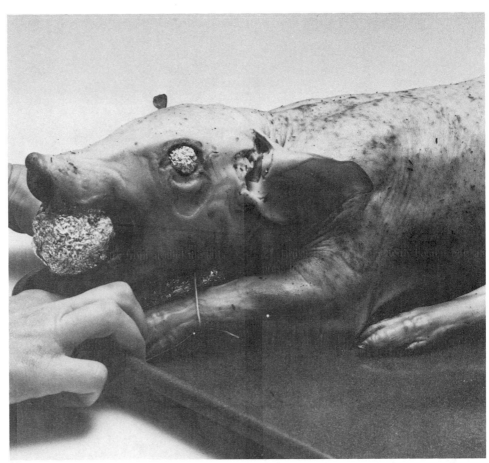

12 Place the pig on a baking sheet and put aluminum foil under the chin so the head is in a pleasing position.

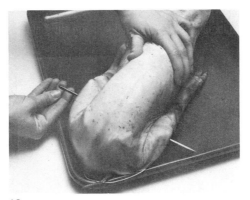

13 Use the trussing needle as a skewer and push it through the hind legs to hold them in place.

14 Put a piece of foil under the tail end. Put the end of trussing string next to the tail and fold up the foil. This makes it easy to find and pull out the string and protects the tail.

Stuff, roast, and carve, continued

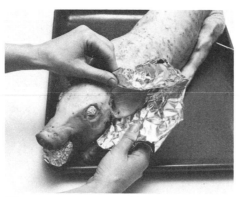

15 Wrap foil around the ears.

16 Brush the pig lightly with oil.

17 Cook the pig in a 325-degree oven for about two and one-half hours, or until internal temperature is 185 degrees. Baste every twenty minutes with the pan drippings.

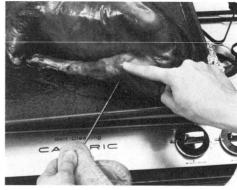

18 Remove the trussing needle. Remove the foil and put an apple in the pig's mouth and cherries in its eyes. Present the garnished pig at the table on a serving platter (see color photograph).

19 Take the pig out to the kitchen because it is easier to carve on a cutting board. Lay the pig on its side and cut the trussing string under the chin.

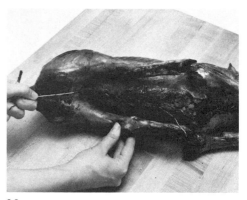

20 Pull out the length of string that closed the cavity.

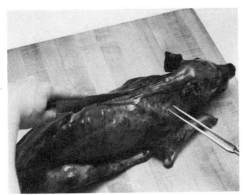

21 Make an incision down the length of the backbone with your carving knife.

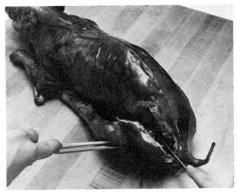

22 Cut off the hind leg by cutting in at an angle to sever the joint where the leg joins the body. Cut all the way back to the tail.

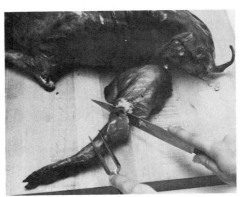

23 Divide the leg at the joint.

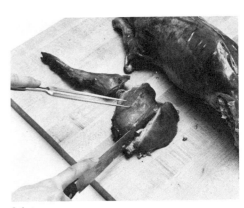

24 Divide the thigh.

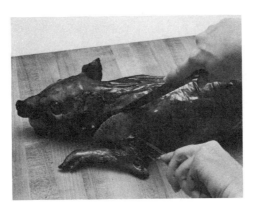

25 Cut off the foreleg, following the shoulder blade, and divide at the joint.

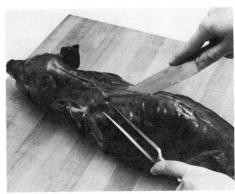

26 Cut down next to the ribs along the incision on the backbone. Use your fork to steady the pig.

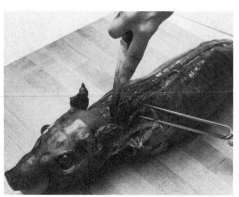

27 Cut behind the head from the backbone incision down under the chin.

28 Cut from the point where the foreleg was severed back to the tail.

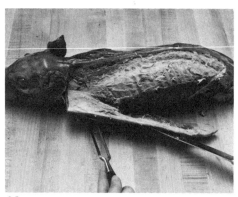

29 Lift off the loin, which is a thin layer of meat.

30 Cut off the belly, which is mostly skin.

31 Cut on either side of the ribs to remove a thin strip of meat between each rib.

32 Pull off the soft rib bones with your fingers.

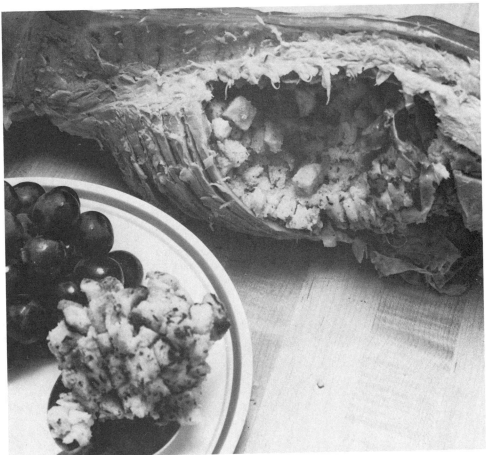

33 Spoon out the stuffing and serve with the carved legs, loin, belly, and rib meat.

VEAL

Cut pocket in breast and stuff

A relatively inexpensive cut of veal can be enhanced by any number of stuffings. Don't use a bread stuffing, however, because it will expand too much in the pocket. Leave the bones in the breast to flavor the roast, which should be braised.

1 Place the breast bone side down. With a boning knife, make a small incision in the widest side of the breast right next to the bone.

2 Hold the meat with one hand and push your knife all the way in along the bone.

Cut pocket in breast and stuff, continued

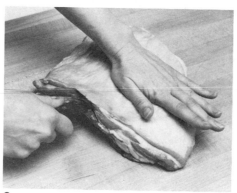

3 Keeping your knife next to the bone, carefully move the blade to the right with an arc motion.

4 Turn the knife over and cut to the left.

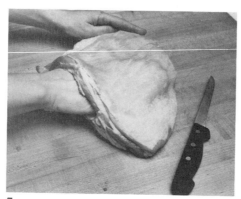

5 Put your hand in the pocket and use your fingers to loosen the meat further.

6 Lift the top flap and loosely stuff the pocket. I'm using a mixture of rice, prosciutto, chopped vegetables, and herbs.

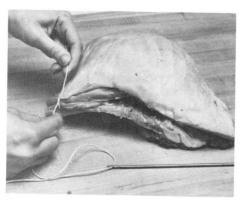

7 With a trussing needle and string, make a stitch in the boniest end of the veal and tie it.

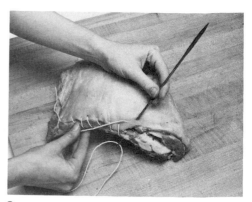

8 Sew the length of the pocket using an overhand stitch.

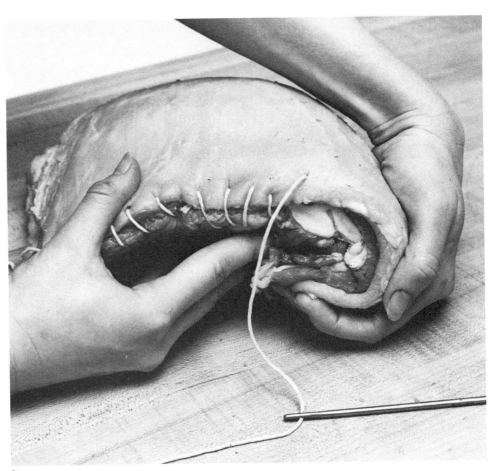

9 Turn the rounded meaty end under.

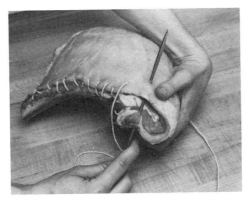

10 Sew through the two thicknesses of veal.

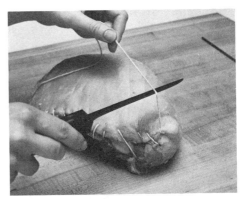

11 Tie a knot at the end. Cook according to recipe directions.

Bone loin and roll with the fillet

This is an extremely luxurious and elegant roast that should be reserved for your most discriminating friends. The loin has a T-shaped bone with a fillet on one side and the loin on the other.

1 Place the loin meaty side down. With your boning knife, cut down along the edge of the fillet following the chine bone.

2 Pull the meat toward you and release the fillet all along the chine bone.

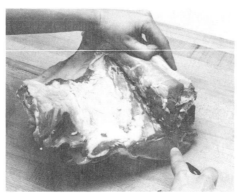

3 The fillet is attached by a membrane to the meat beneath it. Follow that membrane with your boning knife to release the fillet.

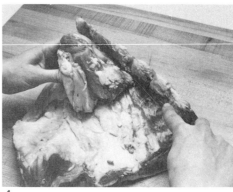

4 Use your fingers and your knife to pull the fillet out.

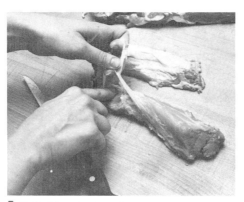

5 Pull off any fat from the fillet. A sinewy chain of meat that runs along the fillet can be pulled off with your fingers.

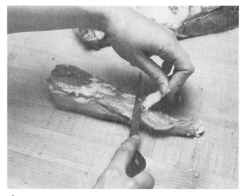

6 Lift up the tendon on the fillet, scrape it from the flesh with your knife, and remove.

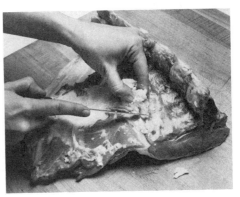

7 Scrape the meat off the sinewy chain, which has a large membrane running through it, and reserve.

8 Remove the fat from the bone side of the loin so you can see the bone structure underneath.

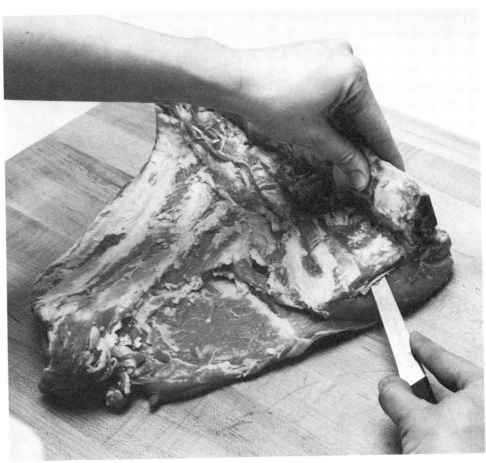

9 Cut under the end of the T-bone to loosen it. Keep your knife next to the bone so that you do not cut into the flesh.

Bone loin and roll with the fillet, continued

10 Cut down just to the flesh between each rib.

11 Starting at the rib ends, carefully work your knife under each rib while lifting up on it.

12 When the rib is released from the flesh, pull it back over the chine bone and twist it off. Repeat with the other ribs, three in all.

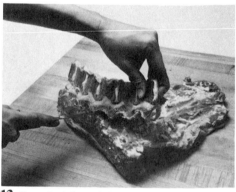

13 Turn the loin and follow with your knife under the bumpy vertebrae to loosen the chine bone.

14 Turn the loin around and, from the opposite side, continue to cut under the chine bone to release it.

15 Trim off any remaining fat and sinews from the loin.

16 Turn the loin over and cut off the layer of fat.

17 Under the fat is a membrane that should be removed. Pull it up and scrape it from the flesh in small pieces.

18 Keep scraping off the membrane, which is tedious but necessary because the membrane will not break down in the cooking.

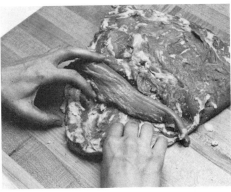

19 Place the fillet and any scraps of meat from the sinewy chain on the thin end of the loin.

20 Roll the thin flap of meat over the fillet.

21 Roll into a compact roast.

Bone loin and roll with the fillet, continued

22 Tie the roast once lengthwise. Then make ties at two-inch intervals along the length of the roast. It can then be roasted or braised.

VARIETY MEATS

Clean and precook brains

Brains, which come in pairs, have the most delicate texture and flavor of all the variety meats. Calf's brains are the most desirable. They are always simmered briefly to firm the texture before further cooking.

1 Soak the brains in cold water for several hours, changing the water frequently to remove any blood. Drain and carefully pick over the brains to remove any membranes and fibers.

2 Put the brains in cold water with vinegar and seasonings. Bring to a boil, then lower the flame and simmer for a few minutes.

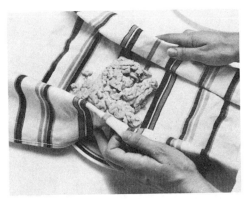

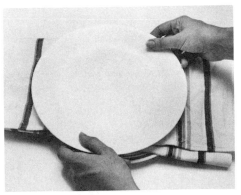

3 Drain and put the brains on a kitchen towel on a plate.

4 Cover with the towel and put another plate on top to firm the meat. Refrigerate until ready to cook as desired.

Trim kidney

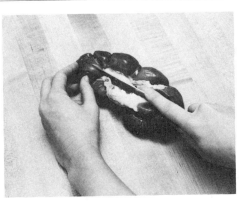

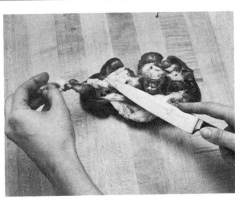

1 Cut through the kidney lengthwise to the core.

2 Pull and cut out the hard core of fat in the center.

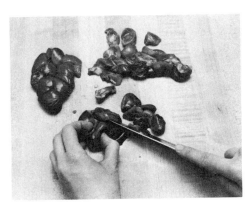

3 The kidney can be broiled whole.

4 Or it can be sliced.

Trim and slice liver

If you buy a whole calf's liver, you can trim and bake it whole, or slice it to the thickness you prefer. Uncooked liver can be frozen, but its texture will not be as good as when it is fresh.

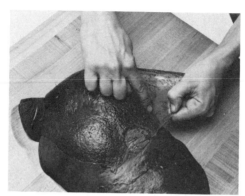

1 With your fingers, pull off the thin skin that covers the liver.

2 Put the liver in the freezer for about ten minutes to make it firm. Hold the end with one hand and slice at a slight angle. A sharp knife should glide through; don't push down.

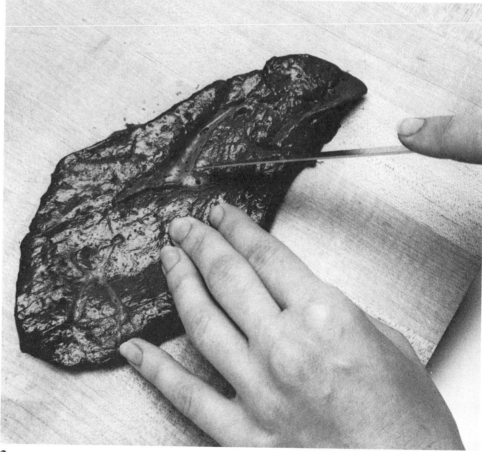

3 Remove any veins and arteries from each slice using a sharp knife.

Pick over chicken livers

Pull and cut off any veins and connective tissue in the livers.

Trim and weight sweetbreads

Sweetbreads are the thymus gland of the calf and occasionally lamb. Like brains, they are always simmered briefly before further cooking. Acidulated water is used to whiten them. They should then be weighted to give them a firmer texture.

1 Soak the sweetbreads in cold water for an hour, changing the water frequently to get rid of any blood.

2 Simmer the sweetbreads in water and lemon juice for fifteen minutes and rinse under cold running water to stop the cooking. Carefully pull off any membranes and tendons.

Trim and weight
sweetbreads, continued

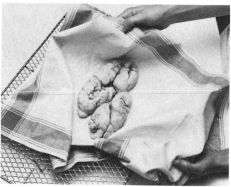

3 Put the sweetbreads on a kitchen towel on a cake rack and cover with the towel.

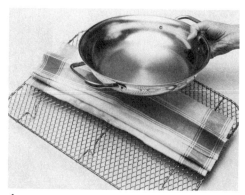

4 Weight the meat with a heavy pan and refrigerate for several hours until ready to cook.

Peel, trim, and slice
tongue

It is easier to peel tongue after it has been partly or fully cooked, depending on the recipe.

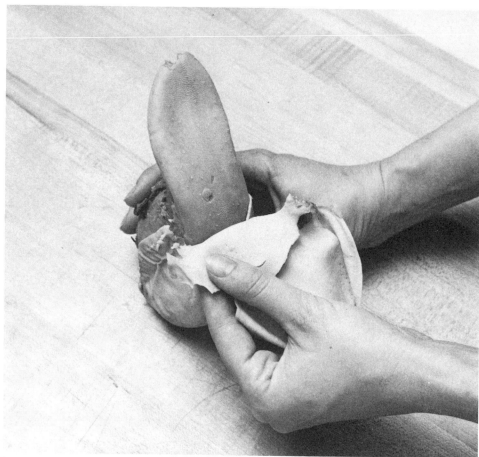

1 Make a small incision at the tip of the tongue and peel off the skin like a glove.

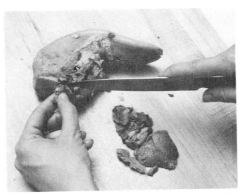 

2 Trim off rootends and any small bones at the base of the tongue.

3 Thinly slice the tongue at a slight angle.

3
POULTRY

GENERAL

Clean and season cavity

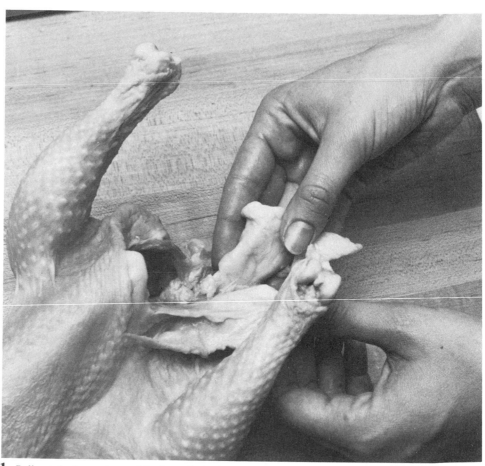

1 Pull out the large pieces of fat from the body cavity and discard. Check to be sure the red spongy lungs have been removed.

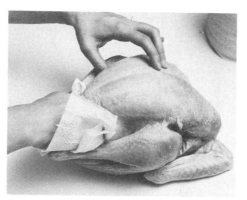

2 Wipe the outside and the body and neck cavities with damp paper towels.

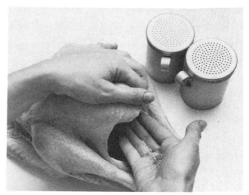

3 Rub the body cavity with salt and pepper. Sprinkle with herbs if desired.

Cut off wings

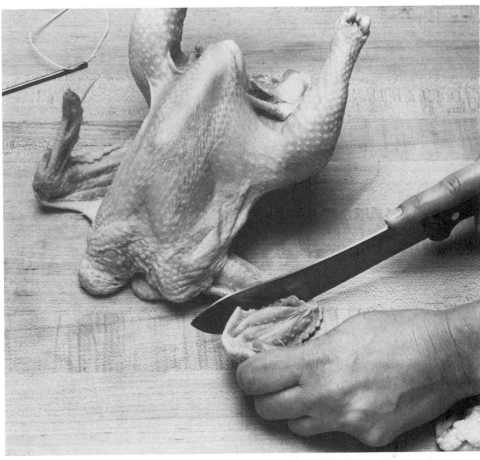

To make it easier to truss the bird and to show off the breast to advantage, cut off wings at the second joint. The one exception is turkey, which has meaty wings.

Remove wishbone

Removing the wishbone facilitates carving a roasted fowl. Otherwise, the wishbone stops your knife when slicing the breast.

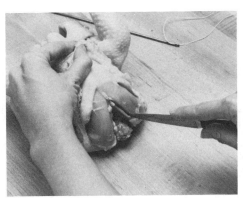

1 Open the neck to expose the wishbone. Cut in behind it using the tip of a sharp knife.

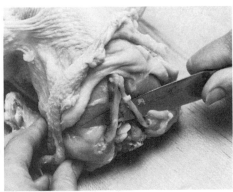

2 Insert the knife behind the wishbone and cut down, freeing it at the bottom.

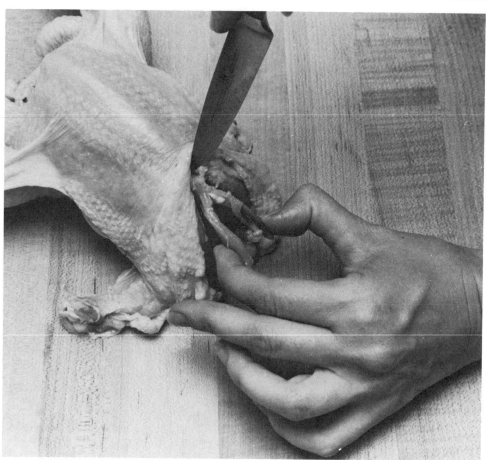

3 If necessary, release the wishbone at the top with your knife. Remove the bone.

Stuff under skin

This is a good way to distribute the flavor of a stuffing throughout the bird as it is next to the meat.

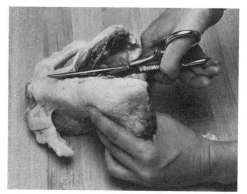

1 Cut off wings at second joint and remove wishbone. Turn the bird on its breast and, with heavy poultry shears, cut through the center of the backbone. You want the skin to stay attached because it looks neater.

2 Turn over (skin side up) and press down with the heel of your hand to break the breastbone and flatten the bird.

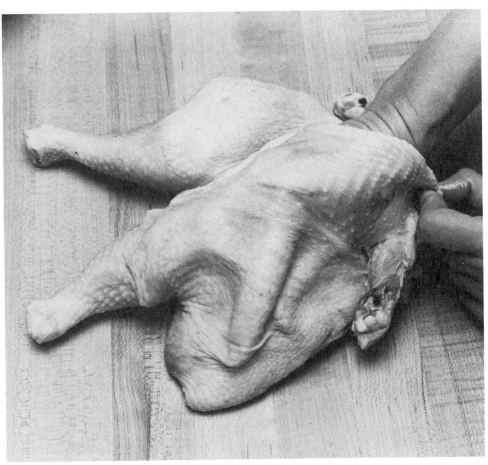

3 Lift the skin at the neck opening and very carefully separate it from the meat by inserting your fingers. Move your fingers all over the body and down into the legs without breaking the skin.

4 Take a handful of stuffing and push it all the way under the skin so it is evenly distributed. Cover the entire area where the skin is separated from the meat.

5 Cut a small incision in the thin skin next to each thigh.

Stuff under skin, continued

6 Turn the bird over and insert each drumstick through its opening, pulling the skin up over each leg.

7 Push the bird together to reshape it.

Stuff cavities and skewer closed

Stuffing expands as it cooks so don't pack it in too tight. You will get a doughlike texture if you do. I like to use two different kinds of stuffing—one in the body cavity and another in the neck.

1 Hold the bird up by the tail and spoon the stuffing into the body cavity. Shake it down but keep it loosely packed.

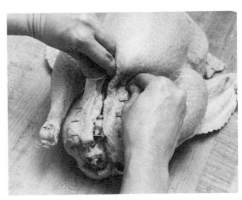

2 Put the bird on its back and fold the tail into the cavity.

3 Push several skewers through from one side of the cavity to the other to close it all the way. Keep the tail inside.

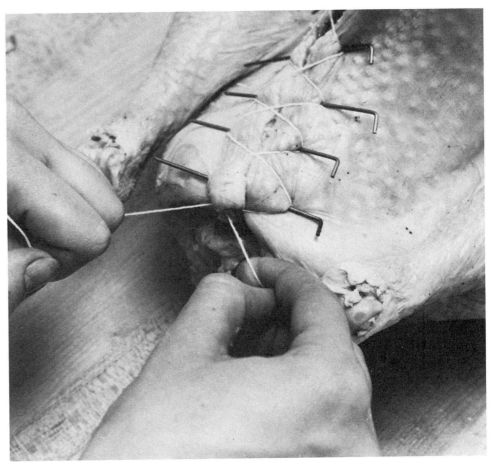

4 Lace trussing string diagonally around the skewers from one side to the other and tie firmly.

Stuff cavities, continued

5 Turn the bird on its breast and put a small amount of stuffing into the neck cavity.

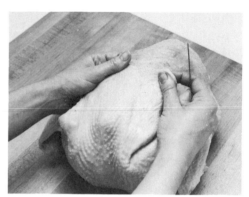

6 Pull the neck skin up over the back.

7 Skewer the neck skin to the backbone.

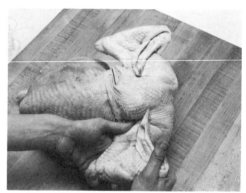

8 Turn the wings under the back, if it is a turkey, and truss the bird with a large needle.

Truss with needle

This method produces a good looking, evenly cooked bird.

1 Thread a long trussing needle with a length of string. Push the legs forward toward the neck and push the needle through the first joint, the body, and out through the corresponding joint on the other side.

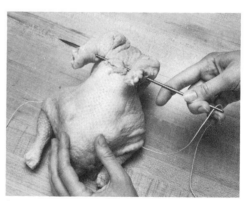

2 Turn the bird breast side down. Pull neck skin over the cavity and hold the wings up. Insert the needle under the bone in one wing, through neck skin and a little of the body, and out through the other wing.

3 Turn the bird on its side and tie the two ends of string firmly but not too tight. The bird will swell slightly during cooking.

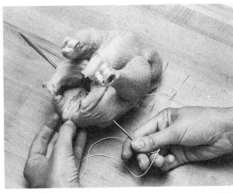

4 Push the tail into the cavity. Thread the needle with another length of string and insert it at the thigh joint. Push the needle through the body cavity, pinning the tail down, and out the other side.

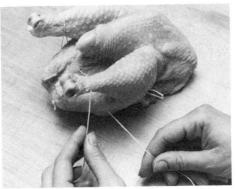

5 Loop the string around the end of one drumstick, push the needle back through the tail skin, and loop the string around the end of the other drumstick.

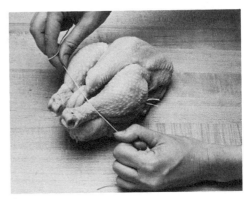

6 Tie the two ends firmly.

Truss with string only

This method can be used on all fowl but will not produce as compact a bird as trussing with a needle. However, it's better than nothing at all.

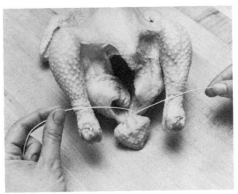

1 Remove the wishbone but leave the wings attached. Loop a length of string under the tail and cross it over on top.

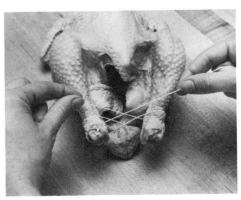

2 Loop string over and under each leg.

**Truss with string only,
continued**

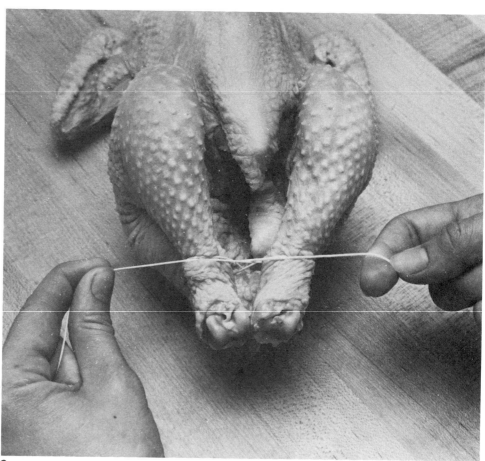

3 Pull legs tightly together. Leave one end of string free.

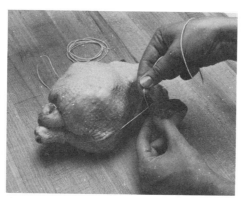

4 Turn the bird on its side and pull one end of string along the back and loop it around one wing.

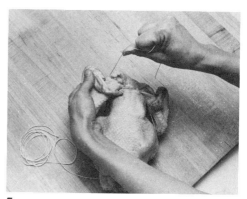

5 Turn the bird on its breast and pull the string across the neck flap and around the other wing.

6 Come around the other side and tie the two ends with even tension.

7 The bird is then ready to be cooked.

Arrange on spit

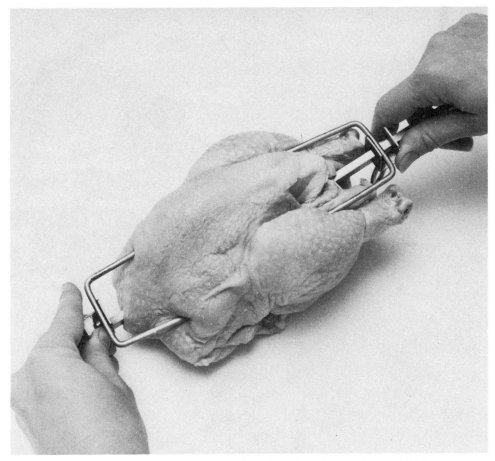

Truss the bird and put the skewer through the body cavity and out through the neck. Stick prongs into thighs at one end, into the breast at the other. Tighten to hold bird securely.

Brown whole bird

Poultry is browned to give it color and seal in the juices before it is braised. This is unlike cooking poultry for stock where you want the juices to be drawn out into the liquid.

1 Put the trussed bird in a large pan with hot oil or oil and butter. Brown on one side, holding the bird with wooden spatulas so as not to break the skin.

2 Turn with the spatulas and brown back, other side, then the breast.

3 The bird should be browned evenly all over before proceeding with further cooking.

Shred

This is a technique that is used for stir-fried Oriental dishes. The small pieces cook quickly and evenly.

1 Place a skinned and boned breast in the freezer for fifteen minutes just to firm it. Hold the meat flat with the palm of one hand and cut into thin slices, knife blade parallel to the board.

2 Keep the slices stacked and cut down through them into thin shreds.

Test for doneness

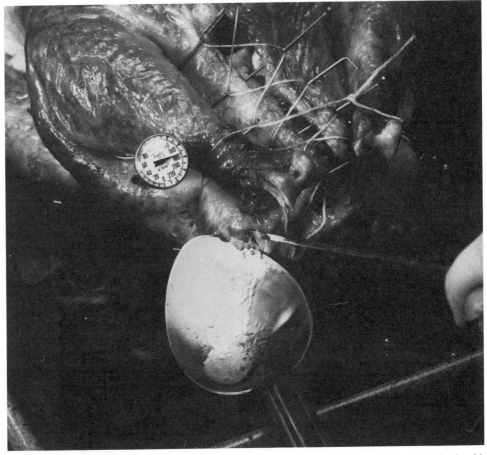

Insert an instant thermometer into the thickest part of the thigh without touching a bone. It should register 170 degrees when poultry is done. I also puncture the thickest part of the meat with a skewer to see if the juices run clear, not rosy.

CHICKEN

Disjoint

You save money and get the pieces you want if you disjoint a chicken yourself. It is a relatively simple technique to learn.

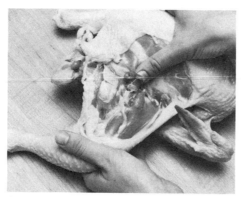

1 With the bird breast side up, slit the skin between the leg and the breast. Pull the leg away from the body to expose the ball and socket.

2 Using a sharp knife, cut through that joint to sever the leg and thigh. Repeat on the other side.

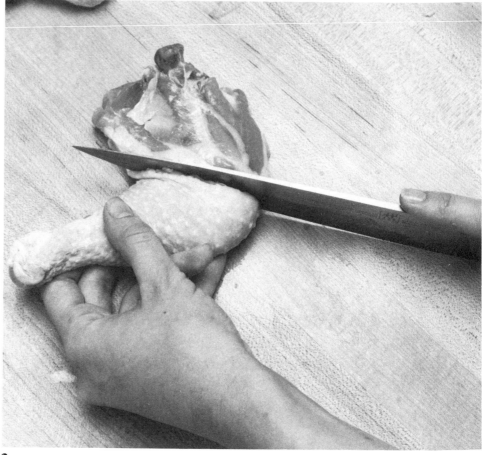

3 Divide the thigh from the leg by bending it (skin side down) to feel the joint. Cut through at that point.

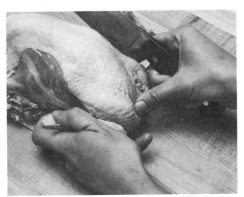

4 Press the wing against the body to find the shoulder ball and socket.

5 Cut through at that point, taking a small piece of breast with the wing. Repeat on the other side.

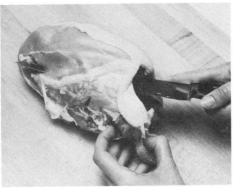

6 Insert your knife through the body cavity and pierce the thin area on one side between the shoulder joint and the rib cage. Cut toward you, parallel to the backbone. Repeat on the other side.

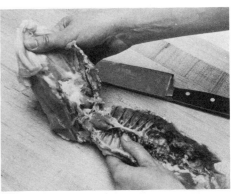

7 Push the breast away from you, separating it from the back.

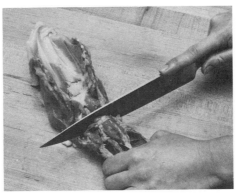

8 Cut through between the breast and the back. Use the backbone for stock.

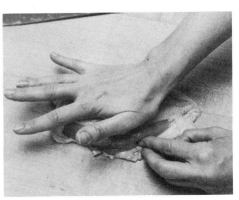

9 Flatten the breast, skin side up, by pressing with the heel of your hand.

Disjoint, continued

10 Turn the breast skin side down. Using steady pressure, cut through the center of the breastbone and slice the breast in two.

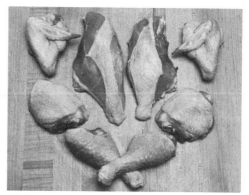

11 You will have two wings, two thighs, two legs, and two breast pieces.

Split for broiling

By removing the backbone and the breastbone, the bird can be flattened so that all surfaces will be evenly exposed to the flame. You will need a heavy chef's knife and a boning knife.

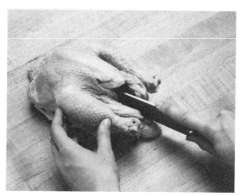

1 Remove wings at second joint. Place the bird on its back and insert a heavy sharp knife in the body cavity. Cut along one side of the backbone and sever it at the hip joint.

2 Open up the bird and cut along the other side of the backbone to free it.

3 Cut through the white membrane on either side of the breastbone.

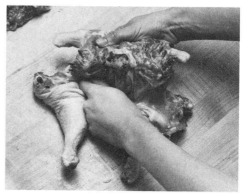

4 Turn the bird around and grasp the top of the breast in each hand. Bend the breastbone until it snaps.

5 Pull out the breastbone and cartilage.

6 Cut the chicken into halves.

7 Using a boning knife, make a small incision in the thick flesh where the thigh meets the drumstick. This helps to flatten the bird so it will cook evenly.

Split for broiling, continued

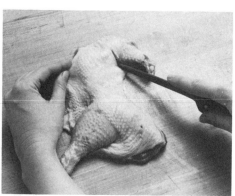

8 Turn the bird over. Cut the tendon at the joint of the wing and the shoulder, which keeps the wing from sticking out and burning.

9 You can broil or grill the halves or cut them into quarters.

Bone breast

Boning a breast is a simple procedure and one that will save you money after the initial investment in a good quality boning knife.

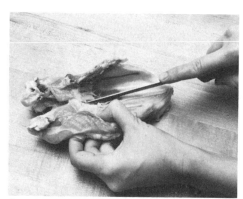

1 Put the breast skin side down and slit the membrane that covers the breastbone.

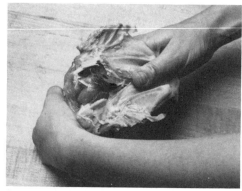

2 Bend the breast away from you to break the bone and cartilage.

3 Remove the breastbone with your fingers.

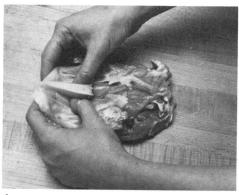

4 Push with your thumbs on either side of the remainder of the breastbone.

5 Pull it off.

6 Cut under the ribs on either side of the breast and remove. Be careful not to pierce the flesh.

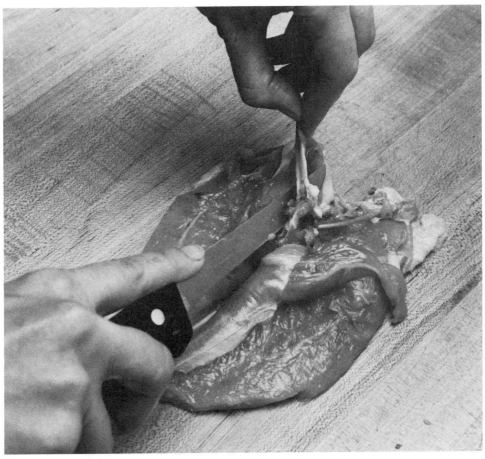

7 Pull up the wishbone and cut through it to remove.

Bone breast, continued

8 Turn the breast and cut off the membrane that runs up the middle. Do this very carefully because this is the thinnest part of the breast.

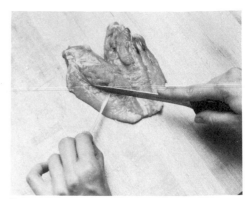

9 Remove the large tendon from the fillets by grasping one end and pulling it toward you. Gently scrape it away from the flesh with your knife.

Stuff breast I

I prefer the second method of stuffing breasts because I think it is pretty. But guests seem to like the surprise element in the first and assume it is difficult to do, which is isn't.

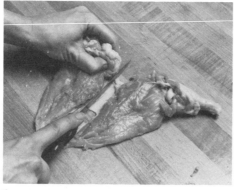

1 Disjoint a chicken but leave the wings attached to the breast. Bone the breast and cut off the wings at the second joint. Cut the breast into halves.

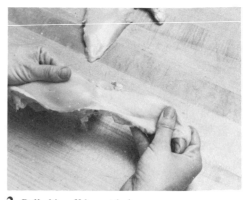

2 Pull skin off breast halves.

3 Remove the tendon from the fillet by pulling it up and carefully scraping it off with your boning knife.

4 Scrape the meat back from the end of the wingbone. This is only for aesthetics.

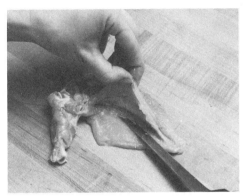 

5 Cut a pocket in the breast, being careful not to cut all the way through.

6 Stuff the pocket (I'm using herbed butter that was frozen to the desired shape) and close with the flap.

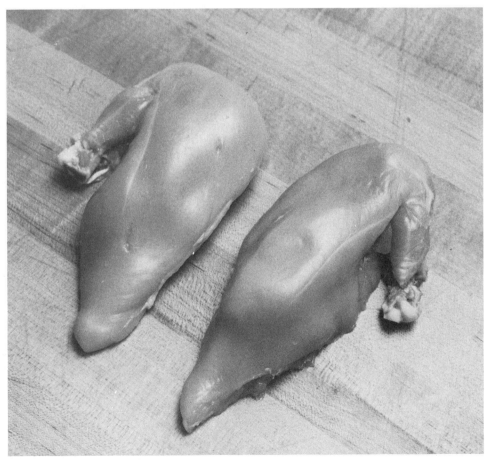

7 The stuffed breasts do not need to be tied because the chicken flaps will stick together when chilled before cooking.

Stuff breast II

1 Cut a boned and skinned chicken breast in two and pound it between pieces of plastic wrap. Start at the center and move out toward the edges to thin the breast evenly.

2 Place filling (I'm using ham and steamed asparagus tips) at one end on the rougher side of the breast and roll.

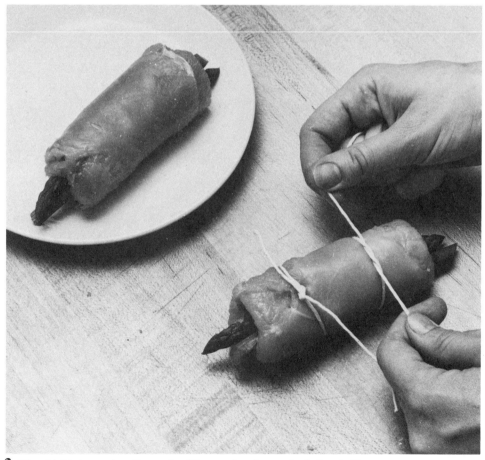

3 Tie with kitchen twine. Brown the fillets to give them color before baking.

TURKEY

Carve

This is an attractive way to carve a turkey (stuffed or not) for a buffet because you can slice the breast, put the slices back in place, and re-cover with the skin. It is also good for the holiday bird; slice only part of the breast and then cover with the skin to keep the remainder moist. Always carve only one side of the bird at a time so it won't dry out.

1 With a sharp knife make a shallow incision just through the skin down the length of the breast.

2 Cut through the skin around the side of the breast.

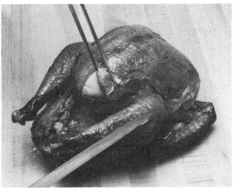

3 Hook your carving fork into the skin at the tail end.

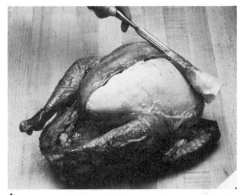

4 Using the fork, roll the skin all the way back to the neck.

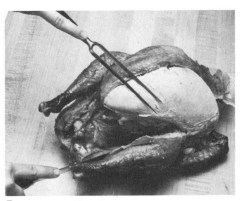

5 Hold the bird steady with your fork and cut off the leg and thigh.

6 Cut through the ball and socket that joins the leg to the thigh.

Carve, continued

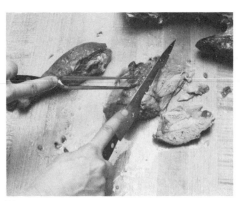 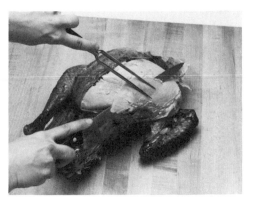

7 Slice the meat off the thigh.

8 Cut thin slices of meat off the side of the breast.

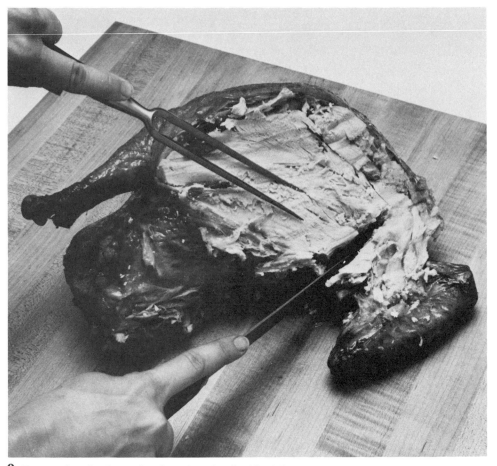

9 Remove the wing by cutting through at the shoulder joint.

Fillet breast

Turkey can masquerade as veal in many recipes calling for scaloppine. It will obviously save money if you bone and fillet a breast of turkey yourself.

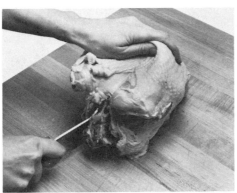

1 Insert a sharp knife into the neck opening and cut down on either side of the backbone.

2 Remove the backbone.

3 Turn the breast over and slit the membrane that runs down the length of the breast.

4 Cut through the bones at the top of the breast, up around the wishbone.

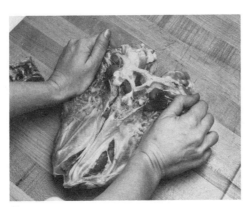

5 Push down on either side of the breast with your hands to flatten it.

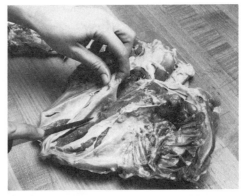

6 With a boning knife, cut down on either side of the breastbone to loosen it. It is much deeper than the bone in a chicken breast.

Fillet breast, continued

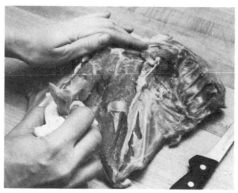

7 Pull up on the breastbone to remove it. Hold it with a paper towel because it is very sharp.

8 Lift up and cut next to the rib bones.

9 Detach the rib bones at the shoulder blade. Repeat on the other side.

10 Remove the portion of the wishbone that is still in the breast.

11 Remove the small fillets from either side of the breast by lifting them up with one hand and running the fingers of the other up and down the length of the fillet.

12 Butterfly each small fillet by cutting through the center, blade parallel to the board. Do not cut all the way through.

13 Open up the fillet and cut out the tendon by pulling up on it with one hand and carefully scraping it off the flesh with a boning knife.

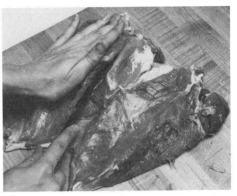

14 Push down on the breast meat with one hand and, with blade parallel to the board, start to cut off a thin slice.

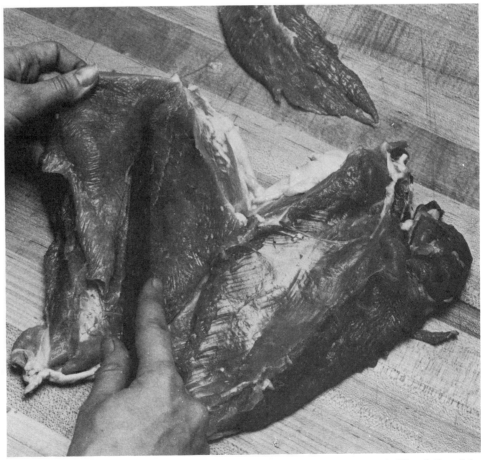

15 Open out the slice and cut through to detach it. Continue until the entire breast is filleted. Pound the turkey slices and the small fillets between pieces of plastic wrap.

Bone and stuff for galantine

A galantine is a very elegant pâté in which ground meats and seasonings are rolled in duck skin and poached. Obviously, boning the duck is time-consuming but well worth the effort because a galantine is a sensational buffet dish or first course. And it is all made ahead and refrigerated.

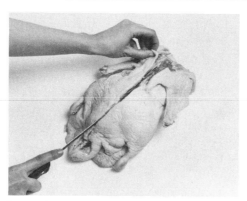

1 Cut off wings at second joint and remove wishbone. Put the duck breast side down and, with a boning knife, cut through the skin all the way down the middle of the backbone.

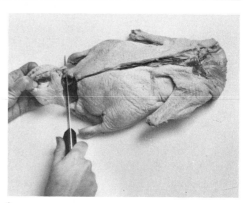

2 Cut off the tail.

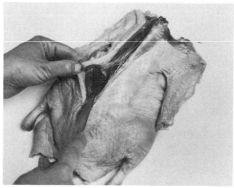

3 Stay close to the backbone and loosen the flesh partway down with your knife. When you come to a small oyster-shaped piece of meat, cut around it next to the backbone, leaving the oyster attached to the skin.

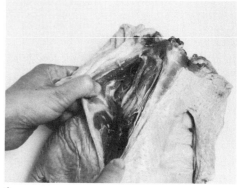

4 Start at the shoulder and cut next to the rib cage down to the oyster-shaped piece of meat to loosen the flesh from the carcass.

5 Pull out the wing. To the right of the knife is the shoulder blade bone. Keep that bone to your right and cut through the ball joint that connects the wing to the shoulder.

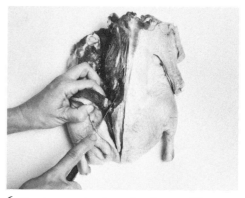

6 Continue cutting down the rib cage. When you get just below where you cut around the oyster of meat, sever the ball joint between the thigh and the hip with the point of your knife.

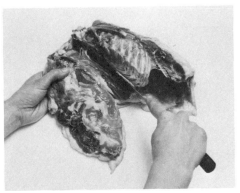 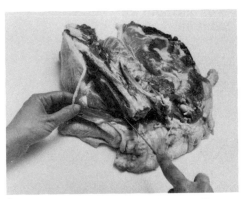

7 Cut under the rib cage just until you reach the breastbone. Don't try to detach it because the skin is very thin there.

8 Turn the bird with neck facing you. Repeat steps 3 through 7.

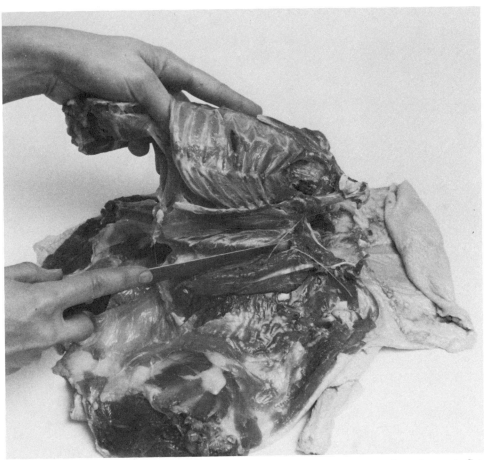

9 After both sides are loosened, lift up the carcass and cut the breastbone away from the meat. Cut through the cartilage, leaving some attached to the flesh. It is easier to remove it later without piercing the skin.

Bone and stuff for galantine, continued

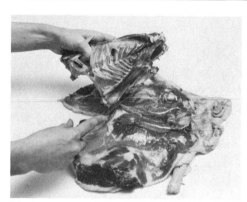

10 Cut off and remove the whole carcass.

11 Put a paper towel under the wing so it won't slip and put the wing bone on end with the tip up. Cut around the tip to loosen the skin from the bone.

12 Holding the tip, start to scrape the skin and flesh from the bone.

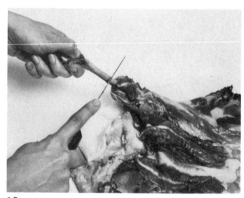

13 Pull up on the bone and continue to scrape and loosen the flesh. The skin will be turned inside out.

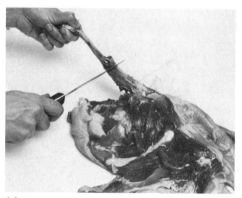

14 Cut off the skin around the knobby end of the bone and pull the bone out. It will have a piece of skin on the knob. Repeat the process with the other wing bone.

15 Go down to the thigh and cut through the flesh covering the thigh bone.

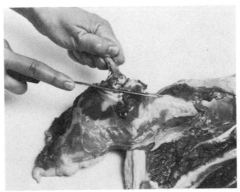

16 Carefully scrape and pull up on the thigh bone as you did with the wings. Cut through the ball joint between the thigh and the drumstick and remove the thigh bone. Repeat the process with the other thigh bone.

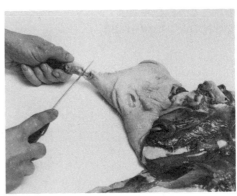

17 With skin side out, cut around the end of the leg bone to loosen the skin.

18 Chop off the knobby tip with a cleaver.

19 Grasp the knobby end of the leg bone from inside and scrape and lift up on the bone. It pulls out easily because the knob was chopped off the other end. The meat will be inside out. Repeat with the other leg.

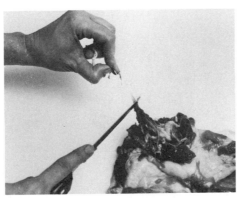

20 While the leg meat is inside out, pull off as many tendons and sinews as possible.

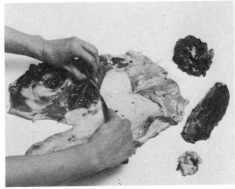

21 Use the tip of your knife and your fingers to remove breast and all possible meat from the skin. Set aside for the stuffing. Do this very carefully so you do not pierce the skin.

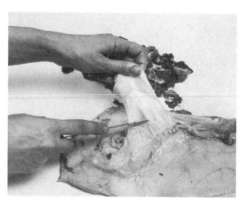

22 Pull and scrape off as much fat as possible without piercing the skin.

23 Scrape the meat off all sinews and discard the sinews. This is time-consuming but important because the sinews will not break down in the poaching.

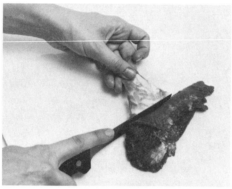

24 Remove the membrane from the breast meat.

25 Chop the duck liver into tiny pieces for the stuffing.

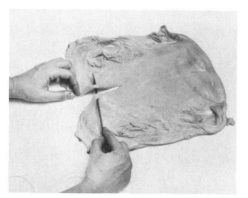

26 Turn the duck skin side up so stitches will be on the outside and easily removed. Using a trussing needle and soft string, sew about two inches of the tail together.

27 Turn the skin over on a clean dish towel that has been rinsed in water and wrung out.

28 Pull up the leg skin that is inside out and fold it to cover a hole, if there is one. Do the same with the wing skin. Trim skin at neck and tail ends and use it to patch any other holes.

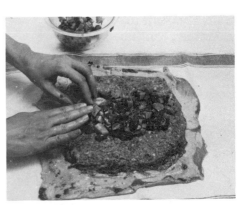

29 Pat a rectangle of stuffing inside the duck skin to within an inch and one-half of the edge. Top with a smaller rectangle of chopped meats (including the liver) and pistachio nuts.

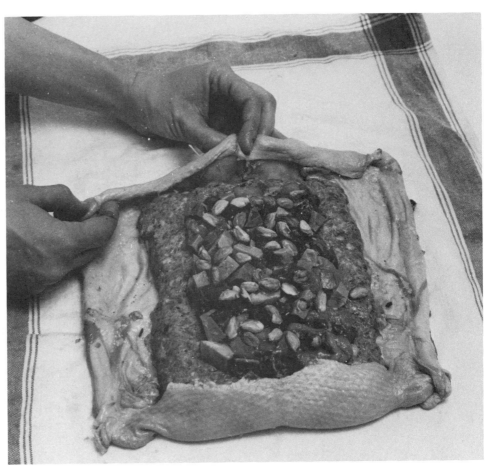

30 Fold up the edges of the skin and trim off excess. The skin should be just long enough to cover the edges of the stuffing.

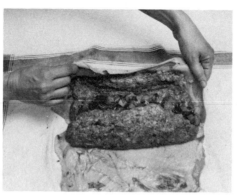

31 Very carefully lift one end of the duck skin and fold the stuffing over the chopped meats. Bring the skin back and do the same with the other side.

32 Moisten your fingers and pat the stuffing into a loaf shape.

33 Fold the neck and tail skin over the stuffing.

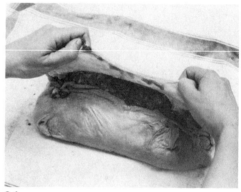

34 Fold the long sides of the skin over the stuffing.

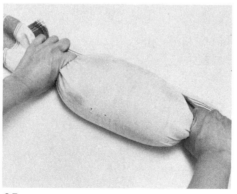

35 Roll the galantine tightly in the dish towel and twist the ends.

36 Tie the ends and tie the galantine in several places along its length. Don't tie it too tight or it will bulge.

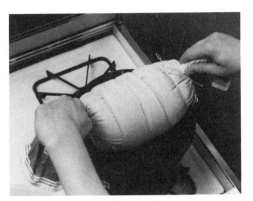

37 Lower the galantine into boiling stock in a heavy pot just large enough to hold it. Simmer about an hour and a half.

38 Remove the galantine and put it in a colander to drain. It will have shrunk from the towel.

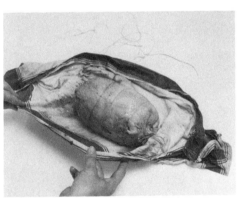

39 Untie the galantine and rinse out the towel.

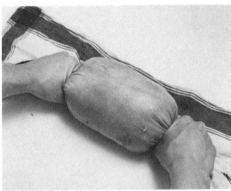

40 Rewrap the duck tightly in the towel to keep it compact and refrigerate for twenty-four hours. The galantine can then be sliced and served like pâté.

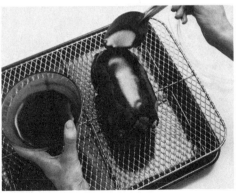

41 For a more elegant presentation, unwrap the galantine after refrigeration and place it on a rack over a roasting pan. Spoon a thin coating of brown chaudfroid sauce (or aspic) over it. The sauce should have an oily consistency.

42 Let each layer cool and spoon another layer over, turning the galantine so it is evenly coated. Strain the sauce that drops into the pan and reuse it. See color photograph of finished galantine.

Stuff for dodine

I prefer a dodine to a galantine because it is more fanciful, but the principle is the same. With a dodine (sometimes called a bal-lotine), the meat and legs are left on the skin and the stuffed duck is roasted rather than poached. It is good either hot or cold.

1 Follow the instructions for boning a duck for galantine through step 14. Put the skin in a bowl and season the meat. I'm using thyme, allspice, salt, pepper, bay leaf, brandy, and Madeira.

2 Fold the skin over the meat and refrigerate for twenty-four hours.

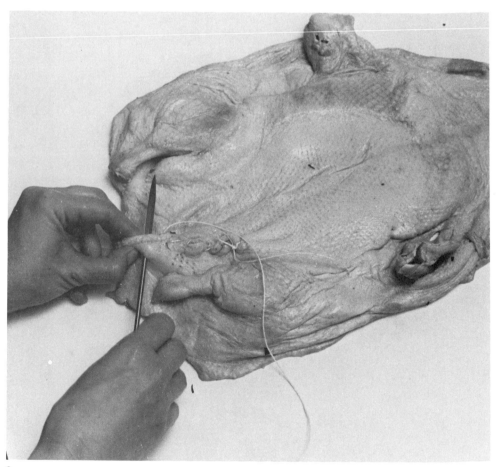

3 Sew the tail cavity skin side up with a trussing needle. I use an overhand stitch so that the string can be pulled out in one piece.

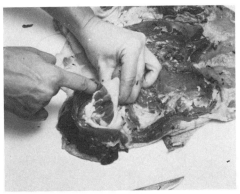

4 Turn the duck skin side down and patch any holes with excess neck skin. There may be a hole where the wing was removed.

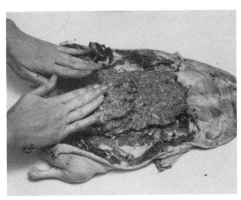

5 Moisten your hands and pat half the stuffing onto the duck.

6 Top with strips of meat (you can take off some of the breast meat from the duck for this, but don't remove it all).

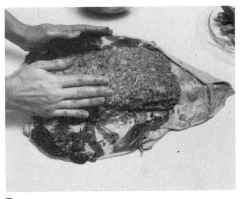

7 Cover with the rest of the stuffing.

8 Push stuffing into the thigh cavities.

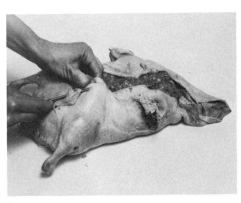

9 Sew up the length of the duck with an overhand stitch.

**Stuff for dodine,
continued**

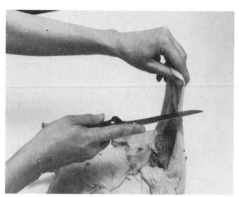

10 Pull up the neck skin and cut off excess.

11 Sew the neck skin to the body.

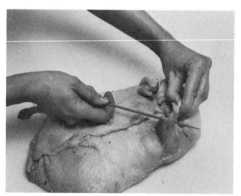

12 Put the needle through the wings.

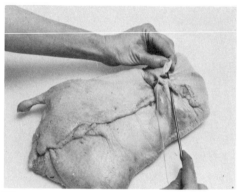

13 And sew them together. This closes up the bird and gives the breast a realistic look.

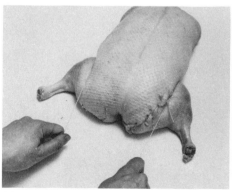

14 Turn the bird over and put string under and up over the thighs.

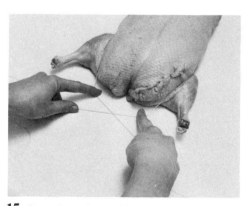

15 Cross the string and loop it under the legs.

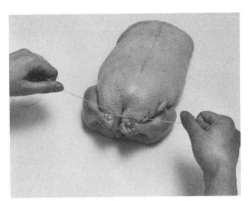

16 Pull and tie the legs up into a realistic shape.

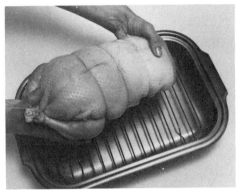

17 Tie around the duck in several places to lengthen it and make it compact. Place it on a rack in a roasting pan.

18 Prick the skin with the trussing needle along the lower part of the thigh and the breast where there is the most fat.

19 Bake in a 375-degree oven for fifteen minutes, then at 350 degrees for one and one-half hours. Prick the skin in the thigh to see if the juices run clear. If they are at all rosy, cook longer. See color photograph of cooked dodine.

Prepare for Peking duck

A crisp brown skin is the goal for this Chinese specialty. Inflating the duck gets air between the skin and the flesh, which makes it easier to slice the skin. Choose a duck with a long neck and as small a neck and tail opening as possible. We used a Long Island duckling bought in a Chinese market, which comes with the head partly severed. You can slit the neck yourself by making an incision just large enough to insert two fingers so that you can loosen the skin.

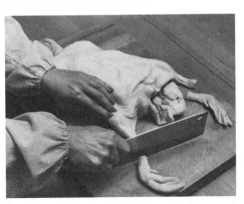

1 With a cleaver, chop off feet at the bottom of the drumstick and discard.

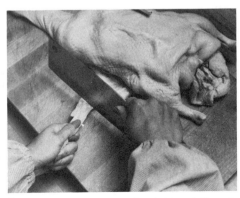

2 Cut off wing tips at the first joint and discard.

Prepare for Peking duck, continued

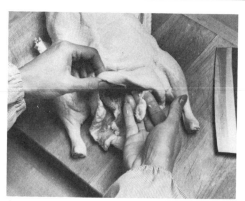

3 Remove excess fat from the body cavity and discard.

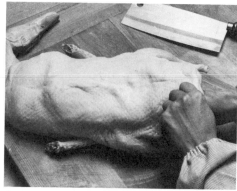

4 Through the tail end, very carefully run your fingers between the skin and meat to loosen the skin all over the body.

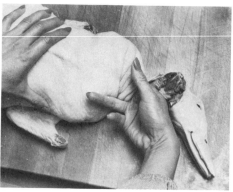

5 Insert your fingers into the neck opening and loosen the skin all the way down to the wings and over the breast.

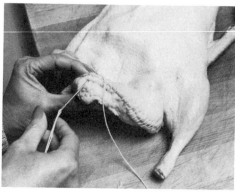

6 With a darning needle and fine string, sew across the tail cavity with very fine stitches.

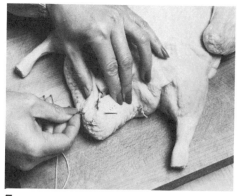

7 Turn the duck over and sew the tail opening where the oil sac was removed if the duck was purchased in a Chinese market. There can't be any holes where air will escape.

8 Insert a flexible straw down into the neck between the skin and the meat and pull the skin tightly around it.

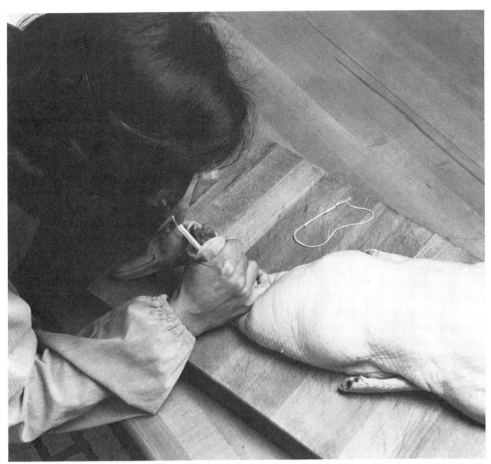

9 Inflate the duck by blowing through the straw. If there are any leaks, sew the skin and inflate the duck again.

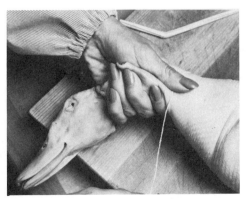

10 Hold the neck skin tight like a balloon.

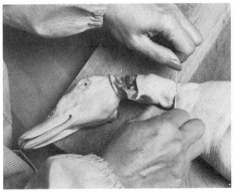

11 Tie the neck so no air escapes.

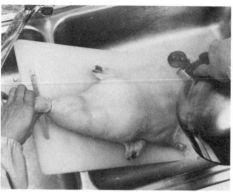

12 Place the inflated duck breast side up on a cutting board in the sink. Pour boiling water over it, turn, and repeat on the back. This seals the skin and makes it taut.

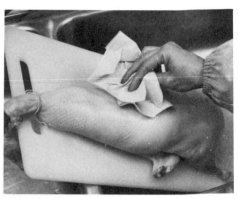

13 Wipe off any moisture with paper towels.

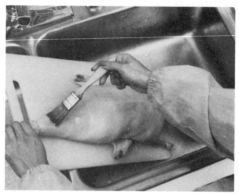

14 Brush the duck with a mixture of one-half cup red wine vinegar, four tablespoons honey, and one cup water.

15 Lift the duck and make sure all sides are coated with the marinade.

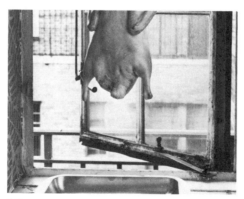

16 Hang the duck by the neck in a cool, well-ventilated spot for six to eight hours. You want it to be thoroughly dry. Put a pan under it to catch any drippings.

17 Put duck breast side down on a rack in a roasting pan. Cook in the center of a 350-degree oven for fifteen minutes. Turn the duck on its back and roast one hour, or until the skin is mahogany brown. Do not baste.

18 Remove the duck and pierce the tail cavity so that fat and juices run out.

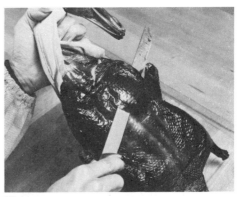

19 Hold the duck by the neck and slice off the crisp skin in pieces about two inches square. This must be done quickly or the duck will deflate and be difficult to carve.

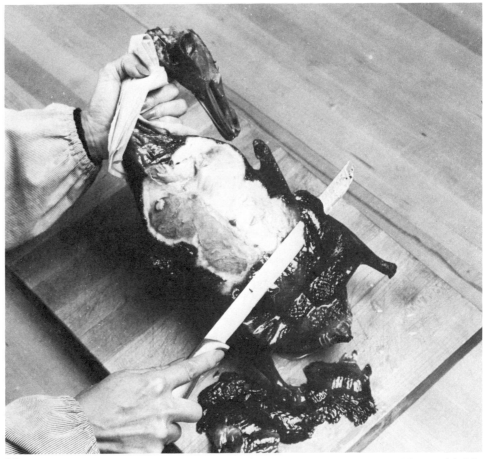

20 Continue to slice off all the skin, which is served on Chinese pancakes with scallions and hoisin sauce. The meat is sliced and served as a separate course in a Chinese meal.

GAME BIRDS

Hang

Game birds are hung to season them, increasing their flavor and tenderness. Hanging also makes plucking the bird easier. But it is not essential.

1 Cut a small incision at the anal opening of the bird.

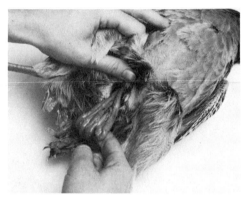

2 Reach in through the hole and hook your finger around the intestines. Pull out and discard because the intestines deteriorate quickly.

3 Tie a string around the neck and hang the bird in a cool spot—no warmer than 45 degrees—for three days to a week.

Pluck

Dry plucking is the best method, but if the feathers have set in, scald the bird to open the pores.

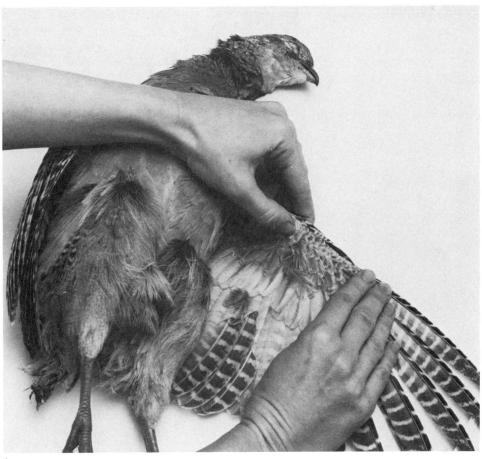

1 Find the joint of the wing tip by bending the feathers back.

2 Cut through and discard. This makes it easier to handle the bird while plucking it.

3 If the feathers do not pull out easily, heat water in a large pot to 180 degrees. It should not be boiling.

4 Immerse the bird and turn it in the water for about thirty seconds, just until water gets into all the feathers.

5 Start plucking the feathers from breast, pulling these out with your fingers in neat rows in the direction they grow.

6 Remove all the feathers from the rest of the body.

7 Remove the pinfeathers with a small sharp knife.

8 Hold the bird over a flame to singe off any down that's left.

Draw

A bird obviously must be eviscerated before cooking. The trick is to remove the organs without breaking them so that no bitter or toxic fluids run into the cavity.

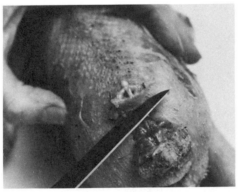

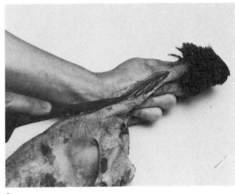

1 Using a sharp knife, cut out the triangular oil gland at the base of the tail. This is important with all wild fowl because it has a strong oily taste.

2 Hold the neck firmly and slit it down the back. Don't slit it down the front because you want the skin to fold over the neck opening.

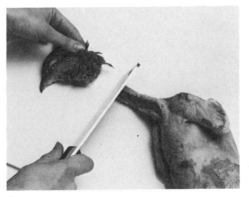

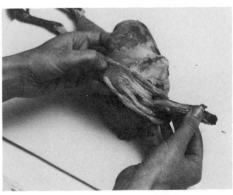

3 Cut off the head with a cleaver or other heavy knife.

4 Pull the neck down, separating it from the skin.

Draw, continued

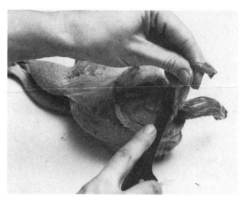

5 Pull up and cut off the esophagus.

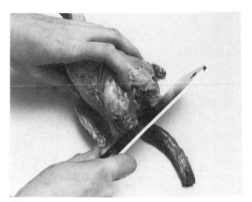

6 Cut off the neck close to the body.

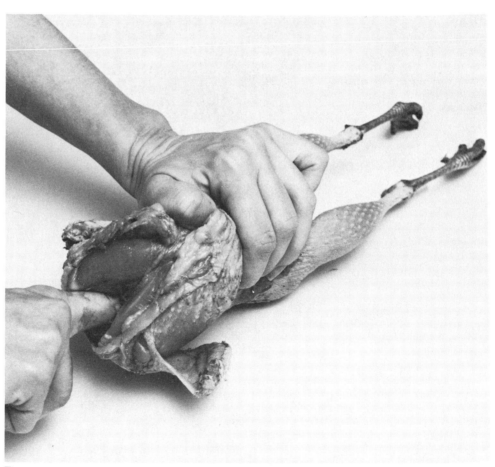

7 Put your finger inside the neck opening and run it all around the perimeter to loosen the lungs.

8 Do the same thing around the perimeter of the body cavity to loosen all the organs.

9 Reach in and very carefully pull out all the organs in one piece. Wipe the inside of the bird with a damp towel.

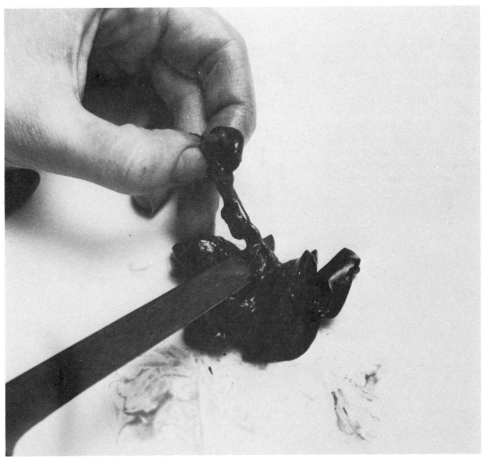

10 Cut the gallbladder, which is a small round gland, away from the liver and discard. If it has broken, the bird should be thoroughly rinsed out and the liver discarded because it will be bitter.

Draw, continued

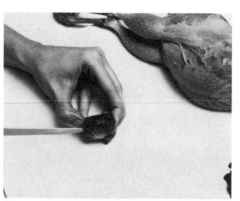

11 Cut into the fleshy side of the gizzard until you reach a white, paperlike pouch.

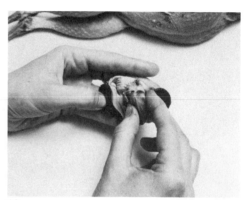

12 Pull out the pouch and discard, saving the gizzard. The pouch contains pebbles and other debris the bird has swallowed.

Bard

Many game birds tend to be lean and should be covered with a thin layer of fatback to keep them moist and give flavor. (Thin leaves of fatback are called bardes in French.) The feet are often left on the game bird because they indicate its age. Big spurs (the bony growth on the leg) mean that the bird is old and should be braised, not roasted.

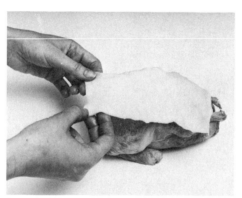

1 Place a layer of fatback over the trussed bird so that breast and legs are evenly covered.

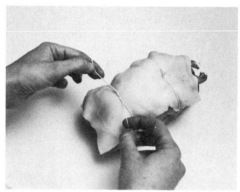

2 Tie in two or three places, depending on the size of the bird.

4
FISH
AND SHELLFISH

GENERAL

Recognize a fresh fish

There are several things to look for when buying fish, one of which is impossible to photograph. A fresh fish has a sweet clean smell—definitely not a strong odor.

1 Look at the eyes. They should bulge slightly and be bright and clear. If the eyes are cloudy and sunken, do not buy the fish. Also, the scales should be shiny and tight against the skin.

2 Look into the gill, the flap just behind the head. It should have a rosy red color.

Scale

A fish knife has a blade that is serrated on one side for scaling. The other side is an all-purpose blade. But you can do an acceptable job of scaling with the back of a short-bladed kitchen knife. It will be easier if you dip the fish in cold water before scaling.

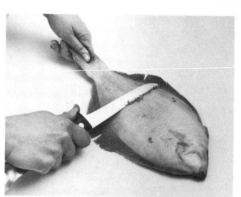

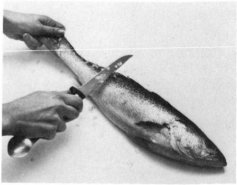

1 For flatfish, such as sole or flounder, hold the scaling knife almost parallel to the white skin. (The dark skin will be removed later.) Hold the tail and work toward the head with short pushing strokes.

2 For roundfish, such as bass, snapper, and sea trout, hold the knife at an angle and scale from tail to head on all sides.

Remove fins I

The fins on a flatfish do not go deep and can be cut off with fish or poultry shears. You can also use this method on a roundfish when the form is important, as in a whole poached fish.

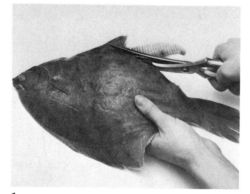

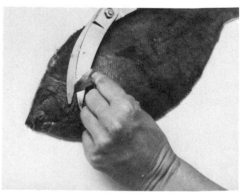

1 Cut off the fins around the perimeter of the fish and trim the tail.

2 Cut off the small fins near the gills.

Remove fins II

For roundfish, it is best to use the following method because the dorsal and ventral fins have fairly deep bones. If the fins are cut just along the edge, stumps of bones will be left in the fish.

1 Make a shallow cut along both sides of the dorsal fin.

2 Pull the fin from the tail toward the head.

3 Remove the whole dorsal fin. Repeat with the smaller fins on the ventral side.

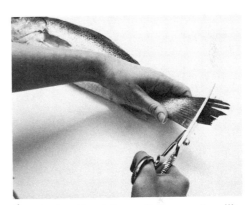

4 Trim the tail and the small fins near the gills.

Skin flatfish

Flatfish are usually skinned on the dark side only. Roundfish are rarely skinned whole. The fish must be fresh, not frozen, so the skin can be pulled off without tearing the flesh.

1 Make a shallow slit on a diagonal behind the head.

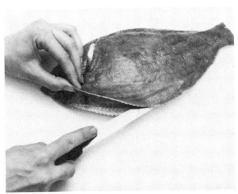

2 Put the tip of your knife under the skin and cut around the perimeter of the fish from head to tail.

Skin flatfish, continued

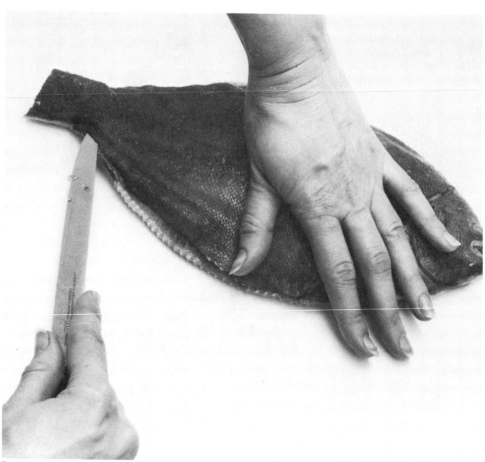

3 For the moment leave skin at the tip of the tail because the fish is very thin there.

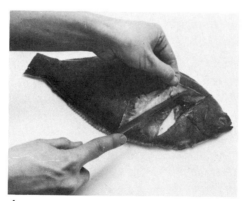

4 Carefully separate the skin from the flesh at the slit by the head. Pull up just enough skin so you can get a firm grip on it.

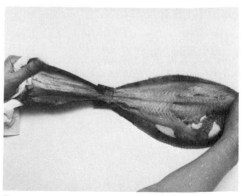

5 With a paper towel grasp the skin and pull it off from head to tail, holding the head with the other hand. Trim off the skin at the tail.

Gut flatfish

This is an easy job because the entrails of a flatfish are all just behind the head. The fish should first be skinned on the dark side.

1 Cut behind the head on the diagonal, following the line of the head.

2 Pull off the head and the entrails will come with it.

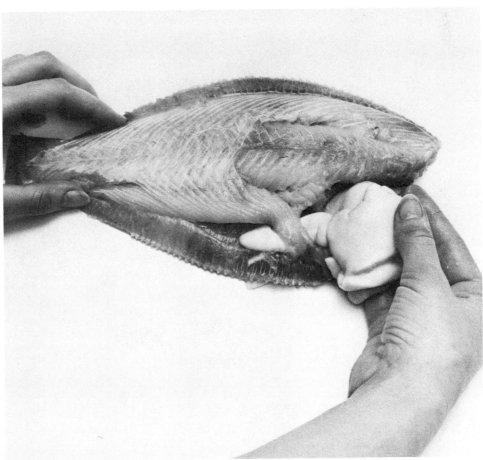

3 Pull out the roe if there is any and sauté it separately. It's delicious.

Gut roundfish I

If you don't want the head on the fish, this is the easiest way to clean it.

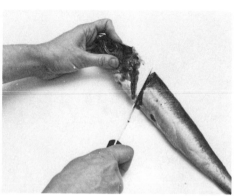

1 Cut off the head just below the gills using a sharp knife.

2 Slit the belly of the fish from the head to the anal vent.

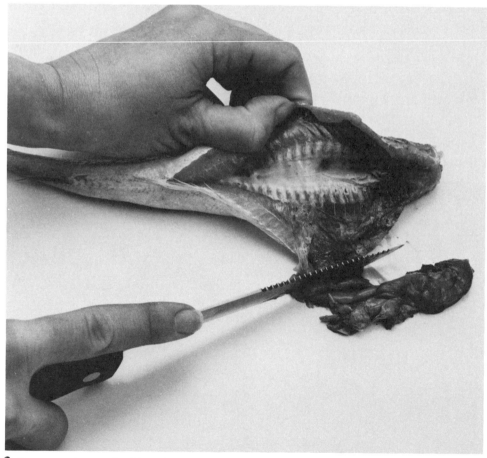

3 Scrape out the entrails. Rinse the cavity of the fish under cold running water.

Gut roundfish II

Use this method when you want to leave the head on, which adds flavor to the fish, and if you don't mind the fish being slit up the belly. This is the way a fish is usually gutted in a fish store.

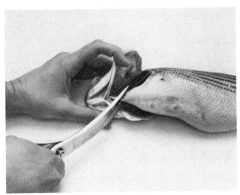

1 Open up the gills and cut through the bone that holds the head to the body under the gills.

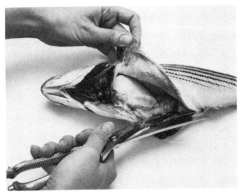

2 With shears, cut down the belly to the anal vent.

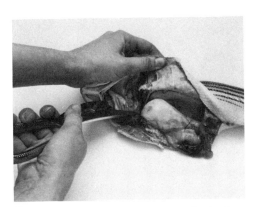

3 Grasp the gills with your shears and twist them out.

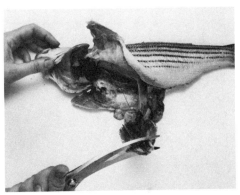

4 The entrails will pull out with the gills. Rinse the cavity of the fish with cold water.

Gut roundfish III

Use this method when the form of the fish is important, as for poaching. The entrails are pulled out through the gills, leaving the belly intact.

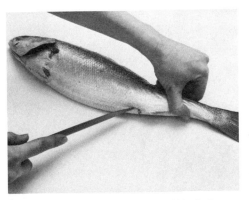

1 Make an incision about one-half inch deep at the anal vent where the entrails are attached.

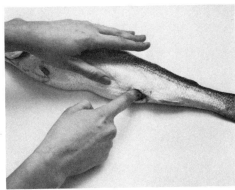

2 Stick your finger in the incision and loosen the entrails.

**Gut roundfish III,
continued**

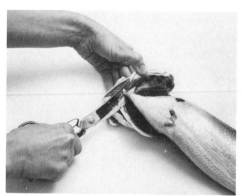

3 Cut through the bone under the gills.

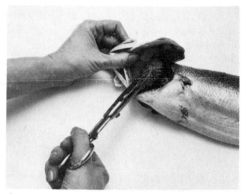

4 Grasp the gills with your shears.

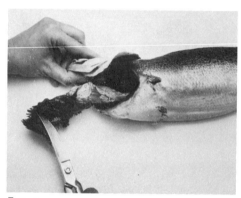

5 Pull out the gills and entrails in one piece.

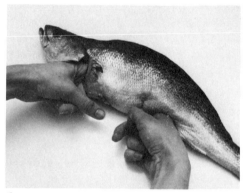

6 Put your fingers in both openings to be sure you have removed all the entrails.

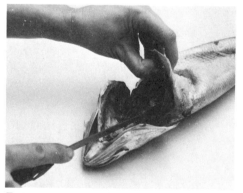

7 From the opening at the head, run your knife along either side of the spine to puncture the blood sacs. Rinse the cavity of the fish with cold water.

8 The gutted fish—in this case a trout.

Fillet a flatfish

If you are going to fillet fish frequently, it is worth investing in a sole filleting knife, which has a long flexible blade. Otherwise, use any sharp knife. A very firm fish can be skinned on both sides before filleting it, which makes it easier to see the line that divides the fillets. I have filleted one side with the skin off, the other with the skin on, to show both techniques.

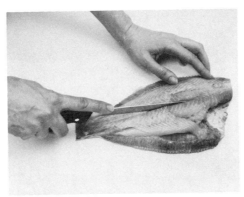

1 Place the fish with the white skin side down (the dark skin has been removed). Cut down the center of the fish with the point of your knife. There is a natural line that separates the fillets.

2 Cut around the perimeter of the fish, only as deep as the remaining fin bones where there is no flesh.

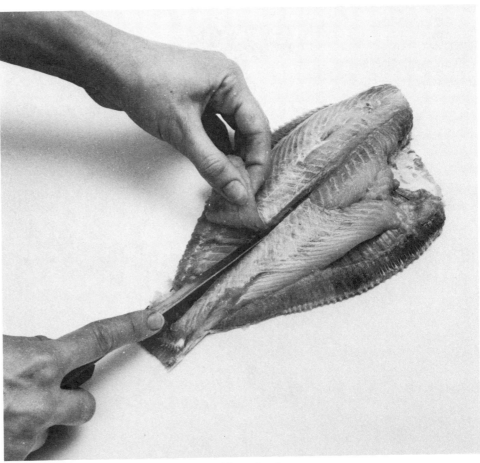

3 Loosen the fillet at the tail and lift it up with one hand.

Fillet a flatfish, continued

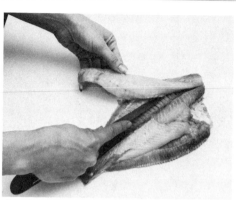

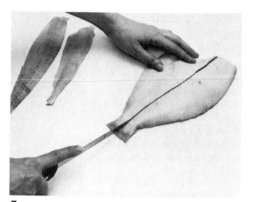

4 Working from the center out to the edge, use the tip of your knife to release the fillet from the rib bones. Keep your blade next to the bones. Repeat with the other fillet.

5 Turn the fish over and cut down the center of the white skin.

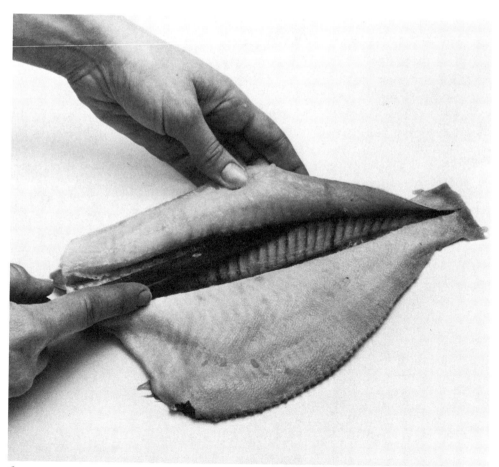

6 Remove the fillets from this side, keeping your knife close to the rib bones and working from the center out to the edge.

Fillet a roundfish

This is not a difficult procedure. The only thing to watch for is in step 4 when the rib bones curve around.

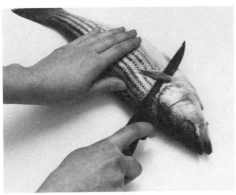

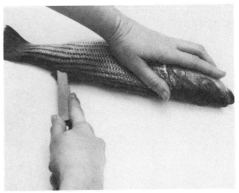

1 Cut at an angle behind the head and small fins just down to the bone.

2 Holding the fish firmly with one hand, cut down the back from the head to the tail. Use only the tip of your knife and keep it pressed against the small bones that project from the backbone.

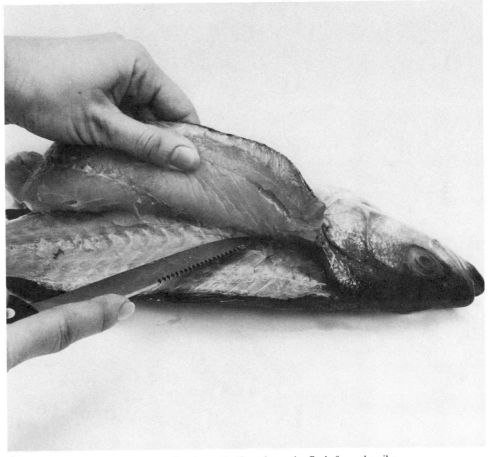

3 Lift up the fillet and, with the tip of your knife, release the flesh from the ribs.

4 When you get to the center of the side of the fish, the rib bones bulge up and around toward the belly.
Move your blade up and follow the ribs around.

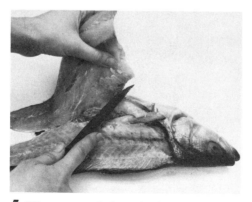

5 When you reach the ends of the ribs, cut off
the fillet.

6 Turn the fish over and remove the fillet in the
same way, cutting behind the head and down the
back.

Skin a fillet

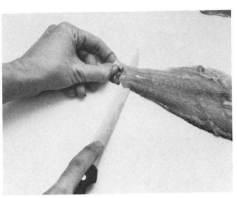

1 Place the fillet skin side down. Grasp the tail with one hand and cut down to the skin.

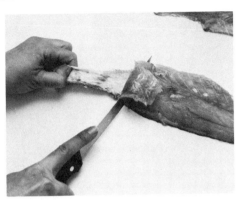

2 Slide the knife along the skin toward the head, detaching the fillet.

Roll fillets

Flounder or sole fillets are particularly suited to this preparation.

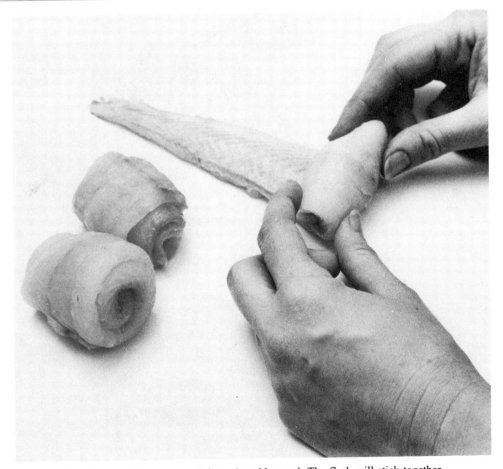

Place the fillet skinned side up and roll from the widest end. The flesh will stick together.

Butterfly

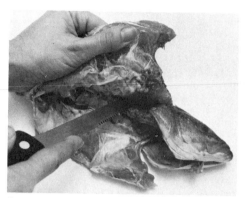

1 Open up a fish that has been gutted through the belly and sever the ribs along the backbone. Be careful not to cut through the fish.

2 Close the fish and hold it firmly with one hand. Insert your knife and continue to cut along the backbone down to the tail.

3 Lift the top flesh and cut it across the tail just to loosen it but don't sever the tail.

4 Hold the fish open and sever the ribs on the under side of the backbone. Continue to cut along the backbone down to the tail.

5 Cut through the backbone at the head.

6 Cut under the bone down to the tail.

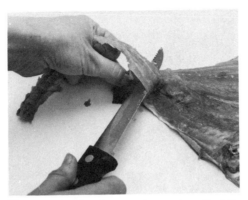

7 Lift up the backbone and sever it at the tail. Cut out the small rib bones at the outside of the two fillets.

8 If you are going to stuff and bake the butterflied fish, leave the head on. For broiling or for sweet and sour dishes, cut it off.

Stuff whole fish

Some people prefer to leave the bone in the fish and stuff it through the belly because the bone adds flavor to the fish. I think it is more appetizing, however, when the bones are removed. This technique is similar to filleting a fish but the fillet is not detached. The fish I am using has been scaled and finned. Wrap the fish in cheesecloth rather than tying it because the string will leave marks on the skin.

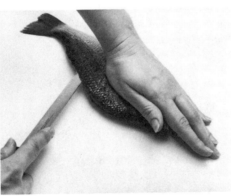

1 Holding the fish firmly with one hand, cut down the back from the head to the tail. Use only the tip of your knife and keep it pressed against the small bones that project from the backbone.

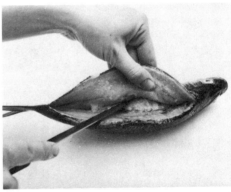

2 Lift up one side of the fish and, with the tip of your knife, release the flesh from the ribs. Be careful to go up over the ribs where they curve toward the belly.

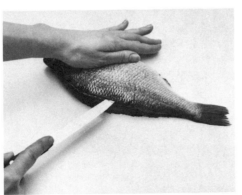

3 Turn the fish and cut down the other side of the backbone.

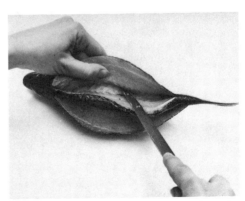

4 Open the fish and release the ribs from the flesh.

Stuff whole fish, continued

5 Using fish or poultry shears, cut through the bone at the head.

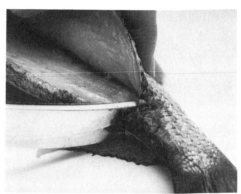

6 Cut through the bone just above the tail.

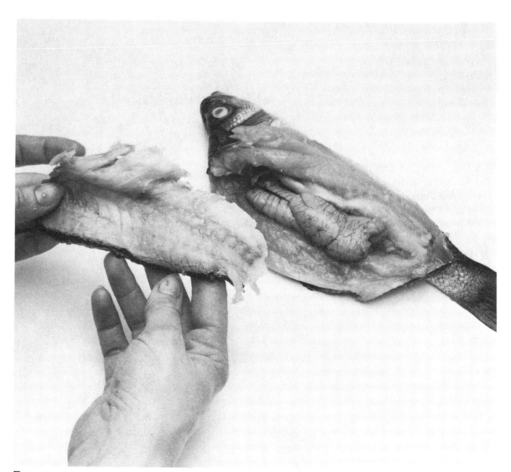

7 Remove the backbone and ribs in one piece.

8 Remove the roe, if any, and the entrails.

9 Cut out the gills on either side of the head. Rinse the fish well before stuffing.

10 Open up the fish and spoon in the stuffing.

Stuff whole fish, continued

11 Put the fish on a piece of cheesecloth large enough to enclose it and rub the fish with oil. This will prevent the skin from sticking to the cheesecloth.

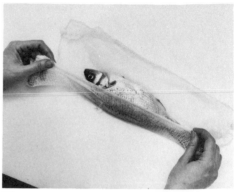

12 Wrap the cheesecloth around the fish, to keep the belly closed, and bake it according to recipe directions. See color photograph of cooked fish.

Poach whole fish

Ideally, a large fish for poaching should be gutted through the gills. However, if you buy your fish already cleaned, it will probably be gutted through the stomach and the bone under the gills will be cut. Tie the head to keep it from falling to the back, and wrap the fish in cheesecloth to keep the belly cavity closed. The cheesecloth also helps in removing the fish from the poacher.

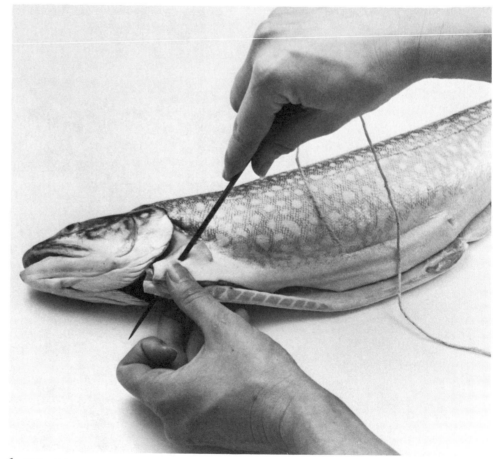

1 If the fish was gutted through the belly, push a trussing needle with a length of string through the bony part of the fish under the chin.

2 Put string behind the gills on either side.

3 Cross the strings over the head.

4 Tie the strings under the chin.

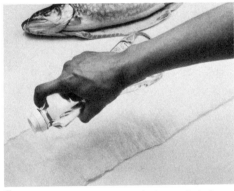

5 Oil a double thickness of cheesecloth large enough to enclose the fish. The oil will make it easier to stretch the cheesecloth and will keep the skin from sticking to it.

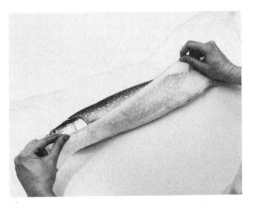

6 Wrap the whole fish in the cheesecloth.

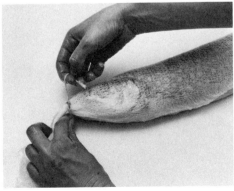

7 Twist and tie the ends.

Poach whole fish, continued

8 Strain the court bouillon and put the vegetables in the bottom of the poacher. Place the rack over the vegetables. They will flavor the fish but won't cling to it.

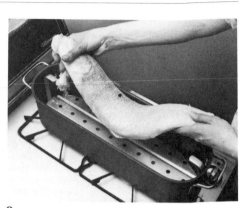

9 Place the fish on the rack.

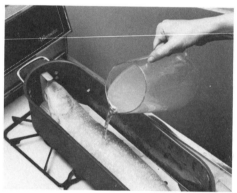

10 Pour lukewarm court bouillon over the fish to cover it. Bring just to a simmer, cover, and cook over low heat for fifteen to twenty minutes, or according to recipe directions. Never let the broth boil.

11 Lift the fish out of the poacher, drain, and place it on a large platter or serving board. Unwrap the cheesecloth and pull out the string around the head.

12 Pull off the skin from the top side.

13 Lift up the fish and pull out the cheesecloth. Cut the fish into serving pieces or decorate the top of the fish.

Steam fish I

A fish poacher makes an excellent utensil for steaming a whole fish. You can also improvise by putting the fish on a rack in a roasting pan. The important thing is to have the rack about an inch above the boiling water. And the steamer must be tightly covered with a lid or heavy-duty aluminum foil.

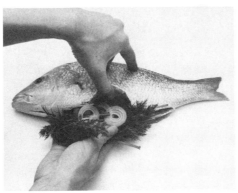

1 Put seasonings in the cavity of the fish.

2 Turn two custard cups upside down in a fish poacher.

3 Pour in water (and court bouillon if you wish) about three-quarters of the way up the custard cups and bring to a boil.

Steam fish I, continued

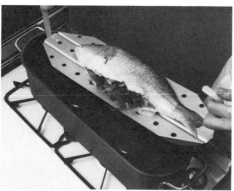

4 Place the fish on the rack and rest the rack on top of the custard cups.

5 Cover the pan with heavy-duty aluminum foil and steam according to recipe directions. (You can also bend down the handles of the poaching rack and cover with the lid.)

Steam fish II

A wok is a good steaming utensil for a small fish, a fillet, or for steaming the fish with a sauce. Use the wooden steamer rack made for woks, or place two chopsticks parallel in the wok.

1 Place a whole fish or a fillet on a plate and season the cavity.

2 Bring the water to a boil in the bottom of the wok and place the plate on the rack. Add sauce if you wish.

3 Cover the wok with the lid or with heavy-duty aluminum foil. Cook according to recipe directions.

Test for doneness

Fish cooks quickly and should be watched so that it doesn't become dry. Remove the fish from the oven when it loses its translucency. Put a fork or toothpick into the flesh to see if it flakes.

Cut cooked fish for serving

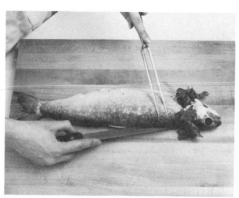

1 Using the tip of your knife, cut through the skin down the back. Steady the fish with your fork held flat against the body.

2 Slit the skin across the tail.

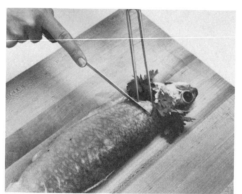

3 Slit the skin behind the head. (Slit the skin up the belly unless the fish was gutted through the belly, as this one was.)

4 Starting at the head, roll the skin back with a fork or your fingers and discard.

5 Cut down the center of the fish just to the bone, separating the two fillets.

6 Cut the fish crosswise down to the bone into serving pieces.

7 Lift each piece off with a wide-bladed cake server or spatula.

8 Lift up the tail with your fork and release the bone from the underside with your knife. Then lift off the whole skeleton in one piece.

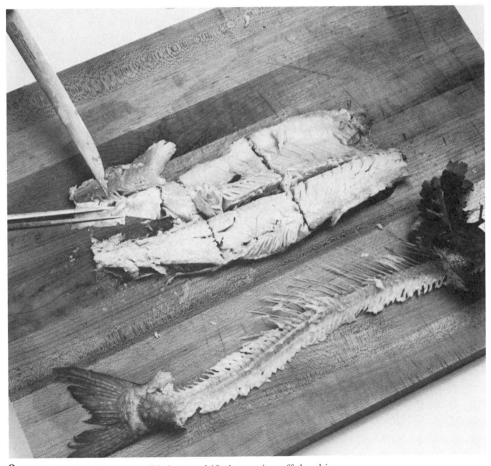

9 Cut the underside as you did the top. Lift the serving off the skin.

Decorate cooked fish

This is a pretty way to serve a whole fish for a buffet. It can first be poached and cooled to room temperature in the poaching liquid.

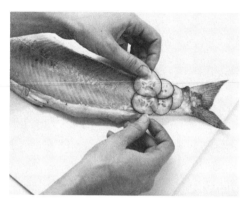

1 Remove the skin from one side of the fish. Starting at the tail, place paper-thin slices of unpeeled cucumber across the fish.

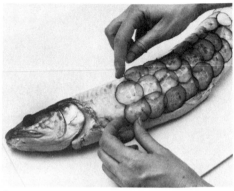

2 Continue all the way up to the head, creating the illusion of scales. Place a small piece of black olive over the eye.

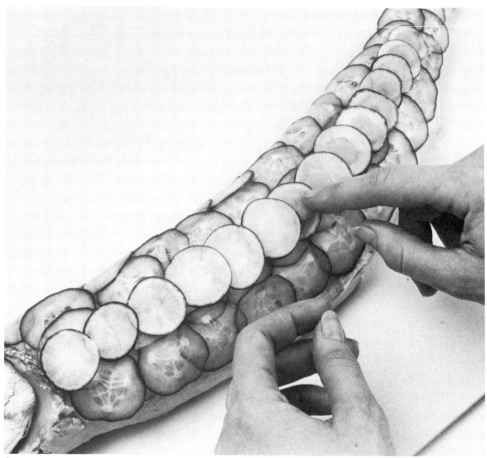

3 Place a row of thin unpeeled radish slices down the center of the fish.

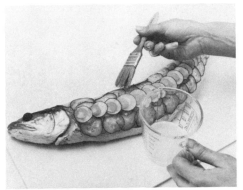

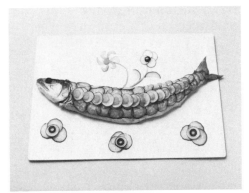

4 Brush the cucumber and radish slices with a light layer of aspic.

5 Decorate the serving board with vegetable cutouts to resemble flowers or any pattern you choose. Brush with aspic.

Wrap fillet in puff pastry

This is an attractive way to present individual or larger servings of fish. Use your imagination in decorating the pastry.

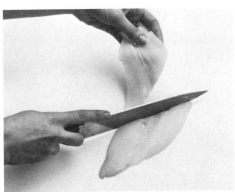

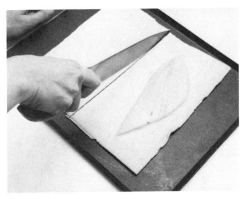

1 Cut a whole fish fillet in two, cutting at an angle so you get a rough fish shape with each piece.

2 Roll out puff pastry into a rectangle large enough to enclose the fillet. The pastry should be one-quarter inch thick. Place it on a baking sheet and cut it in two.

3 Spread fish mousse or any stuffing on top of the piece of fillet.

4 Lay the other piece of fillet on top.

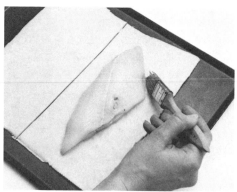

5 Brush the pastry around the perimeter of the fillet with water.

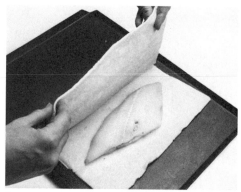

6 Place the other half of the pastry over the top.

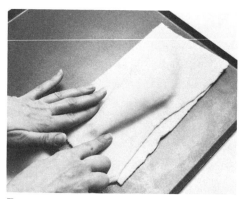

7 Seal the pastry around the fish by pressing with your fingers.

8 Cut around the fish, leaving a one-quarter-inch border to keep the pastry tightly closed. Cut out a tail at the end.

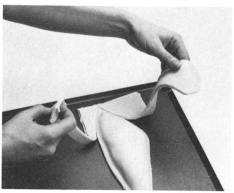

9 Remove excess pastry and roll out for decorations.

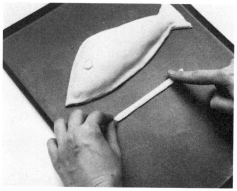

10 Cut out scraps of pastry and moisten them with water. Use a small circle for the eye.

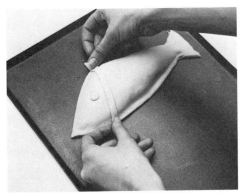

11 Lay a strip of dough behind the eye to create the appearance of a head.

12 Brush the pastry with egg beaten with a little water.

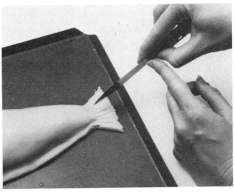

13 Use a knife to decorate the tail and the strip behind the head.

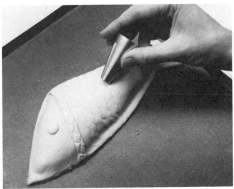

14 Use a metal pastry bag tube to make scalelike marks down the length of the fish. Bake it at 350 degrees for fifteen minutes, or until pastry is brown.

Wrap fillet in paper

Kitchen parchment, which is more porous than foil, is the best for this moist and delightful fish presentation. You can make individual or larger servings.

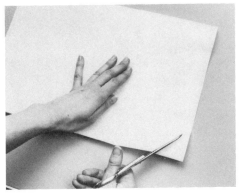

1 Cut out a large rectangle of parchment and fold it in half.

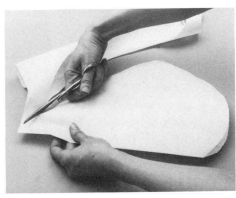

2 Starting at the fold, cut out a half-heart shape.

Wrap fillet in paper, continued

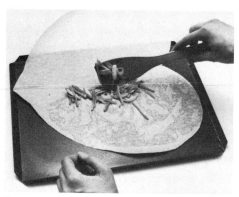

3 Open up the paper and place it on a lightly oiled baking sheet. Spoon sautéed vegetables on the paper near the center fold.

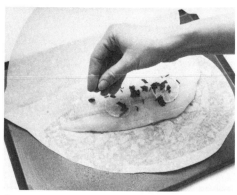

4 Place the fish fillet on top and add lemon slices, herbs, and seasonings.

5 Cover the fish with the other half of the paper.

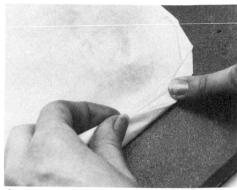

6 Seal the edges of the paper by folding the edges over and pleating them all the way around from the fold. If the edges aren't tightly sealed, the paper won't puff.

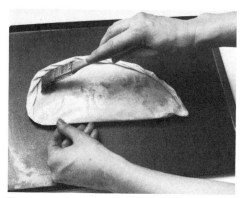

7 Brush the top of the paper package with vegetable oil. Bake it in a 375-degree oven for fifteen minutes.

8 When the fish is cooked, open the paper and serve on individual plates.

Cut fish into steaks

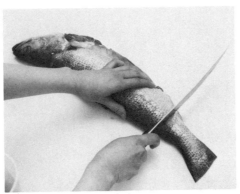 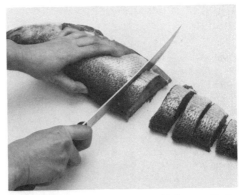

1 Put a finned and gutted roundfish on its side. With a sharp heavy knife, cut through the flesh and bone just above the tail.

2 Cut into steaks of uniform thickness all the way to the head.

3 The steaks can be baked or broiled.

Chop for quenelles or mousse

Quenelles and fish mousses used to be tedious to make even in professional kitchens. Today, however, a food processor makes light work of the chopping. A blender can be used, but the fish or shellfish will have to be added in several batches and scraped down frequently.

1 Cut the fish or shellfish into one-inch pieces and put into the container of a food processor. You can process about three-quarters of a pound of fish at a time. Add seasonings and egg yolks if called for.

2 Turn the machine on and off for about thirty seconds, or until fish is coarsely chopped.

3 Using a rubber spatula, scrape down the mixture from the sides.

4 Add egg whites or cream, according to the recipe, and process another thirty seconds, or until mixture is smooth.

5 If the recipe calls for whipped cream, put the fish mixture in a bowl set over ice and stir in the cream.

Shape and poach quenelles I

Quennelles are gossamer ovals of finely chopped and seasoned fish or seafood that are served with any number of sauces. This is the traditional way to shape them. The only trick to cooking them is to have the water barely simmering over low heat. If the water boils, the quenelles will fall apart.

1 Have a pan of salted water or stock ready with the water just barely simmering. Dip two spoons in the water. Pick up a heaping spoonful of the fish mixture with one spoon.

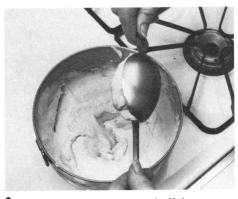

2 Use a second spoon to round off the top.

3 Run the second spoon under the quenelle inside the first spoon.

4 Drop the quenelle into the simmering water. Poach about five minutes, turning once.

Shape and poach quenelles I, continued

5 Remove the cooked quenelle with a slotted spoon and drain briefly on a towel. Serve hot with a sauce.

6 If you are preparing the quenelles ahead, remove them from the poaching liquid and drop them into ice water. Drain and refrigerate for later use.

Shape and poach quenelles II

Quenelles can also be shaped with a pastry bag into rounds or small cylinders.

1 Outfit a pastry bag with a plain tip and fill the bag with the quenelle mixture. Pipe out into small rounds or cylinders.

2 Carefully pour boiling water into the side of the pan, not over the quenelles. The quenelles will float when they are done.

CLAMS

Open

A clam knife, which has a sharp edge and a rounded tip, is essential for opening hard-shell clams. (Don't use those gadgets that mangle the clam meat.) The task will be easier if the clams are well chilled because the muscle that joins the two shells tends to relax. Be sure to save all the delicious clam liquor in the shell.

1 Hold the clam securely in the palm of one hand and curve your fingers around the blade of the clam knife. Insert the side of the blade next to the hinge. Wedge the blade between the two sides of the shell.

2 Turn the clam and work your knife around to the other side of the hinge. Then pry open the shell and scrape the clam from the top shell.

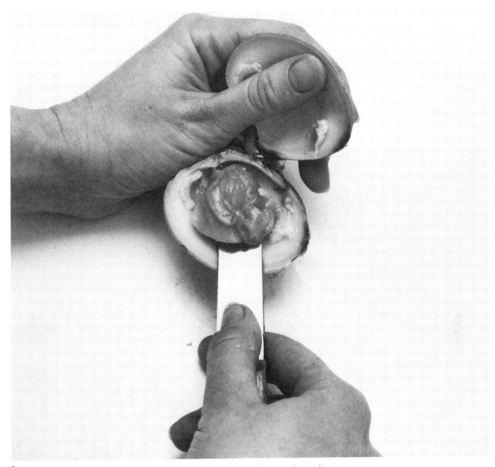

3 Run your knife under the clam on the bottom shell to release it.

HARD-SHELL CRABS

Prepare for stuffing

1 The female blue crab, called a she crab, is considered sweeter than the male and often has delicious roe. The tail of a female is wide; the male's is a narrow strip. For either sex, the tail is called the apron.

2 Put your fingers under the upper shell to pry it off.

Prepare for stuffing, continued

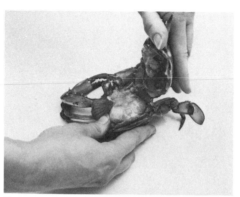

3 Detach the top shell, keeping the crab body whole.

4 Scrape out the liver from the top shell.

5 Scrape out any remaining liver and roe from the body.

6 Cut out the soft, shell-shaped gills on either side.

7 Pull out the sand sac from between the eyes.

8 Pull off any strands on the apron, but leave the apron attached.

9 Fold the apron under the body for extra support. Stuff the body cavity and bake, or steam the crab and serve it cold stuffed with salad.

SOFT-SHELL CRABS

Prepare for cooking

Soft-shell crabs are regular blue crabs that are caught just after they have shed their hard shell, which they do several times before they reach maturity. They can be sautéed, broiled, or fried.

1 Lift up the shell on either side of the tail (called the apron) and scrape out the spongy, shell-shaped gills on both sides.

2 Pull the apron down and cut it off at the body.

Prepare for cooking, continued

3 Using shears or a knife, cut off the eyes on the front of the head.

CRAYFISH

Prepare for cooking

1 If you have time, put the live crayfish in a bowl of cold water with one tablespoon nonfat dry milk. Let them sit for several hours to clean out the intestinal tract.

2 If you want to cook the crayfish without soaking them, twist the center fin of the tail.

3 Pull out the fin and the intestinal tract will come out with it. The crayfish can then be cooked according to recipe directions.

4 If you want just the crayfish meat, break off the tail.

5 Pull the meat out of the tail. There is almost no meat in the body. Use the tail shell and body for soups or sauces.

EEL

Clean and skin

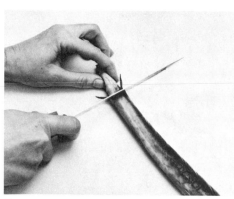

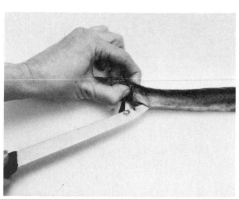

1 Put the eel on its back and cut under the head just through the bone. Don't sever the head.

2 Put the point of your knife into the incision and slit the skin down the belly.

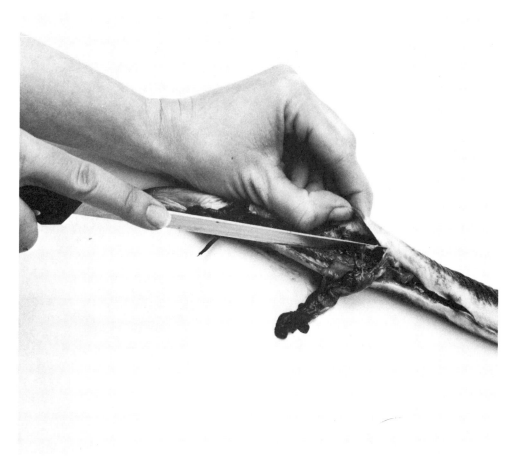

3 Open the belly and scrape out the intestinal tract.

4 With the tip of your knife, cut through the skin around the head.

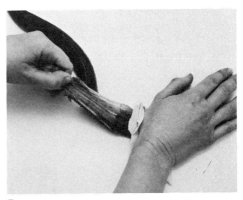

5 Hold the head of the eel firmly with a paper towel. With the other hand, pull hard on the skin.

6 Pull off the skin in one piece down the length of the eel.

7 The skinned eel is ready to be cut crosswise into serving pieces and sautéed, fried, or cooked according to recipe directions.

CONCHS

Remove meat from shell

Conchs (pronounced konks) will be tough unless they are cooked in simmering water before they are opened.

1 Put the live conchs into boiling water. Reduce the heat and simmer until the conchs retreat into their shells—about fifteen minutes.

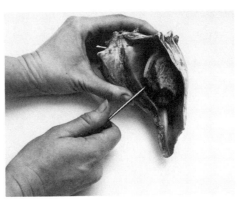

2 Immediately drain the conchs and insert a screwdriver into the shell and loosen the meat.

Remove meat from shell, continued

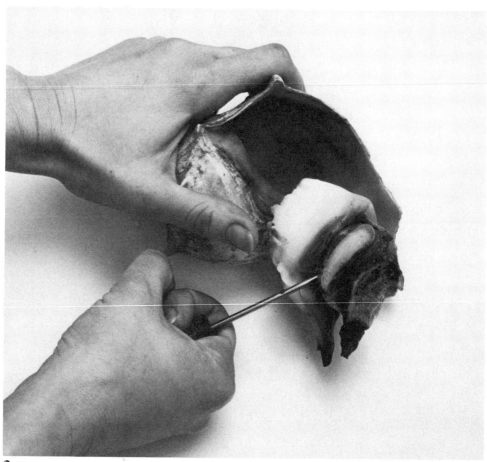

3 Remove the conch meat from the shell.

4 Remove the tentacles and trim any black part off the meat.

5 If you are going to fry the conch or use it in chowder, slice the meat.

LOBSTER

Determine sex

Female lobster are prized because they tend to be meatier and because they often contain a pinkish red roe called coral. It is delicious eaten with the lobster or cooked in a sauce.

1 Place the lobster on its back and hold the tail. Check the two small feelers where the tail meets the body. If the lobster is female, the feelers will be soft.

2 If the lobster is male, the feelers will be stiff.

3 The female, on the left, has a wider, meatier tail than the male.

Split for broiling or baking

1 Put the lobster on its back. Using a sharp heavy knife, cut through the body just above the tail.

2 Cut down the length of the tail through the meat and shell.

3 Turn the lobster and cut through the rest of the body but not through the back shell.

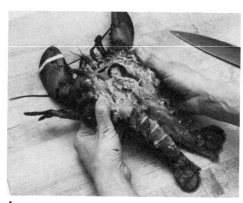

4 Pull the body apart with your hands so it can lie flat.

5 Cut out and discard the sand sac between the eyes.

6 Remove and discard the intestinal vein that runs down the tail.

7 Scrape out the grey green liver, called tomalley, and any roe. Use for a sauce.

8 Put a toothpick through one side of the tail and curl it up to attach it to the top of the tail.

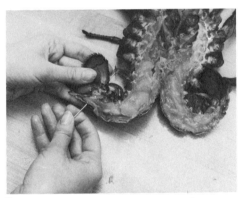

9 Repeat with the other side of the tail.

10 The lobster can be broiled or baked.

Cut up live

Lobster is cut up in the shell for sautés or stews in many of the world's cuisines. The lobster shell adds a great deal of flavor to the finished dish.

1 With a sharp heavy knife, cut through the body and head to divide it.

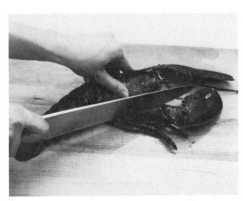

2 Cut off the large claws and the small ones on either side.

Cut up live, continued

3 Cut the tail from the body.

4 Cut the tail crosswise into several pieces.

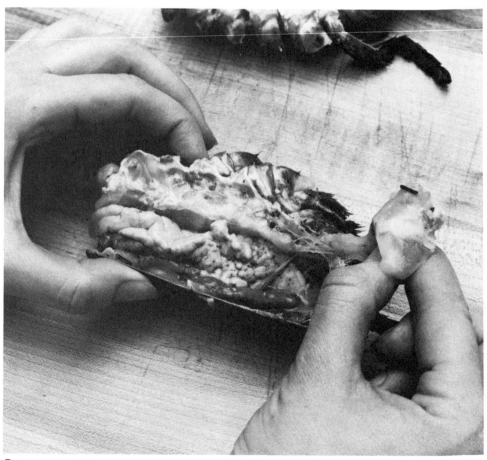

5 Remove and discard the sand sac from between the eyes.

6 Scrape out the liver and any roe and use for sauce.

7 The cut up lobster.

Cut up after boiling

The lobster can, of course, be served whole or split after boiling, which is the best way of all. But if you want only the cooked meat, cut and crack the cooked lobster and remove the meat.

1 With a sharp heavy knife, pierce the lobster between the eyes.

2 Hold the lobster upside down and let the liquid drain out.

3 Break off the tail from the body.

4 Break off the end of the tail.

Cut up after boiling, continued

5 Push the tail meat out in one piece.

6 Turn the tail meat over and make a shallow incision down the length of the tail.

7 Remove and discard the intestinal tract.

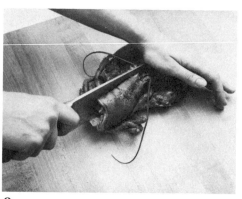

8 Cut the body in two.

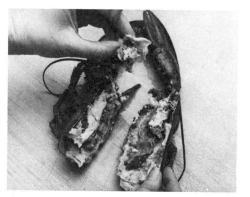

9 Remove and discard the sand sac between the eyes. Scrape out and reserve the liver and any roe.

10 Smash the large claw with a meat pounder or nut cracker.

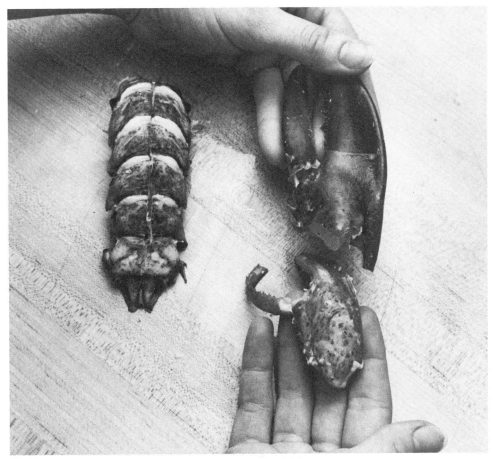

11 Pull out the claw meat in one piece.

MUSSELS

Clean

Mussels are abundant but neglected in America, which is a pity because they are high in protein and low in fat. This is in addition to their delicious taste. Mussels do, however, need to be thoroughly cleaned before cooking. And they must be alive.

1 If any mussel is not tightly closed, check to see if it is alive by putting the tip of your knife into the shell. If the mussel is alive the shell will close immediately.

2 Pull up and cut off the beard, using a knife or kitchen shears.

3 Scrape off any barnacles with your knife.

4 Put the mussels in cold water and rub the shells together to remove any grit that clings to them.

5 Drain the mussels and put into fresh water. Add a handful of salt and let the mussels soak for a few hours. The salt will draw the sand out. Rinse thoroughly before cooking.

Cook and trim

Mussels are never served raw. They cook very quickly in a small amount of white wine in a covered kettle. Seasonings such as shallots, garlic, parsley, and pepper are usually added to the wine.

1 The mussels are done when they open, which should take about five minutes. Discard any that do not open.

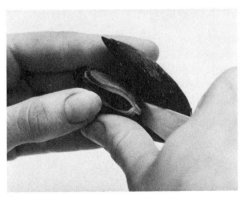

2 Unless you are serving the mussels in the broth in which they cooked, cut under the mussel to release it from the shell.

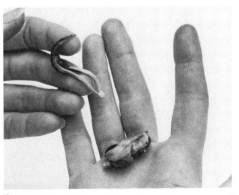

3 Pull off and discard the stringy brown edge of the mussel if you are using it for salad. It isn't necessary, just neater.

OCTOPUS

Clean

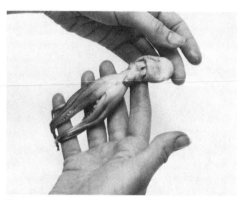

1 This is a small octopus, but the technique is the same with a larger one.

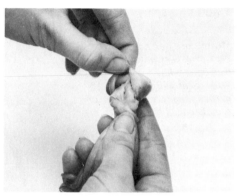

2 Pull up the flap over the head and turn it inside out over your index finger.

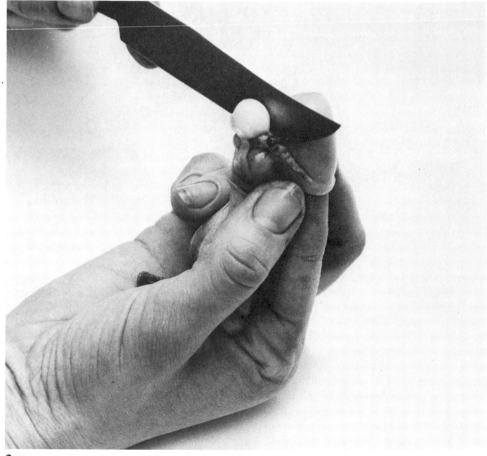

3 Cut around the bulbous yellowish white sac that is exposed.

4 Put your finger down on the cutting board and cut off the yellow and darker ink sacs and attached membranes around the head.

5 The cleaned octopus, which can be sliced crosswise and cooked in a variety of ways.

OYSTERS

Open

Oysters are easier to open than clams, but you still need a special knife. An oyster knife has a short blade with a pointed tip. It often comes with a guard to protect your fingers. The task is easier if the oysters are well chilled because their muscles relax.

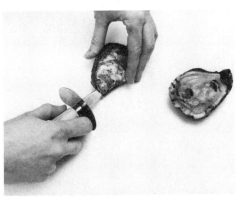

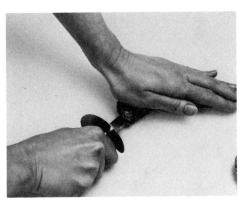

1 Start near the hinge and work the tip of your knife into the oyster.

2 Push down on the oyster with the heel of your hand and move the knife back and forth.

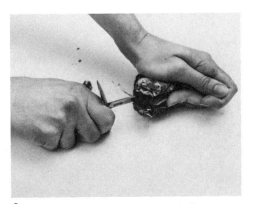

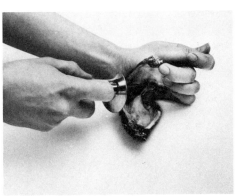

3 Turn the knife to pry open the shell.

4 Pull up the top shell and loosen the oyster with your knife.

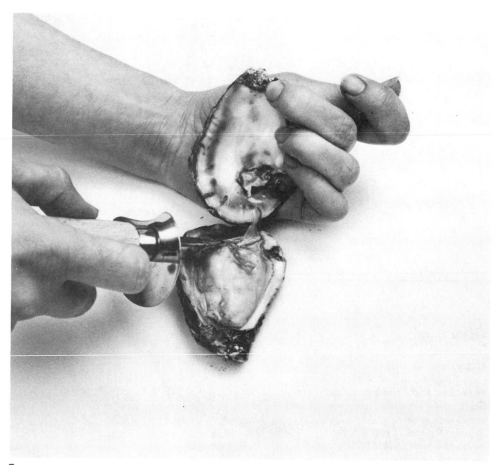

5 Scrape the oyster off the top shell and loosen it from the bottom shell.

SCALLOPS

Open

Scallops are seldom sold in the shell in America, but if you live along either coast you can harvest and open your own, which is easy to do. For reasons no one seems to understand, Americans eat only the white muscle.

1 Use a short-bladed oyster knife and push the point into the scallop.

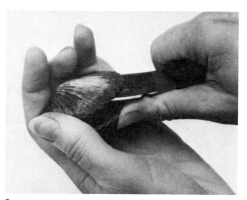

2 Push the knife into the scallop, scraping the muscle from the top shell.

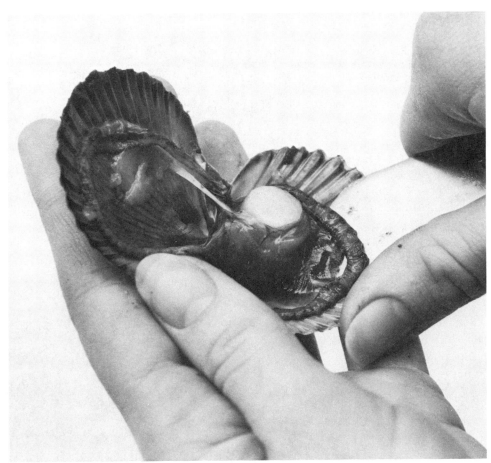

3 Run your knife under the scallop on the bottom shell.

4 Pull off and discard all but the white muscle.

5 The opened scallop has a translucent, shiny appearance, an indication of its freshness.

SEA URCHIN

Open

Sea urchins (called oursins *in French) have a sweet fresh smell and taste. They make unusual and delicious party fare.*

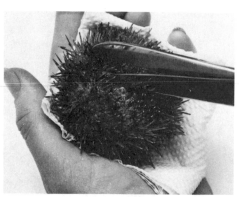

1 Protect your hand with a paper towel and hold the prickly shell with mouth facing up. Cut through the soft part around the mouth.

2 Cut around the top perimeter of the shell.

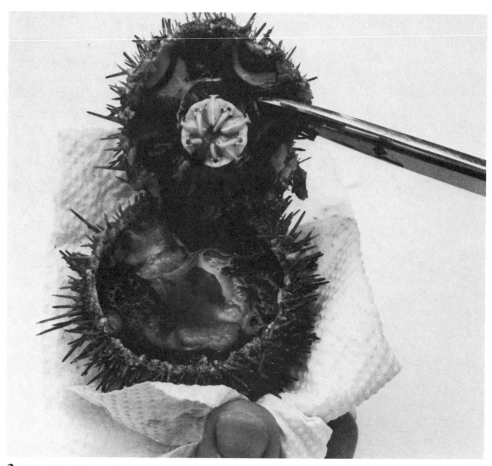

3 Lift off and discard the top of the shell.

4 Spoon out and discard the dark innards.

5 The golden roe that covers the sides of the shell is what is eaten.

SHRIMP

Peel and devein

Shrimp can be peeled before or after cooking, although the shells do add flavor. The dark vein that runs down the back of the shrimp is not harmful. It is removed mostly because it is unattractive.

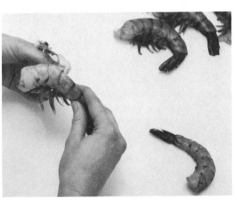

1 Pull off the soft shell with your fingers.

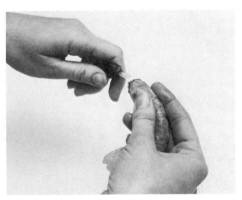

2 The tail can be left on or pulled off.

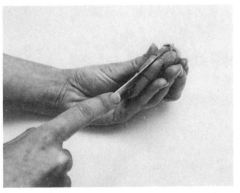

3 Make a shallow cut down the back of the shrimp.

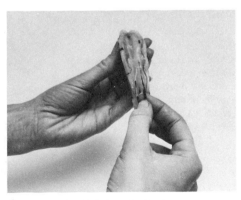

4 Pull out the dark intestinal vein.

Butterfly

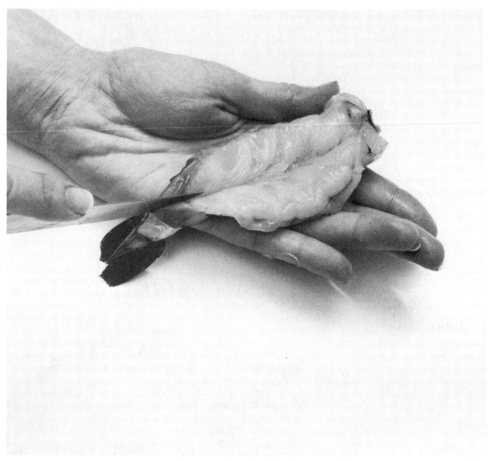

Cut down the back almost but not completely through the flesh. The shrimp will then lie flat for grilling or stuffing.

SNAILS

Stuff shells

Most of the snails we eat are terrestrial although cookbooks usually put them with shellfish. Canned snails are more readily available than fresh and the shells can be boiled and reused many times.

1 Put the canned snails in a sieve and rinse them under warm water to remove the brine in which they are packed. Simmer them in broth for about twenty minutes.

2 Push a small amount of softened butter, usually seasoned with garlic, parsley, salt and pepper, into the shell.

3 Push the snail into the shell.

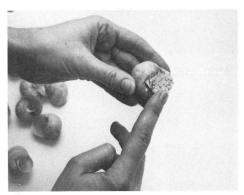

4 Press a small amount of seasoned butter on top to seal it. Bake in snail platters or on a baking sheet.

Remove cooked snails

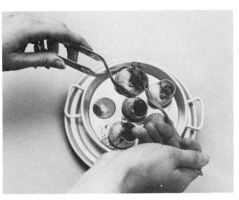

1 Pick up a snail shell with special tongs made for this purpose.

2 Pull out the snail with a small fork. Pour the butter onto the platter and soak it up with bread.

SQUID

Clean

Squid, which is popular in Italy, Spain, and the Far East, can be baked or fried and is delicious stuffed and sautéed. The body and the tentacles are the edible part, although squid is sometimes cooked whole in its own ink.

1 Grasp the head and tentacles of the squid and pull them away from the body.

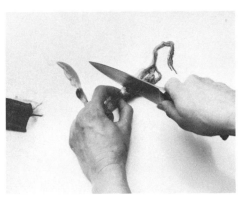

2 Cut off the tentacles. Discard the head and the ink sac.

Clean, continued

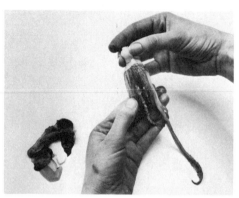

3 Pull off the ball of cartilage attached to the tentacles.

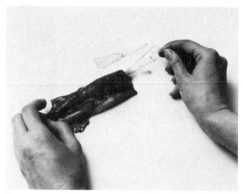

4 Reach into the body and pull out the soft bone that looks like clear plastic. It may come out in pieces.

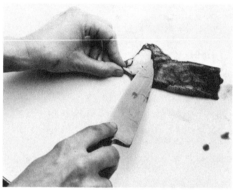

5 Using a sharp knife, scrape off enough skin to be able to grip it with your fingers.

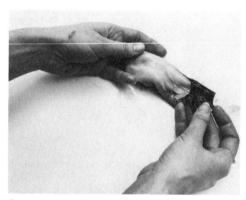

6 Pull off the skin.

7 The body is ready to be stuffed.

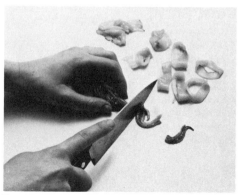

8 You can also slice the body into rings and cut up the tentacles for frying.

Stuff

1 Rinse the body of the squid and dry on paper towels. Chop the tentacles for the stuffing.

2 Add the tentacles to the stuffing (I'm using chopped spinach, onion, bread crumbs, and melted butter) and fill the sacklike body.

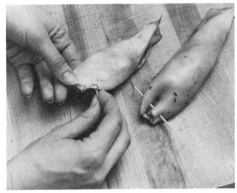

3 Close the top of the body with a toothpick. The squid is then ready to be sautéed or cooked according to the recipe directions.

TROUT

Tie fresh trout

If you have access to very fresh trout, they are delicious prepared as truites au bleu, *which is to say in a court bouillon with vinegar that turns the trout skin a bright blue. They should be gutted through the gills. Tying them is purely for appearance.*

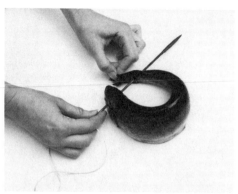

1 Run a trussing needle with a length of string through the eyes and the tail of the trout.

2 Put the tail in the mouth and tie the string loosely.

5
STOCK

Skim

The foam that rises during the early stages of cooking stock is harmless, but it will make the stock cloudy unless removed.

With either white or brown stock, frequently skim the foam that rises to the top using a spoon or skimmer. Add the vegetables to the stock after skimming the surface several times.

Degrease

1 The best and easiest way to degrease stock is to strain and refrigerate it. The fat will rise to the surface and you can scoop it off with a spoon.

2 If you need to use the stock immediately, let it settle for a few minutes and carefully spoon as much fat as possible off the top.

3 Then place two thicknesses of paper toweling over the stock and blot up as much remaining fat as possible.

4 Here is a special cup (sold in cookware stores) that works well. Pour strained stock into the cup, and the fat will rise to the surface after several seconds. Slowly pour off the clear stock, leaving the fat in the cup.

Reduce

Stock gains both body and concentrated flavor when it is reduced. In traditional French cuisine, reduced stock—demi-glace and glace de viande—is used to enrich pan juices and to serve as a base for sauces. Practitioners of the nouvelle cuisine use reduced stock to thicken sauces because they feel that flour masks the flavor.

1 Start with two cups of rich brown stock.

2 Bring to a boil, then lower heat. Simmer gently until the stock is reduced by half and clings to the spoon, which will take about thirty minutes. At this stage, it is called demi-glace.

3 Reduce further over low heat until the stock has a jellylike consistency, which will take another fifteen minutes. At this stage it is called glace de viande.

4 Two cups of stock have been reduced to about one-fourth of a cup. Both demi-glace and glace de viande can be frozen.

Clarify

For consommé, jellied soup, and aspic, stock should be absolutely clear and free of cloudy sediment. Clarifying is the way to produce this sparkling result.

1 The stock must be completely free of fat and at room temperature. Use a wire whisk and beat the egg whites until frothy. Gradually pour in degreased stock, whisking gently but constantly.

2 If you want to add seasonings—finely chopped tarragon, leeks, carrots, or lean meat—do it after all the stock has been added to the egg whites.

3 Pour the mixture into a saucepan and stir very slowly but continuously over moderate heat. Use a spoon rather than a whisk; you want to keep the egg whites in motion but not disturb them too much.

4 As soon as the mixture turns cloudy, stop stirring and turn the heat as low as possible.

5 After about one-half hour, the egg white (and seasonings, if you've added them) gather on the top of the stock.

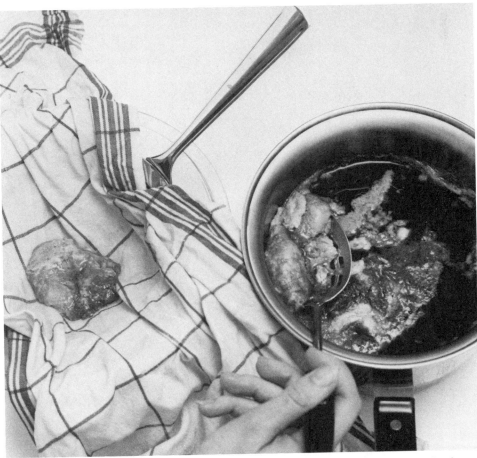

6 Rinse a very clean kitchen towel or several layers of cheesecloth in cold water and wring it out. Place it in a fine-meshed strainer over a bowl. With a slotted spoon, very carefully lift out egg whites (and seasonings) and put them into the towel.

7 Ladle the broth and any remaining egg white into the bowl.

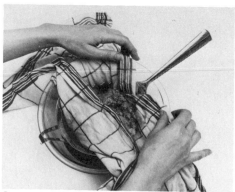

8 Lift the towel carefully, making sure no egg whites fall into the bowl.

9 Close the ends of the towel and twist them gently over the strainer.

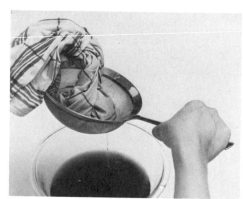

10 Lift the strainer out of the bowl, leaving the clarified stock.

6
PÂTÉS

PÂTÉS

Assemble, cook, and weight pâté in fatback

A very simple pâté is assembled in a terrine lined with fatback, which insulates and moistens the filling. If you learn the techniques for this, you can make almost any pâté. Weighting after cooking firms the pâté and gets rid of any air spaces. It will keep in the refrigerator for up to a month if you remove the fatback after the pâté is weighted. Wipe off any meat juices and return the pâté to a clean terrine. Pour melted fatback or lard around it.

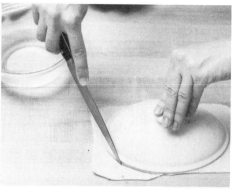

1 Cut fatback to line the bottom and to cover the top of the mold, in this case an oval terrine. Use the cover as a guide.

2 Pat the fatback in with your fingers, pushing it carefully up around the sides.

3 Cut rectangular pieces of fatback to fit all around the sides of the mold, slightly overlapping. Let two inches of fatback hang over the sides.

4 Moisten your fingers and put about a third of the ground meat mixture into the mold. Pat it to get rid of any air bubbles.

5 Lay strips of meat, about one-quarter inch thick—chicken, veal, duck, or ham—over the ground meat mixture. These will form a decorative design when the pâté is sliced.

6 Pat in another layer of ground meat, another layer of strips, and top with ground meat.

7 Pull up the fatback over the filling, and cover the center with the other piece of fatback cut around the lid. Place a bay leaf on top.

8 Cover with a layer of heavy-duty aluminum foil and punch a few holes in the foil.

9 Cover with the lid and place in a larger pan. Pour boiling water about halfway up the mold. Bake at 350 degrees until the internal temperature is 170 degrees.

Assemble, cook, and weight pâté in fatback, continued

10 Remove the terrine from the water bath and cut out a piece of cardboard, using the mold as a guide.

11 Put the cardboard on top of the foil and weight the pâté with about five pounds of material—using cans, a brick, or whatever. Let ripen in the refrigerator for about twenty-four hours.

12 To unmold, put the terrine in a pan of warm water to loosen the fatback on the bottom. Run a knife around the outside of the pâté.

13 Invert the pâté onto a platter and wipe off the meat juices with paper towels.

14 Turn the pâté over. It can now be sliced and served in the fatback. Or you can decorate it with aspic (see following instructions).

Decorate with aspic

This is a more elegant presentation of a pâté cooked in fatback. The trick to working with aspic is to melt only small amounts as you need them. Place over ice water until the jelly reaches a syrupy consistency that is thick enough to coat the terrine and cling to the pâté.

1 Cool the aspic over ice until it is a syrupy consistency. Pour a thin layer over the bottom of the clean terrine. Refrigerate about five minutes, or until set.

2 Remove all the fatback or lard from the pâté. Invert the pâté into the terrine.

3 Pour aspic over the whole pâté, filling the terrine. Chill for several hours, or until set.

4 With a very soft brush, use a patting motion to carefully cover the top of the pâté with more melted aspic. Chill for a few minutes until almost set.

Decorate with aspic, continued

5 Garnish the pâté (I've used scallion greens, a carrot flower, and a tomato rose) and very lightly stroke on more aspic over the garnish. Chill until set and serve the pâté from the terrine.

Assemble and cook a pâté en croûte

This is a slightly more difficult way to assemble a pâté but very elegant. The principles are the same as for any pâté.

1 Thoroughly grease a hinged mold, inside and around the hinges. Remove the bottom if the mold comes with one.

2 Roll out a sturdy pastry (use a pâte à pâté) into a one-inch-thick round.

3 Check to make sure that the pastry at each end is two inches longer than the mold.

4 Brush the side edges of the circle of pastry with water, leaving a dry area of about four inches down the middle.

5 Heavily flour the center and ends but not the side edges brushed with water.

6 Fold the pastry in half with the floured edges toward you and press the moistened edges together, ending up with a somewhat half-moon shape. Pull the corners of the pastry down, ending up with a skullcap shape.

7 Roll the pastry away from you to deepen the skullcap.

8 There will be a space in between the two layers of pastry where the flour keeps it from sticking together.

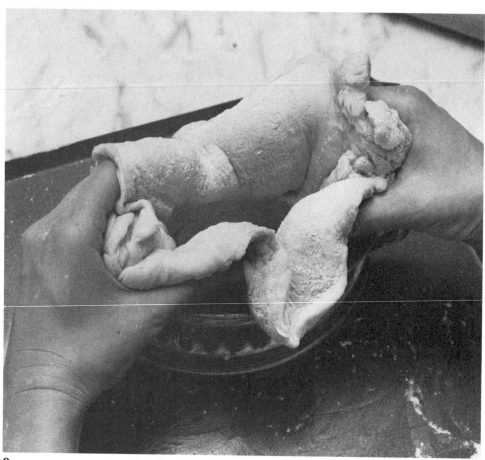

9 Place the mold on a greased baking sheet to catch the juices as the pâté bakes and to support the bottom. Very carefully lift the pastry into the mold, opening it so the floured side faces up.

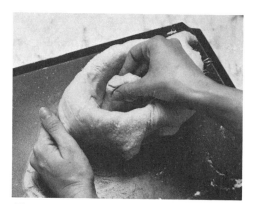

10 Press the pastry into the mold with a piece of dough or your fingers.

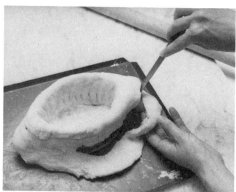

11 Leave a two-inch overhang of pastry, cutting off the excess.

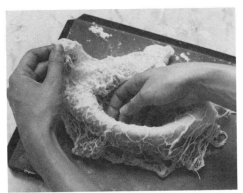

12 Line the pastry with caul fat, or a very thin layer of fatback, pressing it well into the sides. This will keep the pâté moist.

13 Layer ground meats and strips of meat and pull up the caul fat to cover the top.

14 Roll out scraps of pastry and cut out a top for the pâté, tracing around the bottom of the mold for a guide.

15 Brush the rim of the pastry with beaten egg.

16 Fold up the overhanging pastry and pat down. Trim off any excess pastry at each end.

17 Grease a metal pastry-bag tube and insert it into the pastry. This allows steam to escape and prevents the juices from leaking and cracking the crust. If the mold is large, use two such chimneys.

Assemble pâté en croûte, continued

18 Roll out remaining scraps of pastry and cut out circles with the pastry-bag tube.

19 Working at the edge of the table so your knife handle is free, make a scallop design from a center pivot using the back of your knife.

20 Brush the scallops with egg and decorate the pâté. Bake until the interior temperature reaches 160 degrees, putting the thermometer through the chimney. During the cooking, remove juices through the chimney with a bulb baster.

21 Cool the pâté and refrigerate for twenty-four hours. Insert a funnel into the steam hole and pour in about a cup of aspic. You want to fill the space where the pâté has shrunk from the sides.

22 Lift the mold on the baking sheet and tilt it from side to side so that the aspic is evenly distributed. Chill for several hours, or until set. Remove the mold and slice the pâté.

Assemble and unmold vegetable pâté

Vegetable pâtés make nice luncheon dishes or first courses. I've used all vegetables in the pâté with aspic, but you can also combine fish, meat, or poultry with the vegetables. They may also be put in a buttered mold instead of in aspic.

1 Cool the aspic to a syrupy consistency and pour a thin layer into the bottom of a loaf pan. Refrigerate about five minutes, or until set.

2 Put the pan in a bowl of ice and place strips and cutouts of vegetables in a decorative pattern. The vegetables should be blanched and refreshed or steamed. Dry thoroughly.

3 Carefully spoon a thin layer of aspic over the vegetables and refrigerate until set.

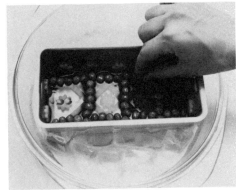

4 Add layers of vegetables—peas, carrots, green beans, turnips, whatever—covering each layer with a little aspic and letting it set before adding the next layer.

5 If you want to decorate the side of the mold with vegetable cutouts, dip them in aspic and press them onto the mold.

6 Fill the mold with aspic and put your knife behind each cutout on the sides so that the aspic gets all around them. Refrigerate for about twenty-four hours, or until set.

7 When ready to serve, dip a thin-bladed knife in hot water and dry. It should be slightly warm. Carefully run the knife around the sides of the pan to loosen the pâté.

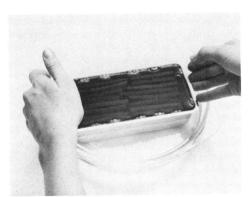

8 Dip the bottom of the mold in lukewarm water for about thirty seconds. Don't have the water too hot or it will melt the aspic.

9 Cover the mold with a plate and invert it.

10 Garnish the pâté and slice.

7
PASTA AND RICE

PASTA

Mix dough

Homemade pasta (noodle dough) has a better texture than commercial varieties and, after practice in rolling it, is not difficult to make. Pasta dough is basically a mixture of flour and eggs—three-quarters to one cup of flour to each egg. Milk is sometimes called for in pasta that will be stuffed. And one or two regional pasta doughs are made with water instead of eggs.

1 Mound the flour on a wood or Formica surface and make a well in the center. Pour the whole eggs into the well. If the recipe calls for milk (or chopped spinach for spinach noodles), add it with the eggs.

2 Hold one side of the flour with one hand so it won't collapse and beat the eggs well with a fork, incorporating some of the flour from the inside of the well.

3 Using one or two fingers, gradually incorporate the flour and the eggs. Move your finger in a circle around the inside of the well, drawing the flour into the eggs.

4 When the eggs are no longer runny, mix the eggs and flour with your fingers, squeezing to make the dough stick together. It will be quite crumbly.

5 With a pastry scraper, gather any crumbs and incorporate as many as you can into the dough. Discard the rest.

Knead and roll by hand

Thinning and stretching pasta dough is tricky because it must be done quickly before the dough dries out. But it isn't difficult. You rapidly roll the pin back and forth while moving your hands from the center of the rolling pin out to the edges.

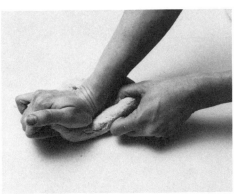

1 On a clean wood or Formica work surface, push the ball of dough away from you with the heel of your hand.

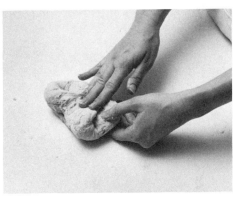

2 Fold the dough toward you.

3 Give the dough a quarter turn and knead it again with the heel of your hand. Fold, turn, and knead until dough is smooth and satiny. It will take about ten minutes.

4 Very lightly oil and flour a long, thin rolling pin.

Knead and roll by hand, continued

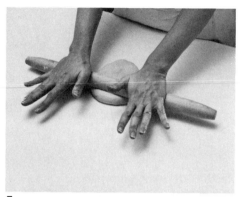

5 With only light pressure, roll the far third of the circle away from you. Give the dough a quarter turn and repeat. Continue until the dough is one-eighth inch thick.

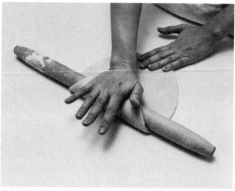

6 Turn the far end of the dough over the rolling pin and roll it toward you, just until the edge of the circle is under the pin.

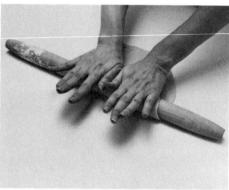

7 Put your hands next to each other in the center of the rolling pin and quickly roll the pin back and forth.

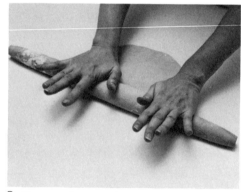

8 Keep moving your hands apart while rolling the pin back and forth.

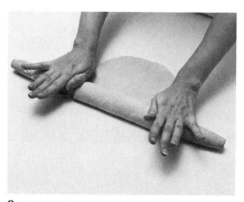

9 Your hands should reach the edges of the pin in a second or two.

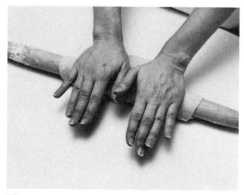

10 Roll more of the dough onto the pin and repeat, moving the hands apart as you roll the pin back and forth. Turn the dough and roll another edge over the pin. Repeat the thinning process until the dough is almost transparent.

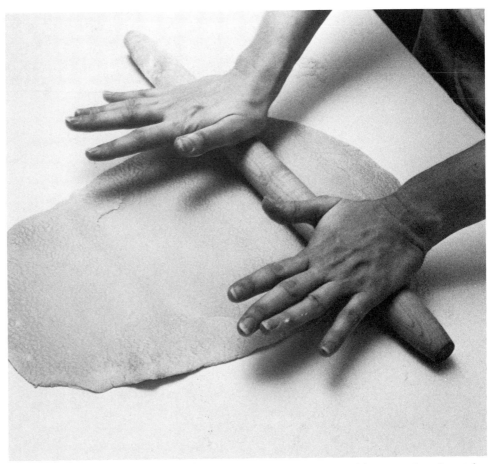

11 Unroll the dough and flatten any bumps with the rolling pin. The dough is now ready to be cut for stuffed pasta, or dried and cut for noodles.

Knead and roll by machine

Although it is much easier to roll noodle dough by machine than by hand, purists maintain that the texture produced by the machine is too smooth.

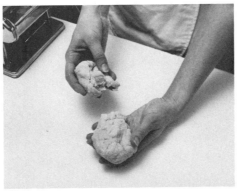

1 Break off a small amount of the crumbly pasta dough.

2 Put the remainder on a soup plate and cover it with another soup plate so it won't dry out.

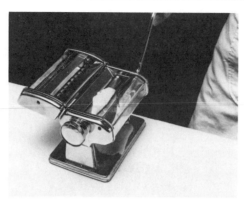

3 Using the widest setting, feed the small piece of dough through the machine.

4 Fold the dough in half.

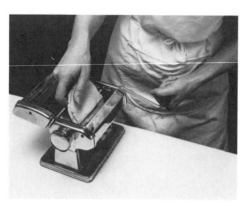

5 Put it through the widest setting again. Fold and repeat until it is smooth and satiny, about eight times in all.

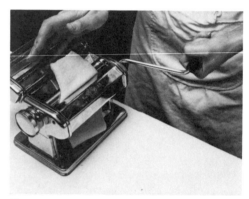

6 Feed unfolded sheets of dough into the machine at progressively narrower settings. If the dough is for stuffed pasta, use it immediately. If it is for flat noodles, dry it according to instructions further on in this chapter.

Shape tortellini

Most stuffed pasta is made from the same basic egg dough. It is the shape, the filling, and the sauce that make each one distinctive. Tortellini are stuffed circles of dough that are pressed into a compact shape. Cappelletti are made the same way, but they are squares of dough rather than circles.

1 Cut kneaded and rolled pasta dough into one and one-half inch strips. Using one strip of dough at a time (keep the rest covered), cut out two-inch circles using the rim of a glass or a cookie cutter.

2 Put one-quarter teaspoon of filling on each circle.

3 Fold the dough over the filling. It won't quite reach the opposite side.

4 Press with your fingers to seal the edges.

5 Put your index finger in the center and bend the pasta around it.

Shape tortellini, continued

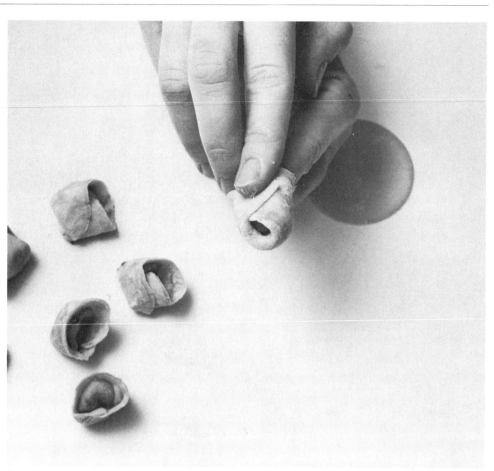

6 Press the two ends together to seal.

Fill and cut ravioli

1 Cut kneaded and rolled pasta dough into two rectangles about four inches wide. Place one-quarter teaspoon of filling for each ravioli in two rows at one-and-one-half-inch intervals along one rectangle.

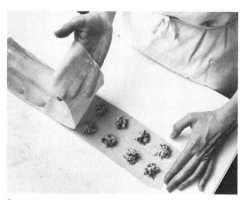

2 Cover with the second rectangle.

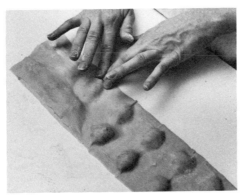

3 Press around the filling with your fingers to seal the dough and get any air out.

4 Cut into squares with a wide pastry wheel that crimps both edges. Run the wheel along outside edges to make the ravioli uniform on all sides.

Fill and cut tortelloni

Tortelloni are like ravioli, but are cut on only three sides.

1 Cut kneaded and rolled pasta dough into strips two and one-half inches wide. Put one-quarter teaspoon of filling for each tortelloni at one-and-one-half-inch intervals down the center.

2 Fold the near edge of dough over the filling.

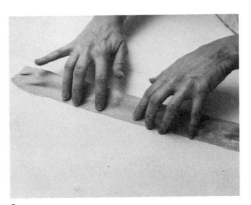

3 Press the edges together.

4 Press the dough together between the filling.

Fill and cut tortelloni, continued

5 Run a narrow pastry wheel down the long side to make the edges uniform. Then cut between the filling.

Cut and parboil lasagna, manicotti, and cannelloni

All these large flat pieces of pasta are parboiled before further cooking.

1 Roll out long rectangles of pasta dough—about four and one-half inches wide. With a pastry wheel, cut eleven-inch lengths for lasagna, six inches for manicotti, and four and one-half inches for cannelloni.

2 Put a few pieces at a time into rapidly boiling salted water and leave them for ten seconds.

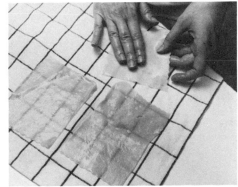

3 Remove the pasta with a slotted spoon and place in ice water to stop the cooking.

4 Dry the pieces on a towel. Assemble the lasagne according to the recipe. Fill and roll manicotti and cannelloni according to the following instructions.

Fill and roll manicotti and cannelloni

1 Put about one tablespoon of filling in the center of each piece of pasta.

2 For manicotti, fold in the short sides.

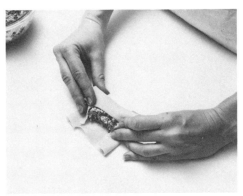

3 Roll the dough around the filling in a neat package. The pasta will stick together if it is fresh.

4 For cannelloni, roll the dough around the filling leaving the ends open.

Dry and cut dough for noodles

Unlike stuffed pasta, flat noodles are cut from dough that has been dried and stretched after it is kneaded. Fettucine, tagliatelle, and tagliarini are all flat noodles that are different only in width.

1 Roll all the kneaded and rolled pasta dough onto the rolling pin.

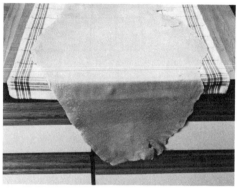

2 Unroll it onto a kitchen towel, letting about one-third hang over the edge of the work surface. Every ten minutes shift it so another third hangs over the edge. The dough should be dry and leathery but still pliable.

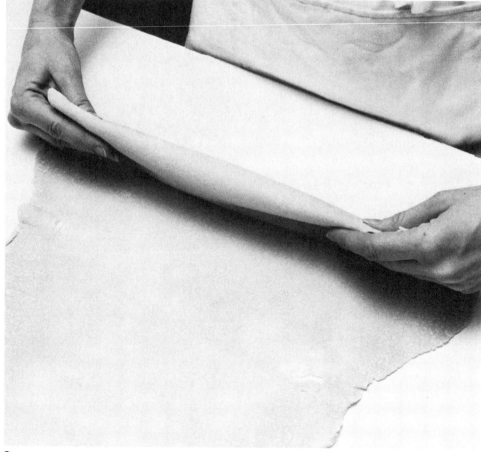

3 Roll the dough onto the rolling pin and unroll it on a clean work surface. Fold the dough loosely over itself into a long flat rectangle about three inches wide.

4 Hold the dough with one hand, fingers curved under. Hold the blade against the knuckles and slice the dough into the desired widths.

5 Unroll the strands and spread them out on a clean surface to dry for five or ten minutes before cooking. (The dried noodles can be stored in a cool spot.)

Cut noodles by machine

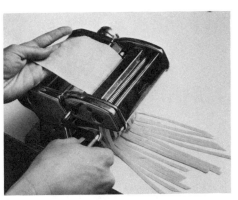

1 Feed kneaded, rolled, and dried pasta dough into the machine set for the desired width.

2 Let the noodles dry for at least five minutes before cooking. They shouldn't be sticky.

Cook noodles and test for doneness

Pasta should be cooked al dente, which means firm to the bite. Homemade pasta cooks in only a few seconds after the water has returned to the boil. Commercial pasta will take longer but not as long as indicated on the packages.

1 Add salt to four quarts rapidly boiling water for each pound of pasta.

2 Add the noodles all at once so they will be done at the same time.

Cook noodles, continued

3 Stir the noodles with a wooden spoon to keep them from sticking together. Let the water return to the boil.

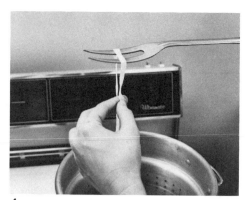

4 Lift up a noodle with a long fork and bite into it or press with your finger to see if it is soft but still firm in the center.

Roll garganelli

Garganelli is a tubular pasta that has a ridged pattern achieved by rolling it on a comb.

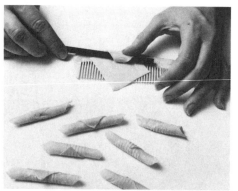

1 Cut kneaded, rolled, and dried pasta dough into one-and-one-half-inch squares. Place a point of each square on a comb that has long teeth and roll the opposite point around a pencil.

2 Roll the pasta around the pencil and down the comb, pressing into it to create the design.

DUMPLINGS

Shape and cook

Dumplings can be cooked in stock, soups, stews, or plain water. The important thing is to have the liquid at a simmer. If it is boiling, the dumplings will disintegrate.

1 Dip two teaspoons into simmering liquid.

2 Dip one spoon into the batter.

3 Run the second spoon under the batter and scoop the dumpling into the simmering liquid.

4 Put a glass cover over the pan so you can see that the liquid is just at a simmer.

5 After ten minutes, remove the cover and insert a toothpick into the dumpling. If the toothpick comes out dry, the dumpling is done.

Shape and cook spätzle

Spätzle are the German version of small egg noodles.

1 Put spätzle dough into a metal colander and hold it over a pan of simmering water.

2 With a wooden spoon, force the dough through the holes in the colander. The spätzle will sink to the bottom.

3 When the spätzle float on the top they are done.

Shape gnocchi for poaching

There are several kinds of gnocchi dough and many ways to cook gnocchi, which are Italian dumplings. But they are usually poached first before further cooking.

1 Outfit a pastry bag with a plain tip and fill the bag with gnocchi dough. Dip a small sharp knife into simmering water.

2 Force the dough through the pastry bag and cut it with the knife when the dough is about three-quarters of an inch long.

Fill and shape won ton

Won ton are the delicate Chinese dumplings served in soups or deep-fried and served with a sauce. Won ton skins are available in supermarkets and Chinese grocery shops, usually in one-pound packages. Buy the thinnest ones possible, and keep the skins covered as you work so they don't dry out.

1 Hold the won ton skin in one hand and put a heaping teaspoon of filling in the center. I'm using ground pork, spinach, scallions, soy sauce, and sesame oil.

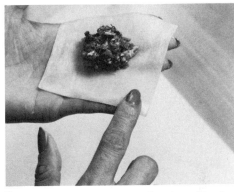

2 Dip your finger in water and moisten the edge of the skin facing you, not the sides.

3 Fold the moistened edge over the filling and press it against the opposite edge.

4 Press the sides of the won ton together.

Fill and shape won ton, continued

5 Fold the moistened seam toward you slightly.

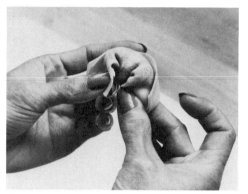

6 Bend the sides of the won ton around the filling, bringing the folded corners together. The open corners stand free.

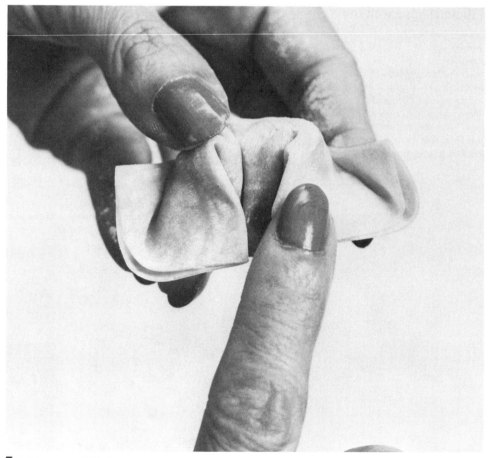

7 Moisten one folded corner.

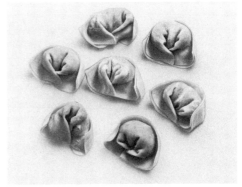

8 Press the folded corners together.

9 If the filling was cooked, the finished won ton can be wrapped in foil and frozen. Or they can be frozen in the cooked soup. Keep those you are going to cook immediately covered with plastic wrap so they don't dry out.

Fill and shape shiu may

Chinese dumplings come in many shapes and with a variety of fillings. Shiu may, which are among the prettiest, are steamed.

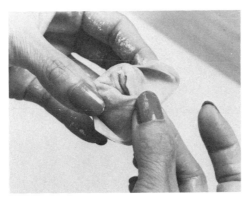

1 Cut won ton skins into circles.

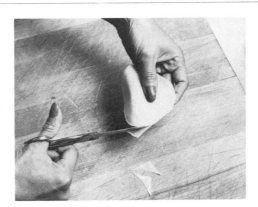

2 Hold the skin in one hand and place one teaspoon of filling in the center.

3 With your fingers, gather together the edges of the won ton skin, forming a pouch.

4 Pinch and pleat the edges.

Fill and shape shiu may, continued

5 Encircle and press the dumpling gently around the middle using the thumb and forefinger so that the filling mounds slightly and the dumpling has a pinched waist.

6 Garnish the shiu may with a sprig of fresh coriander.

7 The completed shiu may ready for steaming.

Fill and shape jao-tze

This delicately pleated northern Chinese dumpling is fried, steamed, or boiled. The skin can be made with a flour and water dough or you can use commercial round wrappers available in Oriental markets.

1 Holding the skin in one hand, place one heaping teaspoon filling in the center of the wrapper. Dip your finger in water and moisten the perimeter of the wrapper.

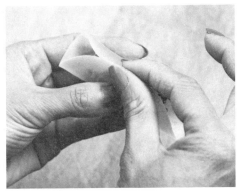

2 Bring up the edges and press together in the center, leaving the ends open.

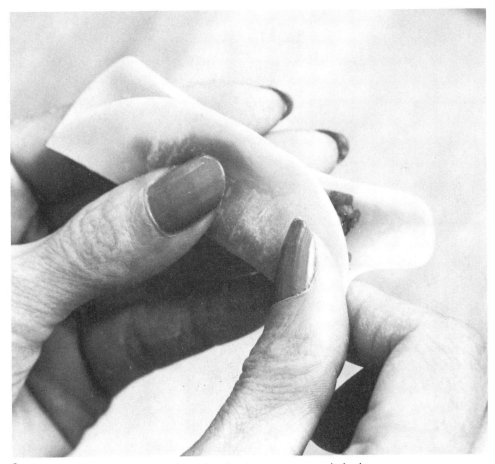

3 Pinch the edges of the right end together, leaving wrapper open in back.

**Fill and shape jao-tze,
continued**

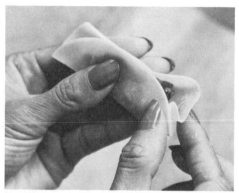

4 Pinch together again, making another pleat with the open wrapper.

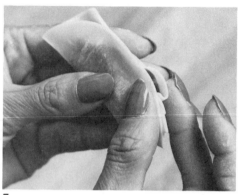

5 Continue to pinch and pleat until all the wrapper on the right side is taken up, usually three pleats. The purpose of the pleats is so the jao-tze will stand up. Repeat pleating on the left side.

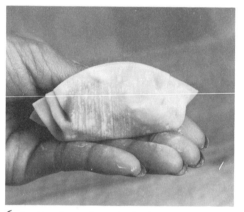

6 Jao-tze shown from the back.

7 Completed jao-tze from the front. Cover with plastic wrap until ready to cook.

RICE

Steam

Everyone swears by his own method of cooking rice. I find that steaming it produces the fluffiest rice with every grain separated. You can steam brown rice in the same way; just boil it initially for five minutes longer than white rice.

1 Pour rice into a large amount of rapidly boiling salted water.

2 Cook at a rapid boil for seven to eight minutes.

3 The rice should feel firm to the touch.

4 Drain the rice through a sieve and run cold water through the sieve to remove excess starch. Put in a steamer over boiling water, cover, and cook for fifteen minutes.

5 The cooked rice will be fluffy and well separated.

Boil

This method produces grains that stick together, which is preferred in Oriental cooking so that it is easier to eat with chopsticks. Before cooking, put rice in a sieve and run cold water over it to remove excess starch.

1 In a heavy saucepan, combine one and one-half cups water with each cup of rice.

2 Let it come to the boil and stir with a wooden spoon.

3 Boil uncovered about ten minutes or until the rice forms craters, called fish eyes.

4 Lower the heat and cover the rice. Cook over very low heat for about twenty minutes.

5 The finished rice will be quite sticky.

Cook risotto

Short-grained arborio rice produces the best risotto because the grains can absorb a lot of liquid without becoming soft. The trick to making risotto is to add the liquid in small amounts and to stir it constantly so the rice does not stick to the pan.

1 Sauté onion in butter and olive oil until translucent but not colored.

2 Add rice and stir to coat all the grains. Bring stock to a simmer on another burner.

3 Ladle one-half cup of stock into the rice. Start over medium heat.

4 Stir constantly until rice absorbs the stock. Adjust the heat if the stock seems to be evaporating too quickly.

Cook risotto, continued

5 Add another one-half cup of stock and stir until it is absorbed. Continue adding small amounts of stock and stirring.

6 When the risotto is almost done, it will be creamy but the rice will still be firm in the center.

7 Stir in any meat, vegetables, herbs you wish. I'm using sautéed zucchini.

8 Add one-quarter cup of stock and stir until it is absorbed.

9 Add a generous amount of Parmesan cheese. Stir and serve immediately. Risotto gets gummy if it sits.

Cook pilaf

Pilaf, the traditional rice dish of Turkey, Syria, and Persia, is best when made with a long-grain rice called basmati, which is available in specialty food stores. But any good long-grain rice can be used. Meat, poultry, or seafood and seasonings are added.

1 Sauté chopped onion in butter until onion is soft.

2 Add rice and stir to coat the grains with the butter. Bring liquid to a boil.

3 Add raisins or chopped chicken livers to the rice and onion and mix well.

4 Add twice the amount of boiling liquid as rice. Cover and cook over very low heat for about twenty minutes.

Cook pilaf, continued

5 Uncover and pull the rice from the side of the pan to see if all the liquid is absorbed. If not, cook for a few minutes longer. Spoon into a bowl and stir in nuts, raisins, parsley, or whatever.

Form in ring mold

1 Generously butter the ring mold.

2 Pack the cooked rice (I'm using pilaf) into the mold and smooth the top.

3 Put a serving plate over the top of the mold.   **4** Invert the mold onto the plate.

5 Garnish with toasted almonds, parsley, and raisins, if desired.

8
EGGS

GENERAL

Test for freshness

Break an egg onto a plate to see if it holds together. If it is thin and watery, it is not fresh. The yolk will vary in color, but it should be plump and well centered. Never buy cracked eggs because harmful bacteria can enter through the crack.

Separate

Either of these methods is satisfactory for separating eggs. Using your hand is a safer way, however, because you are less likely to pierce the yolk. In either case, be sure that no yolk falls into the whites because the smallest particle of yolk will keep the whites from whipping properly.

1 Have two bowls ready, one for the yolks and one for the whites. Crack the egg sharply in the center on the edge of a bowl; then carefully pull the shell apart with you fingers.

2 Pour the yolk back and forth from one shell to the other until all the white has dropped into the bowl.

3 You can also break the egg and pour it into your slightly cupped hand. Let the white fall through your fingers into the bowl.

Beat whites

A large balloon whisk and an unlined copper bowl are the best utensils for beating egg whites because you achieve the greatest volume. The balloon whisk incorporates the air most efficiently; the acid in the bowl reacts with the whites to hold their satiny texture. However, you can use a stainless steel bowl and add cream of tartar for the proper acidity.

1 Before each use, clean the copper bowl with salt and just enough vinegar to moisten it.

2 Use a sponge or soft cloth to scrub the entire surface; then rinse with hot water and dry thoroughly. Both the bowl and the egg whites should be at room temperature.

Beat whites, continued

3 With a balloon whisk, start beating the whites slowly in a circular motion, coming down on the far side of the bowl and up toward you. The purpose is to incorporate air into the whites.

4 Increase the speed and beat in a figure-eight motion, down in the middle of the bowl, under, and up on your side, then down and away from you.

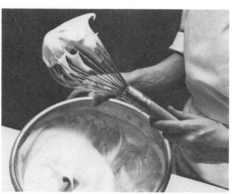

5 Soft peaks will form, which is when you gradually add sugar or sugar syrup for a meringue. Beat faster with a circular under and up motion.

6 When stiff peaks form, stir the whites briefly and use immediately.

7 Put a whole egg on the whites to be sure they are stiff but not dry, the proper consistency for a soufflé or mousse. The egg should rest on top and not sink.

8 Egg whites that have been beaten too long and are too dry will not mix well with other ingredients to perform their leavening function.

Fold in whites

1 Add about one-third of the stiffly beaten egg whites to soufflé or mousse mixture.

2 Cut these whites into the center with a rubber spatula. Pull down, under, and up on the side, folding the whites into the sauce. Give the bowl a quarter turn and fold again. Repeat several times.

3 Add the rest of the egg whites and fold in gently just until the streaks of white are evenly distributed.

Beat whole with fork

For omelets and scrambled eggs, beat the whole eggs until yolks and whites are well blended and frothy.

Beat yolks with sugar until ribbon forms

This is the consistency called for in many desserts, such as soufflés, cakes, custards, and sabayon, or zabaglione.

1 Whisk the yolks in the top of a double boiler until thick and creamy. The water should be at a simmer; if heat is too high the eggs will scramble.

2 Add the sugar very gradually, whisking all the time.

3 After several minutes, the sauce will fall in a ribbon when the whisk is lifted above the mixture.

Add yolks to hot mixture

Here is a method that is safer than beating yolks directly into a hot mixture. By adding a little of the sauce to the yolks first, the yolks are heated gently and are less likely to scramble when they are stirred into the hot mixture.

1 Beat yolks with a whisk until well blended and add a little cold milk or cream, beating to blend. This will prevent graininess.

2 Add a little of the hot sauce to the yolks while beating.

Add yolks to hot mixture, continued

3 Pour the egg yolk mixture into the hot sauce.

4 Stir constantly over low heat until thickened and smooth.

Boil

Eggs are simmered over low heat rather than boiled, although the term "boiled" is generally used. Use very fresh eggs for soft-boiled or eggs mollet. Use eggs that are two or three days old for hard-boiled, because they will be easier to peel.

1 Using a pin, poke a hold in the large end of the egg to pierce the membrane. This will prevent the egg from cracking and make hard-boiled eggs easier to peel.

2 Bring water to a gentle boil, lower eggs into it with a slotted spoon, and reduce heat to low so that the water simmers.

3 Cook a soft-boiled egg, at left, about three and one-half minutes; egg mollet, in center, for six minutes; hard-boiled, on right, for eleven minutes. Plunge eggs to be peeled into cold water.

Scramble

This method produces the creamiest texture I've ever found.

1 Pour beaten eggs into the top of a double boiler set over simmering, not boiling, water.

2 Stir slowly with a wooden spoon, constantly scraping the bottom and sides of the pan.

3 When eggs start to thicken, add one teaspoon of butter for each egg, stirring constantly after each addition.

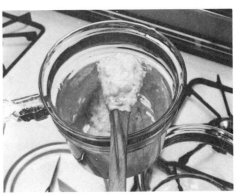

4 When the eggs reach the desired consistency, remove from heat, season, and serve. The length of time for cooking will depend on the number of eggs.

Poach

It is important to get the eggs into the water quickly so you can time them accurately. It helps to crack the eggs and put them on their sides in the egg carton. Then you can break them into the water in rapid succession.

1 If eggs are not perfectly fresh, lower them into simmering water for ten seconds. Otherwise, they will not hold together.

2 Add about two tablespoons white vinegar to four inches of water in a deep casserole. The vinegar helps the whites to coagulate.

3 Break the eggs quickly into the simmering water so they will all cook about the same length of time.

4 When all the eggs are in, hold a slotted spoon parallel to the surface and move it over the top of the water, which will keep the eggs from sticking to the bottom. Cook about three and one-half minutes, or until whites are firm.

5 Remove the eggs with a slotted spoon and put in cold water for a few seconds to remove the vinegar and stop the cooking.

6 Put the eggs on a kitchen towel and trim off any loose white.

7 If you are not serving them immediately, leave the eggs in cold water. They can be stored for several hours, or overnight, and reheated briefly in hot water before serving.

Fry

1 Melt butter in an iron or nonstick pan that you keep just for eggs. When the butter is just frothy but not colored, break an egg into a saucer and slide into the pan.

2 Cook over moderate heat until just set. Turn the egg quickly with a spatula if you want a firmer yolk. This is easier to do in a large pan.

Bake

1 Butter an individual ramekin and place it in a larger pan. Add about a tablespoon of cream, tomato sauce, puréed vegetables, or whatever to the ramekin.

2 Break an egg into the ramekin and season with salt and pepper.

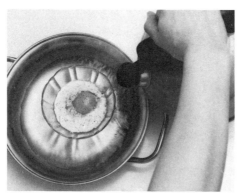

3 Pour boiling water into pan about halfway up the ramekin. Bake in a 375-degree oven for about ten minutes.

4 Remove the ramekin before egg is fully done because it will continue to cook in the dish. The white should be almost set and the yolk slightly runny.

Deep fry

Deep-fried eggs will be golden on the outside and the yolk will be soft like a poached egg. One caution: the oil must be extremely hot for the eggs to cook properly so be careful not to burn yourself when inserting them.

1 Heat oil in a heavy, deep casserole to 380 degrees. Soak a wooden spoon in the hot oil for several minutes so the egg won't stick to it. Break eggs into individual ramekins.

2 Put one egg into a ladle and lower it just to the top of the oil. Pour the egg into the oil.

3 Put the wooden spoon over the egg and gather the white around the yolk.

4 Pull the egg to the side and shape it against the casserole into an oval. It will cook in about one minute.

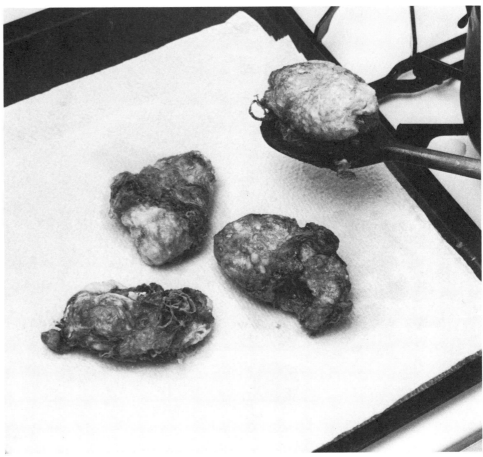

5 Remove and drain on paper towels. Serve with tomato sauce, if desired.

HARD-BOILED

Peel and slice

This Oriental method of slicing hard-boiled eggs produces a neater cut than a knife, and the yolk doesn't get crushed.

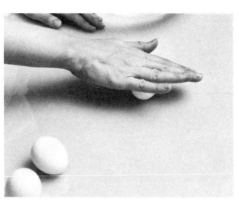

1 Roll eggs on a hard suface to break the shell slightly.

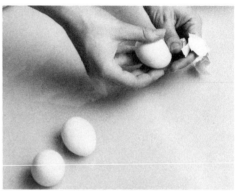

2 Crack and pull off the shell. Eggs that are a few days old will be easier to peel than fresh ones.

3 Wrap a length of thread around the egg lengthwise and cross it at the top.

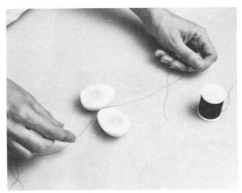

4 Pull the thread and it will cut through the egg.

5 You can also cut through the egg crosswise in the same way.

Sieve yolks

Use sieved yolks for stuffing eggs, over buttered vegetables, in any dish called mimosa, or with caviar if you're lucky.

1 Put a fine-meshed sieve over a bowl and add the yolks. Press down with a wooden spoon all around the sieve.

2 Scrape the yolk off the bottom of the sieve as you go along.

OMELETS

Cook folded omelet

A folded omelet is the exception to the rule requiring low heat for eggs. You want to cook it quickly over high heat. Purists believe an omelet should not be colored, but I like it slightly brown.

1 Heat an iron or nonstick pan that is used only for eggs by rolling it around over the burner.

2 Melt butter in pan over high heat until foamy.

Cook folded omelet, continued

3 When foam starts to subside, quickly pour in the beaten eggs (mixed with herbs in this case).

4 Hold a fork parallel to the pan and quickly stir the eggs four times around. Simultaneously, shake the pan with your other hand.

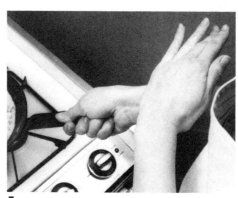

5 Hit your forearm just above your wrist.

6 This action makes the omelet slide to the far edge of the pan. The top should be very creamy.

7 Sprinkle filling on top, if desired. I'm using ham and cheese.

8 Fold over one side of the omelet with your fork, then the other.

9 Lift the pan and invert the omelet onto a plate.

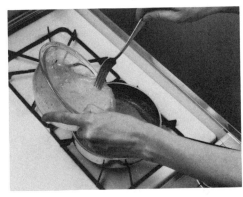

10 The omelet should have pointed edges and the seam should be on the plate.

Cook flat omelet

A flat omelet, or frittata in Italian, is firm, not runny, but it should not be dry. It is cut into wedges and served hot or at room temperature, which makes it good picnic fare.

1 Melt butter over low heat in a heavy skillet or nonstick pan with straight sides.

2 When the butter begins to foam, add half the beaten eggs.

3 Stir briefly over the bottom using a fork.

4 Add the filling—cheese, vegetables, herbs, ham, whatever.

**Cook flat omelet,
continued**

5 Pour the rest of the egg on top, folding down the cooked egg that has risen up the sides.

6 With the fork, continue to pull cooked egg away from the side so that the liquid egg runs out to the edges. Cook about five minutes over low heat.

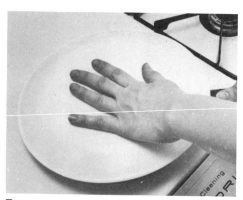

7 Invert the omelet onto a plate.

8 Slide it back into the skillet and cook three minutes longer.

9 Invert again onto a serving plate.

SOUFFLÉS

Dust mold

Butter keeps a soufflé from sticking to the mold. Dusting it adds texture and flavor to the cooked soufflé.

1 Butter the soufflé mold and put in flour, grated cheese, or bread crumbs for an entrée soufflé. For a dessert soufflé, dust with sugar.

Dust mold, continued

2 Tilt the mold so that it is thoroughly coated.

3 Shake out excess.

Tie collar

A collar is used primarily for a frozen soufflé so that it looks as if it puffed up above the mold.

1 Butter a strip of aluminum foil or kitchen parchment and wrap it around the soufflé mold, buttered side in. Leave a two-inch collar standing up.

2 Tie securely with kitchen twine.

Fill mold

For a cooked soufflé, don't fill the mold above the rim or you will have soufflé all over your oven. The egg whites will make it rise and puff up.

1 Carefully pour the soufflé mixture into the mold and fill to just below the rim. For a frozen soufflé with a collar, you can fill the mold above the rim and part way up the collar.

2 Make a slight dome shape in the center with a rubber spatula.

3 Run your finger around the perimeter just below the rim. This will give the cooked soufflé a nice shape. Cook according to recipe directions.

Test for doneness

1 A cooked soufflé will be slightly firm to the touch. It should be creamy on the inside and crisp on the outside.

2 You can insert a skewer or trussing needle into the side of the top of the soufflé (not into the center, which will deflate it). If it comes out slightly moist, the soufflé is done.

3 To serve the cooked soufflé, scoop out a portion of the creamy center and a portion of the crisper side for each serving.

MAYONNAISE

Beat yolks and whisk in oil

This is an easily mastered technique that every cook should practice until it is routine. Homemade mayonnaise has a flavor and consistency superior to any commercial variety, and with a few additions you have such sauces as rémoulade, tartar, and aioli. The only trick is to beat the yolks well initially, so they will incorporate the oil, and to add the oil gradually at the beginning.

1 Using a wire whisk, beat egg yolk with mustard, vinegar, and salt until thoroughly blended.

2 Gradually add oil (a light olive oil, safflower oil, or a combination of both, according to taste) in droplets, beating with the whisk to incorporate the oil with the yolk.

3 When the mayonnaise has thickened slightly and you've added about half the oil, increase the flow to a thin but steady stream, beating constantly.

4 The completed mayonnaise will be quite thick. Taste for seasoning and add lemon juice, if desired.

Correct separated mayonnaise

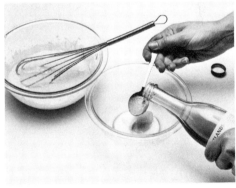

1 The mayonnaise may separate if the oil is added too quickly.

2 Put a teaspoon of mustard and a teaspoon of vinegar (for one cup of mayonnaise) into a clean bowl.

3 Mix with a clean whisk and slowly add the separated mayonnaise, about a teaspoon at a time, beating after each addition.

4 The mayonnaise will thicken again and be like new.

HOLLANDAISE

Beat yolks and add butter

Hollandaise is a basic sauce: Orange juice and zest produce a sauce maltaise; tarragon and vinegar, a sauce béarnaise; tomatoes, a sauce choron. The trick in making it is to keep the water in the double boiler at a simmer, never a boil. Too high heat will cause the eggs to scramble.

1 Put the egg yolks in the top of a double boiler and add cold water (one tablespoon for four yolks).

2 Whisk the yolks and water until the yolks are sticky.

3 Add clarified butter in a very slow stream, whisking constantly. If the sauce doesn't thicken properly, the butter was added too quickly.

4 When the hollandaise begins to thicken, add the butter (up to a cup) a little more quickly. Continue to whisk until thickened.

5 Add lemon juice and serve immediately, if possible. The sauce can be kept briefly in a bowl of tepid water.

Correct separated hollandaise

1 If the sauce is too thick and looks as if it is going to be scrambled or separate, remove the pan from the heat.

2 Put it in a pan of cold water and whisk constantly until it is smooth.

CUSTARD

Cook until it coats spoon

This is the consistency for a light custard, called crème anglaise, used like cream over fruit or as a base for other desserts.

1 Add hot milk in a steady stream to egg yolks and sugar that have been beaten until they form a ribbon. Whisk constantly.

2 Set the pan over simmering water and stir the mixture until the sauce coats a wooden spoon.

Caramelize a mold

Custards are frequently cooked in a mold that has been caramelized to give the custard a brown sweet glaze. Metal molds become coated more evenly and are easier to use because the sugar can be cooked in the mold.

1 Put about three tablespoons of water in a charlotte mold (or any one-quart metal mold) and add one-half cup sugar.

2 Swirl the mold over low heat. Don't stir the mixture.

3 Brush down any crystals that form on the sides using a pastry brush dipped in cold water.

4 After a few minutes, the sugar will begin to color and then become amber. It turns color quickly at this point and will burn if you don't move rapidly.

5 Immediately plunge the mold into a bowl of ice water.

6 Swirl the sugar syrup around in the mold until it is completely coated.

7 Turn the mold over onto a plate and let the excess run out. The mold can sit until you are ready to fill it.

Cook and strain into mold

1 Put a mold into a larger pan and place a fine-meshed strainer on top. I'm using a caramelized mold.

2 Add hot milk by droplets to uncooked beaten egg yolks and sugar. Beat constantly until well blended and smooth.

Cook and strain into mold, continued

3 Carefully spoon off the foam that forms on top, which would toughen the custard.

4 Ladle the custard mixture through the strainer into the mold.

5 Pour boiling water around the mold about half-way up the sides and bake at 325 degrees. Keep filling the pan with boiling water as it evaporates. Cooking time will depend on the size of the mold.

MERINGUE

Shape and decorate vacherin

Meringue should stand in stiff, glossy peaks. For shells such as vacherin, dacquoise or baked alaska, use an Italian meringue made with cooked sugar syrup, which partly cooks the whites and makes a sturdier casing.

1 Place parchment paper on a baking sheet and put four dabs of meringue in the corners to hold the paper down. Using a bowl, outline four circles with a pencil. Mine are about six inches in diameter.

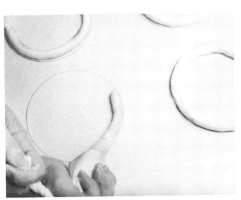

2 Outfit a pastry bag with a plain tube and fill with meringue. Pipe out to outline the four circles.

Shape and decorate vacherin, continued

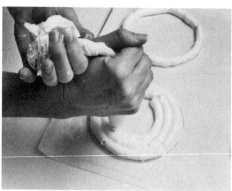

3 Fill one of the circles with smaller and smaller circles to form a base. (Cover any remaining meringue with plastic wrap.) Bake the circles in a 200-degree oven for about one and one-half hours, or until dry.

4 Carefully pry up the rings and cool on open rack. When cool, use leftover meringue and pipe out dabs on the perimeter of the base, about two inches apart.

5 Place a ring on the base, more dabs of meringue, and continue until all three rings are stacked. Return to the 200-degree oven until dabs of meringue are dry, about forty minutes.

 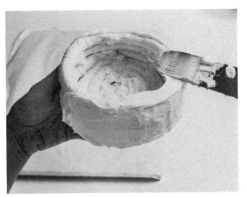

6 Make fresh meringue and frost the shell, filling in any holes between the rings.

7 Smooth the surface with a spatula.

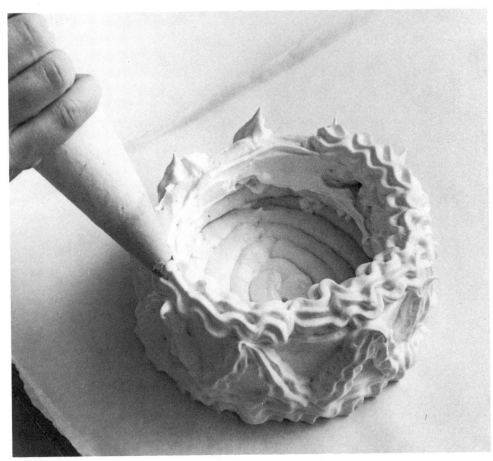

8 Decorate as desired with meringue and return to the oven. Bake another hour, or until completely hard. The shell can be left in the turned-off oven until ready to fill and serve or it can be stored in an airtight container.

Poach

Use a meringue made with granulated sugar rather than sugar syrup. Poached meringues can then be used for oeufs à la neige.

1 Dip a metal or wooden spoon into meringue and round it with another spoon to make an oval shape.

2 Poach about a minute and a half on each side in three or four inches of simmering water or milk.

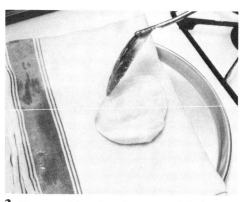

3 Remove with a slotted spoon and drain on a clean kitchen towel.

9
BUTTER

BUTTER

Clarify

This is a simple technique that is used in many cuisines. The purpose is to remove the milky solids from melted butter because the solids burn when heated to high temperatures. Use unsalted butter for cooking because the flavor is better.

1 Cut butter into chunks and melt over low heat. Skim the foam off the top.

2 Pour the clear liquid into a measuring cup, leaving the milky residue. Discard the milk solids.

Mix with flour for thickening

1 Combine equal parts flour and chilled butter and work together with your fingers until thoroughly blended.

2 Break off small amounts to add to sauces for thickening. This is called *beurre manié* in French.

Cut into curls or balls

There are many ways to cut butter decoratively for serving at the table. Here are two of the easiest.

1 Dip a melon-ball cutter into lukewarm water and place it on the cold butter.

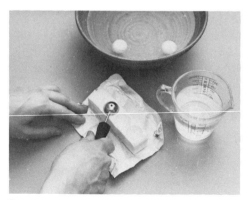

2 Press down, turn, and scoop out a ball. Put the balls in cold water until ready to serve.

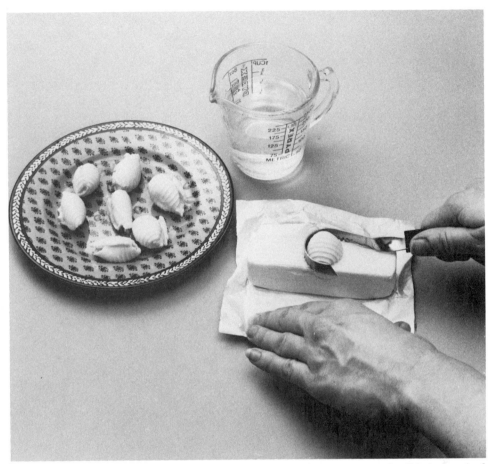

3 Thoroughly chill the stick of butter. Dip a butter curler into lukewarm water and pull it the length of the stick. Refrigerate the curls on a plate until ready to serve.

Cream

Butter is creamed to soften it so you can incorporate sugar or seasonings.

1 Have sweet butter at room temperature. Work it with your hands to soften it.

2 Beat briefly with a wooden spoon until creamy. Don't overbeat or the oil will separate from the mass.

Roll and slice seasoned butter

Herbs, anchovies, mustard, garlic, and shellfish produce interesting and varied flavors when added to butter. Serve over meats, fish, or poultry, depending on seasoning. Seasoned butters are also used to enrich sauces.

1 Cream sweet butter and add seasonings. (I used herbs, lemon juice, salt and pepper.)

2 Spread onto a piece of wax paper.

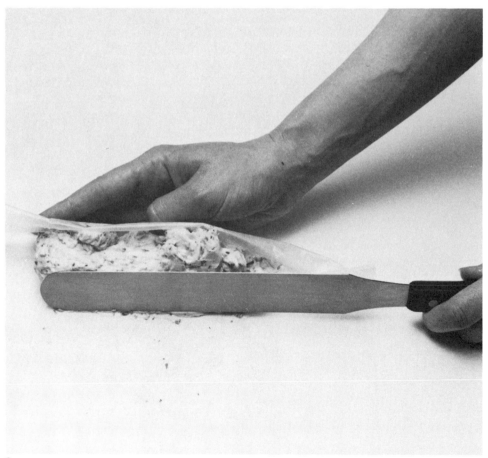

3 Hold up one end of the paper and, with a spatula, push the butter against your hand.

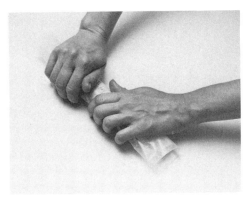

4 Roll the butter tightly in the paper.

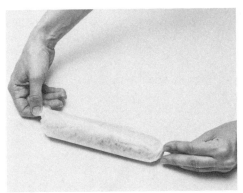

5 Fold up and twist the ends and refrigerate (or freeze).

6 When butter is thoroughly chilled, dip a decorative cutting knife into lukewarm water and slice. Serve the butter over meats or fish, depending on the seasonings.

10
PANCAKES AND CRÊPES

PANCAKES AND CRÊPES

Mix and cook pancake batter

The only trick to making light and delicious pancakes is to stir the batter just to combine the ingredients. Never beat the batter because the pancakes will be tough.

1 Sift the flour, salt, and baking powder into a bowl. Add the beaten eggs, milk, and melted butter all at once.

2 Stir only until the dry ingredients are moistened. The batter should be lumpy.

3 Scrape the batter into a measuring cup to make pouring easier.

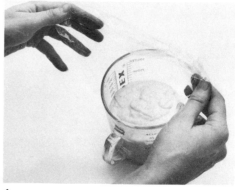

4 If you have time, cover the batter with plastic wrap and refrigerate it for one or two hours. This lets the flour expand and absorb the moisture.

5 Heat the griddle and test it by dropping cold water on it. If the water jumps and sputters, the griddle is the right temperature.

6 Pour a small amount of batter onto the griddle for each pancake.

7 Turn the pancakes with a spatula when bubbles appear on the surface. Cook briefly on the other side until lightly browned.

Mix and cook crêpes

Crêpes are very thin pancakes that are filled with creamed mixtures for luncheon dishes or with sweet mixtures for desserts.

1 Sift the dry ingredients into a bowl. Make a well in the center and break the egg into it.

2 Beat while gradually adding the milk.

3 Add melted butter and beat until the dry ingredients are well moistened. The batter should be smooth.

4 Cover the batter and refrigerate for at least an hour, or even overnight, to let the flour expand.

5 To get just the right amount of butter in the heated crêpe pan, put a piece of raw potato on the end of a fork. Dip the potato in the melted butter and rub it over the bottom of the pan.

6 Ladle a small amount of batter into the pan.

7 Tip the pan so the batter runs evenly all over the bottom.

8 Run the tip of a knife around the crêpe to be sure it isn't sticking.

9 Turn the crêpe by flipping it. Pull the pan sharply toward you and up. This is easy to do with a little practice.

10 Or you can put a small knife under the crêpe and flip it over.

11 When the second side is cooked, stack the crêpes on a plate with the second side up, which will be spotty. This is the side that will hold the filling.

Fill dessert crêpes I

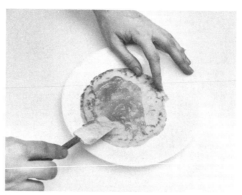

1 Using a small rubber spatula, spread a crêpe with jam.

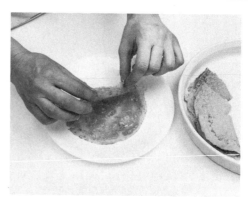

2 Fold it into halves.

3 And then into quarters.

4 Put the crêpes in a buttered baking dish and heat them in a 350-degree oven for ten minutes.

5 Sprinkle the crêpes with powdered sugar and toasted almonds.

Fill dessert crêpes II

1 Put a small amount of pastry cream flavored with strawberries and kirsch on the warm crêpe.

Fill dessert crêpes II, continued

2 Roll the crêpe around the filling, leaving the ends open.

3 Sprinkle with powdered sugar and arrange sliced strawberries over the top of the crêpes. Serve immediately.

Mix and cook Chinese pancakes

Chinese pancakes, called doilies, are sturdy wrappers made of a flour and water dough rather than a batter. They are steamed and served with many dishes, the most notable being Peking duck.

1 Put flour in a mixing bowl and make a well in the center. Add warm water all at once. Add vegetable oil.

2 Mix the dough with your hands until it sticks together.

3 Form the dough into a rough ball.

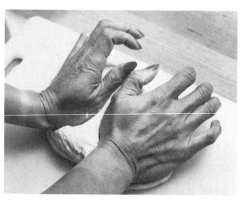

4 Knead the dough a few times.

5 Form it into a ball again and cover it. Let rest about twenty minutes to allow the gluten in the flour to relax.

6 Lightly flour your hands and rub the ball of dough between the palms of your hands.

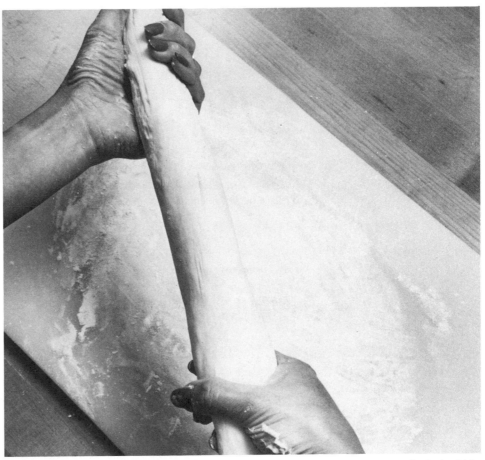

7 When the dough is a long sausage shape, stretch it slightly by pulling with your hands. It should be about one and one-half inches in diameter.

**Mix and cook Chinese
pancakes, continued**

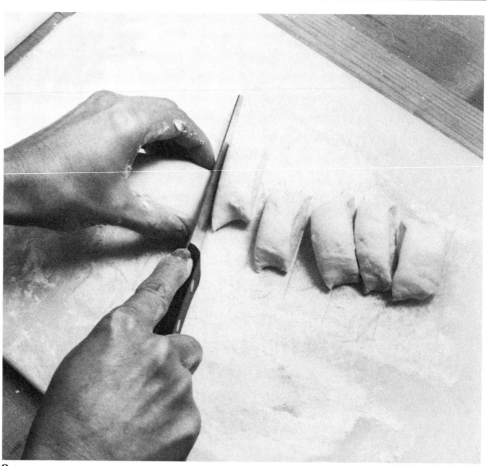

8 Place the dough on a heavily floured board and cut it into rounds about one inch thick.

9 Place the rounds on their sides and flatten them slightly.

10 Brush the tops of the rounds generously with oil.

11 Place one round on top of another, oiled sides together so you can separate them later.

12 Press down on each pair of rounds until it is about three and one-half inches in diameter.

13 Lightly roll each round until it is one-sixteenth inch thick. I'm using a cut-off broom handle for rolling because it is light; too much pressure will make it difficult to separate the pancakes.

Mix and cook Chinese pancakes, continued

14 Heat a nonstick skillet and add a pancake.

15 Cook until it is white on top, about thirty seconds. Turn and cook the other side about thirty seconds, until it is slightly puffed.

16 While the pancake is still warm, pull it apart with your fingers. Continue to cook all the pancakes in the same manner.

17 Stack the pancakes in aluminum foil. Wrap the foil completely around them and steam for twenty minutes.

Shape and cook tortillas

Mexican tortillas can be made with corn flour, called masa harina, which is available in many supermarkets and Spanish markets. Or they can be made with regular flour. They are shaped in the same way. There are special tortilla presses, but it is easy to roll them.

1 Mix warm water into masa harina, stirring with a wooden spoon.

2 Mix the dough with your hands until it sticks together. Add more water, if necessary.

3 Pull off a small piece of dough and rub it between your palms into a ball about one and one-half inches in diameter. Keep the balls covered as you shape them.

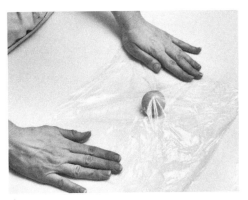

4 Put a ball between pieces of plastic wrap or wax paper.

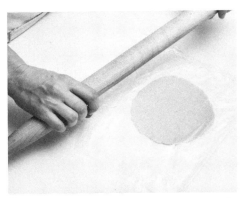

5 Roll the dough until it is about six inches in diameter and one-eighth inch thick. Continue to roll each ball of dough in the same way.

Shape and cook tortillas, continued

6 Cook the tortillas on a hot, ungreased griddle for thirty seconds. Turn with a spatula and cook the other side for one minute. Turn again and cook for thirty seconds.

7 Stack the tortillas in a napkin. They should be soft and pliable for filling.

11
BREADS

YEAST BREADS

Proof yeast

Yeast is a plant cell that needs warmth and sweetness to activate it. The essential thing is to have the liquid at a temperature of about 110 degrees. Test with a candy thermometer until you get the feel—it should be lukewarm, or suitable for a baby's bath. As long as you use dry yeast before the expiration date on the package, it probably will be "alive." But if it has been stored at very high or low temperatures, you should "prove" whether it is still active. Cake (or compressed) yeast is short-lived and seldom used.

1 Put the yeast in a small bowl and add one tablespoon flour and one teaspoon sugar for each package of yeast.

2 Add one-quarter cup lukewarm water.

3 Stir well to combine. Put in a warm place (about 80 degrees) for ten minutes.

4 The yeast will bubble and foam if it is active. It is then ready to be used.

Mix dough

The amount of flour needed for a yeast dough—no matter what the other ingredients—will vary greatly. Flours themselves differ in moisture content, and the humidity in the air will affect their absorption quality. Start with the least amount called for and add more as needed. You can use a heavy-duty mixer with a dough hook or a food processor, but a wooden spoon and a strong arm are just as good.

1 Add lukewarm water to the yeast and mix. Let the yeast sit for a few minutes until it is dissolved.

2 Combine the flour and other dry ingredients in a bowl. Make a well in the center with your fingers.

3 Pour in the yeast mixture.

4 Pour in the liquid.

5 Using a wooden spoon, combine the dry and liquid ingredients.

Mix dough, continued

6 Stir thoroughly with the wooden spoon, gradually adding small amounts of flour as needed.

7 When ready, the dough forms a ball. It will be sticky but should not be so wet that it falls through your hands. If it does, it needs more flour.

Knead

Some people find kneading the most enjoyable part of baking bread because they can take out all their aggression on the dough. For whatever reason, kneading is an essential technique to learn because it distributes the yeast cells evenly through the dough and helps to develop the gluten in the flour, which gives the dough volume. If you knead quickly—about twenty times a minute—the total kneading time should be about five minutes. I prefer to knead on a heavily floured cloth because the cloth absorbs the flour and keeps the dough from sticking. When you flour a board, the dough tends to absorb too much flour. Also, with a cloth you don't need to add more flour as you work.

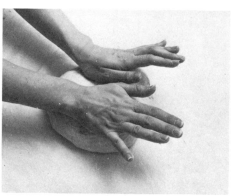

1 Lightly flour your hands and put the ball of dough on a heavily floured cloth—a pastry cloth, linen towel, or even a pillowcase. Start with the heels of your hands in the center.

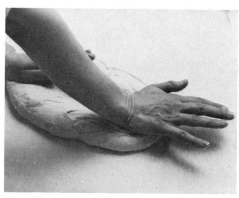

2 Push one hand away from you and the other back, stretching the dough.

3 Fold the dough over.

4 Flip it over.

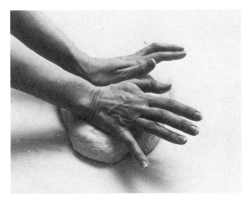

5 Put your hands in the center again.

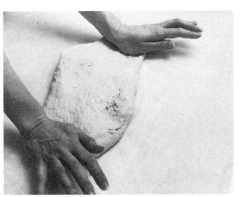

6 Push with the heels of your hands out to the sides.

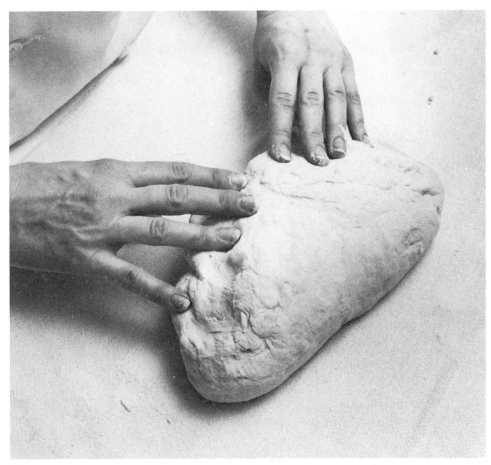

7 Fold the dough, flip it over, and repeat steps 2 through 6 for about five minutes.

Knead, continued

8 Gather the dough into a ball. It should be smooth and elastic and have slight blisters on the surface. If you put your finger in, the indentation should spring back. The dough is now ready to let rise.

Let rise

Rising gives the yeast time to fer-ment and contributes to the texture of the bread. Because yeast needs constant warmth to keep it active, put the bread in a warm, draft-free place. The pilot light in a gas oven provides the right climate, as does an electric oven that has been heated for about one minute and then turned off.

1 Rub the inside of a bowl with vegetable oil or butter. (If you want a hard crust, don't grease the bowl; dust it lightly with flour.)

2 Put in the ball of dough and turn it so that all sides are covered with the fat to prevent the sur-face from drying and cracking.

3 Cover the bowl with plastic wrap or a kitchen towel. Place in a warm place (about 80 degrees).

4 Let rise until the dough is twice its original size, which can take from one to two hours, or even longer. If you stick your finger into the dough, it will leave an indentation and the dough will not spring back.

Punch down

The dough has risen because it is full of carbon dioxide gas. Punching it down lets the gas escape and produces a uniform grain.

1 Punch the dough with your floured fist.

Punch down, continued

2 Pull the dough from the sides into the center.

3 Press it with your fingers to remove any gas bubbles that are left. If the recipe calls for a second rising, cover the bowl and let rise again.

Shape into a loaf

1 Put the punched down dough on a lightly floured surface (preferably marble if there is butter in the dough). Cut it into as many portions as the recipe calls for. Cover the dough you are not working with.

2 Pat each portion into a rectangle a little longer than the loaf pan, which has been buttered and dusted with flour.

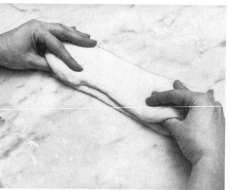

3 Fold the length of dough toward you.

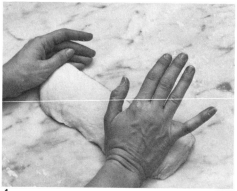

4 Seal the edges with the heel of your hand.

5 Roll the dough so that the seam is on top.

6 Pat down again into a rough rectangle. If the dough seems to resist, cover it with plastic wrap and let it rest a few minutes, which relaxes the gluten.

7 Using the side of your hand, make a trench down the middle of the dough.

8 Fold it toward you again.

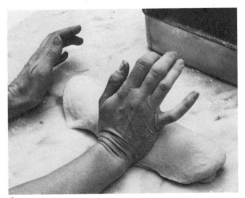

9 Seal the edges with the heel of your hand.

10 Roll the dough so the seam is underneath.

Shape into loaf, continued

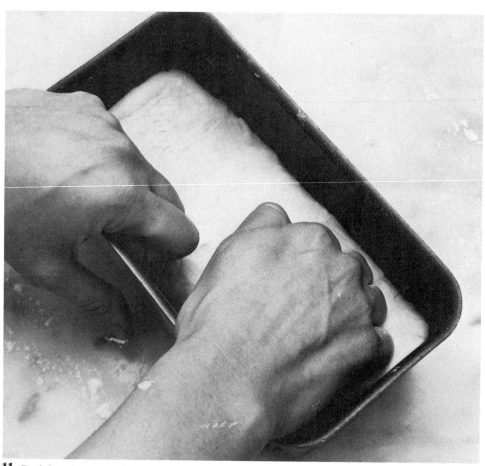

11 Put it into the prepared pan and, using your knuckles, push the dough into the corners of the pan. It should be no more than two-thirds full. Cover and let rise about an hour, or until the dough comes to the top of the pan. Bake according to recipe directions.

Shape into a braided loaf

A braided loaf can be cooked in a loaf pan or on a baking sheet. If you have a soft rich dough, it is best to bake it in a loaf pan so it won't spread out of shape.

1 Divide the dough into three equal pieces. On a lightly floured surface, roll each piece into a rough square.

2 Roll each square of dough into a tight roll.

3 Lightly roll the dough under your hands to lengthen it.

4 Cross two lengths of dough at one end and press the third length over the center.

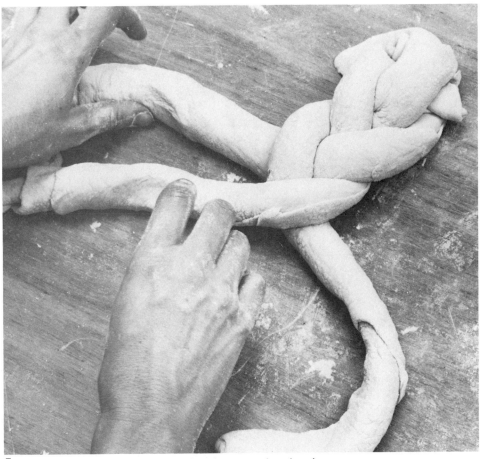

5 Braid the dough by lifting one side into the center, then the other.

Shape into a braided loaf, continued

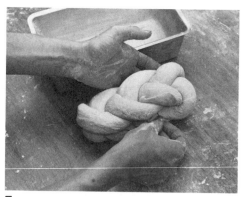

6 Place the dough next to the loaf pan.

7 Turn the ends under so the loaf will fit loosely in the pan.

8 Place the loaf in the greased pan. Cover and let rise until twice its original size.

 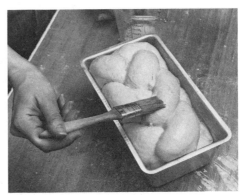

9 If the braid has lost definition, snip it with scissors along the lines of the braid.

10 Brush the loaf with egg beaten with a little water and bake according to recipe directions.

11 The cooked loaf.

Shape into a pullman loaf

This loaf has a flat top and a closer texture than a regular loaf of bread. It is used for sandwiches, Melba toast, and canapés. In French, it is called pain de mie. *There are special covered pans for a pullman loaf, but it is easy to improvise your own.*

1 Shape the dough and put it into a regular loaf pan. Cover the pan tightly with buttered aluminum foil, buttered side down.

2 Put another pan on top of the loaf pan.

3 Put a brick, or other heavy heatproof object, on top. Let the bread rise about an hour, or until it almost fills the pan. Bake according to recipe directions.

Shape into a cylindrical sandwich loaf

A cylindrical covered pan has been introduced that produces a loaf that can be sliced in the food processor. It is obviously a boon for those who make a lot of canapés.

1 Pat the dough into a rough oval shape about the length of the pan, which has been thoroughly greased, including the hinges.

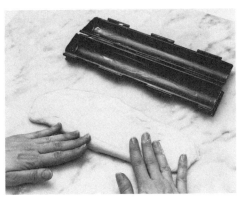

2 Roll the bread, starting with the edge nearest you.

3 Press the seam together with your fingertips.

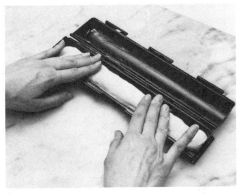

4 Place it seam side down in the pan. Cover with plastic wrap and let it rise until it reaches just above the top of the pan.

5 Close the cover and insert the metal pin through the hinges. Bake according to recipe directions.

6 Finished round and rectangular sandwich loaves.

Shape into long loaves I

There are special pans for baking French loaves of bread, but I use them just for the rising so the loaves have a compact shape. The loaves are then turned out onto a cookie sheet for baking, which produces a more evenly browned crust. Lining the pans with a cloth enables you to turn the loaves out more easily.

1 Cut the dough into halves or quarters, depending on the recipe. Fold each piece in half, cover, and let rest for a few minutes.

2 On a lightly floured board, pat each piece of dough into a rough oval.

3 Fold the dough in half toward you.

4 Seal the edges with your fingers.

5 Place the dough seam side up.

6 Pat the dough again into a rough oval. Cover and let it rest a few minutes if it resists you.

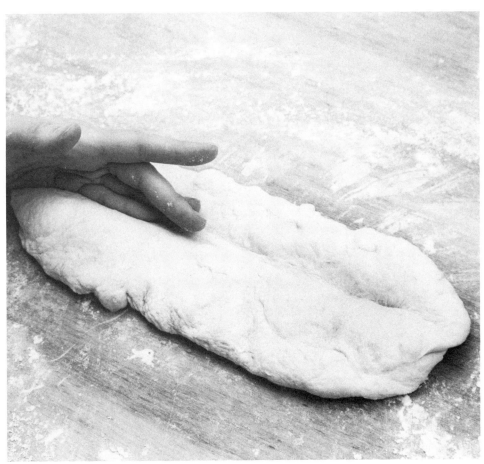

7 Using the side of your hand, make a trough down the length of the dough.

8 Fold the dough in half toward you.

9 Place the dough seam side down and roll it under your hands until it is a long sausage shape.

Shape into long loaves I, continued

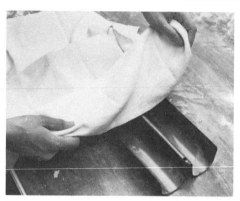

10 Line a French bread pan with a floured pastry cloth or linen towel.

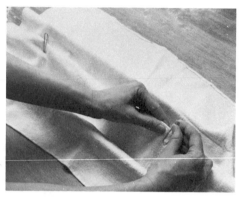

11 Pull up the cloth in the center and put paper clips in three places to hold the fold of cloth above the pan. This will make it easier to turn the loaves out onto the baking sheet.

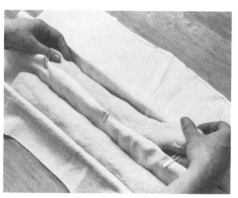

12 Lay the bread in the pan.

13 Cover with a damp towel and let rise in a warm place for about an hour, or until doubled in size.

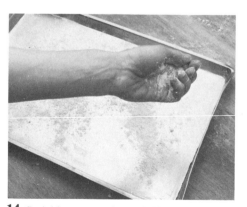

14 Sprinkle corn meal on a baking sheet.

15 Place the bread pan next to the baking sheet and lift up the center fold of pastry cloth.

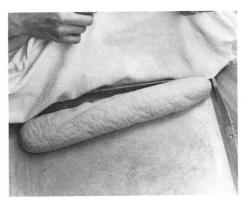

16 Roll the bread onto the baking sheet.

17 Turn the cloth around and roll the second loaf onto the baking sheet.

18 Place the loaves bottom side up. This moister side will be easier to slash.

Shape into long loaves II

This method works well if you don't have French bread pans. Pat and roll the dough into a sausage shape as in the previous instructions.

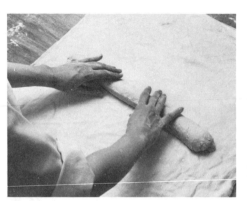

1 Place the loaf in the middle of a floured pastry cloth or large linen towel.

2 Hang the cloth over the edge of a table or kitchen counter and weight it so it won't fall. Let the bread rise until doubled in size. Then roll out onto a baking sheet sprinkled with corn meal.

Shape into a peasant loaf

1 Flour a kitchen towel well and place it floured side up in a round basket, which will shape the loaf while it is rising.

2 Pat out a rough circle of dough and fold it in half, pressing down slightly.

3 Give it a quarter turn and fold it in half again, pressing down.

4 Repeat with a quarter turn and fold it in half.

5 Continue folding and turning until the dough starts to come into a rounded shape.

6 Pat the dough until it forms a ball and is smooth from all the stretching.

7 Twist the edges together where it has been folded. This is called the key.

8 Place the dough, key side down, in the basket and cover with the towel. Let rise about an hour, or until the dough has doubled in size.

Slash and mist peasant and long loaves

Large loaves of bread should be slashed so that steam can escape while they are baking. It is not possible in a home oven to create the true French bread, but by misting during the first fifteen minutes of baking you can approximate the traditional crust. The steam prevents a crust from forming too quickly.

1 About fifteen minutes before you are going to bake the loaves, preheat the oven and put a broiler pan on the floor of the oven. Just before you put in the loaves, fill the broiler pan with boiling water.

2 Put the risen peasant loaf on a lightly floured baking sheet.

**Slash and mist peasant
and long loaves, continued**

3 Using a single-edge razor blade, cut a slash about halfway around the top third of the loaf. Or you can cut a cross in the top of the loaf.

4 Mist the loaf lightly with an atomizer. Don't soak it.

5 For long loaves, make diagonal slashes the length of the loaves.

6 Mist the loaves and mist at three-minute intervals for the first fifteen minutes of baking. If there is any water left in the broiler pan after the initial fifteen minutes, remove the pan from the oven.

7 The finished long loaf.

8 The finished peasant loaf.

Test for doneness

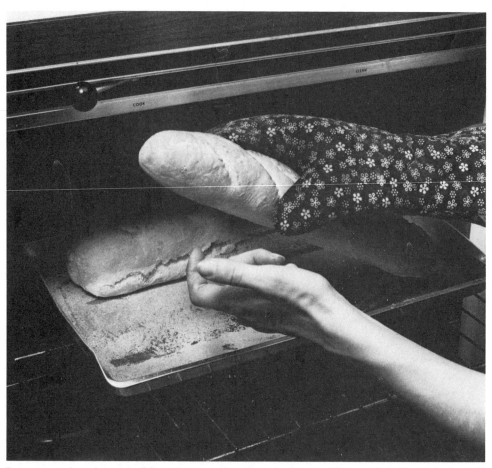

Remove any shaped yeast loaf from the pan and tap it on the bottom. If it sounds hollow, it is done. If not, put it back in the oven, either in the pan or on the oven rack, until it is done.

Shape into bread sticks

1 Pat the bread into a rough circle on a lightly floured board.

2 Using a lightly floured rolling pin, roll out the dough until it is one-quarter inch thick.

3 Using a sharp knife, cut the dough into one-half inch strips.

4 Roll each strip with your hands until it is about a foot long. If the dough sticks, lightly oil your hands.

5 Lay the strips on a nonstick baking sheet or one that has been greased and lightly floured.

Shape into bread sticks, continued

6 Lightly brush the strips with egg beaten with a little water. Cover and let rise until the strips have doubled in size.

7 Sprinkle with poppy or sesame seeds, if desired, and cook according to recipe directions.

8 The finished bread sticks.

Shape into pita

These rounds of Middle Eastern yeast bread puff up when baked, then deflate, leaving a pocket in the center for a filling. Or they can be served just as a bread.

1 Using a pastry scraper or a sharp knife, divide the dough into small equal portions—to make as many pitas as called for in the recipe.

2 Roll each portion under the palm of your hand into a ball.

3 Flatten out the ball with your hands and curve it slightly over your fingertips.

4 Push the edges together on the bottom.

5 Using a rolling pin, roll each ball into a circle about one-quarter inch thick.

6 Cover the rounds with a towel and let rise slightly for about thirty minutes.

Shape into pita, continued

7 Place the rounds on a greased or nonstick baking sheet and bake according to the recipe directions.

8 The finished pitas.

Shape into clover rolls

1 With a sharp knife, cut the dough into the number of pieces called for in the recipe.

2 Roll each portion under the palm of your hand into a small ball.

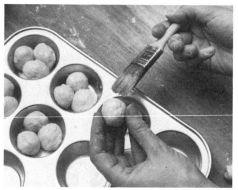

3 Brush each ball with melted butter and place three balls in a buttered muffin tin. Cover and let rise until doubled in size. Bake according to recipe directions.

4 The finished rolls.

Shape into crescent rolls

These can be made with a rich bread dough, or with a dough that has been folded and rolled with layers of butter. The latter produces the delicious croissants of French breakfast fame.

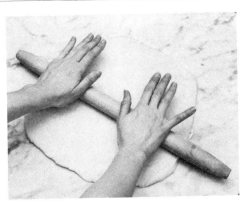

1 Using a lightly floured rolling pin, roll the dough on a lightly floured surface into a large circle about one-eighth inch thick.

2 Cut off the edges of dough to make a neat circle. (I'm using a pizza pan as a guide.) Save the scraps of dough.

3 Using a sharp knife, cut the dough into as many wedges as called for.

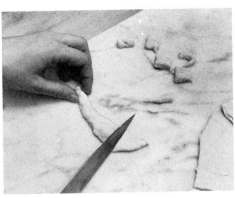

4 Cut the scraps of dough into as many pieces as you have wedges.

5 Use a pastry brush to brush off any excess flour on the dough.

6 Place a small piece of dough on the wide end of the triangle. Mist the point of the triangle with water so it will adhere to the dough when rolled.

Shape into crescent rolls, continued

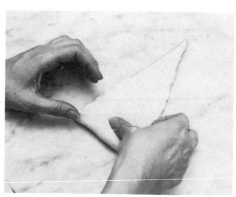

7 Fold the wide end of the triangle over the scrap of dough.

8 Hold the point with one hand and roll the dough with the palm of your hand toward the point.

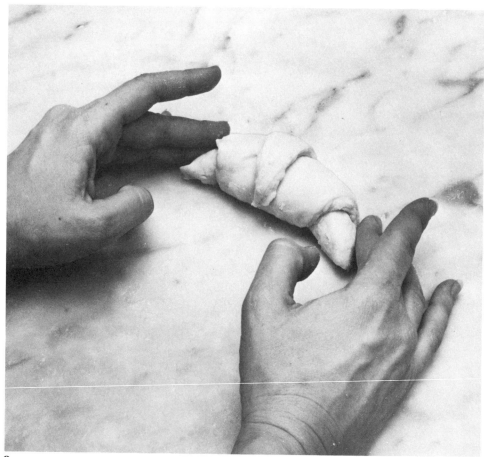

9 Press the dampened point onto the roll and bend the edges slightly into a crescent shape. Place on a greased or nonstick baking sheet and let rise until doubled in size.

10 Carefully brush the top of the crescents with egg beaten with a little water. Don't let the egg glaze overflow into the creases because the rolls won't rise properly. Bake according to the recipe directions.

11 The finished crescent rolls.

Shape into brioche

You can make large or individual brioches in the traditional fluted tins. Or you can bake the dough in a coffee can. Brioche dough is also used to encase foods before baking.

1 Heavily butter a brioche tin.

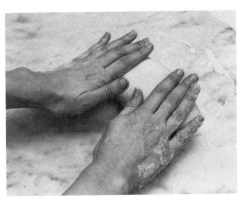

2 Roll the well-chilled dough on a lightly floured surface (preferably marble) into a thick sausage shape.

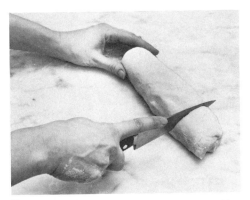

3 Cut off one-third of the dough and set aside.

4 Pat the rest of the dough into a smooth ball.

**Shape into brioche,
continued**

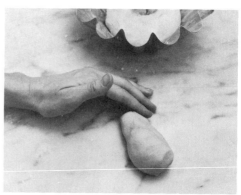

5 Place in the brioche tin and make a hole in the center of the ball with your fingers.

6 Roll the other third of the dough into a cone shape.

7 Place the cone in the hole, pointed side down.

8 Cover with plastic wrap and let rise until doubled in size.

9 Carefully brush the top and the bottom (called the head and shoulders) with egg beaten with a little water. Do not let the glaze run into the crease because the brioche won't rise properly.

10 Use scissors to make four or five cuts between the head and shoulders, which will help the brioche to rise.

11 Bake according to recipe directions. If the brioche seems to be browning too quickly, cover it with aluminum foil.

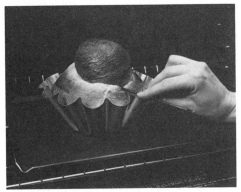

12 Put a trussing needle between the head and shoulders. If it comes out dry, the brioche is done.

13 The finished brioche.

Shape and fill coffee cake

Coffee cakes can be yeast doughs, or quick breads, which are leavened with baking powder and need no rising. They can be shaped in numerous ways; here is just one, made with a yeast dough.

1 Roll the dough into a rectangle about eight by fourteen inches and one-quarter inch thick. Brush the surface with melted butter.

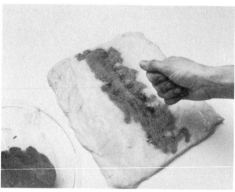

2 Sprinkle the filling down the center third of the dough. I'm using sugar, cinnamon, raisins, and nuts.

3 With a sharp knife, cut one-half-inch strips at a slight angle on either side of the filling.

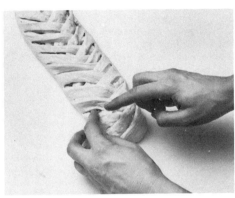

4 Overlap the strips, first one side then the other, the length of the coffee cake.

5 Fold the ends and tuck them under. Cover the coffee cake and let rise about thirty minutes. Bake according to recipe directions.

6 The finished coffee cake.

Cut into croutons I

The croutons shown are the most useful size for soups and salads. They are browned in butter or oil in a frying pan. Use finely textured slightly stale bread.

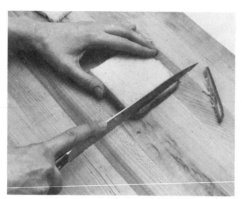

1 Cut off the crusts.

2 Cut into strips.

3 Turn the strips at an angle and cut into diamond shapes.

4 Or cut the strips straight across into squares.

Cut into croutons II

This heart-shaped crouton is used to garnish stews, puréed vegetables, or anything with a sauce.

1 Trim the crusts from the bread and cut each slice in two, forming two triangles.

2 Cut off one corner of the triangle so that it comes to a point in the center.

3 Cut out a small cube from the center.

4 Round off the edges.

5 The finished crouton is then browned in a small amount of butter and dipped in the sauce of the dish with which it will be served.

Slice bread for canapés

Use a finely textured, slightly stale bread for canapés. I'm using the pullman loaf, shown earlier in the chapter, which is flat on top. Cut the bread into long slices so that you can make several canapés at once. If you are using the cylindrical sandwich loaf, slice it in the food processor or with a sharp serrated knife.

1 Cut off the top crust using a long sharp knife.

2 Stand the loaf on end and cut into quarter-inch slices.

3 Continue to cut thin slices, holding the top of the loaf firmly with one hand.

4 When the loaf gets too thin to stand on end, lay it flat and slice it horizontally, holding the bread with the palm of your hand.

5 Trim the crusts.

Decorate canapés I

Canapés can be time-consuming if they are made individually. Decorating a long slice of bread and then cutting it into individual canapés will save time.

1 Spread each long slice with soft butter to keep it moist. I've flavored mine with dill and lemon juice.

2 Lay thin slices of meat—in this case smoked salmon—on the bread.

3 Trim off excess meat.

4 Outfit a pastry bag with a small star tube and fill with seasoned butter. Pipe the butter down the length of the bread on either side.

**Decorate canapés I,
continued**

5 Cut with a sharp knife into triangles or rectangles.

Decorate canapés II

*If you are making a lot of canapés,
have all the meat and garnishes
ready and keep the bread slices
moist in a damp towel.*

1 Spread the bread with softened butter or mayonnaise and cover with meat (I'm using prosciutto). Cut the bread into small rectangles.

2 Put a teaspoon of seasoned butter into a paper cone. Pipe out a simple decoration.

3 Cut a small pickle (cornichon) into very thin slices, but don't cut through the stem end.

4 Place the fanned-out pickle on the canapé.

5 Or pipe out a slightly more elaborate pattern.

6 Slice off a piece of olive.

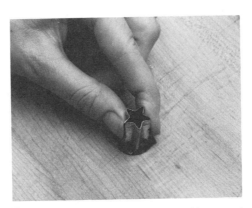

7 Cut the slice into a star shape with a metal canapé cutter.

8 Place the star on the canapé. Cover with plastic wrap until ready to serve.

Decorate canapés III

1 Spread the bread with mayonnaise and cut it into squares. Put small asparagus spears next to the square and cut them the same size as the bread.

2 Pick up the asparagus with your knife and lay it on the bread.

3 Cut strips of pimiento into thin slices.

4 Place them diagonally on the asparagus.

Decorate canapés IV

1 Spread round or square pieces of bread with butter. Hold a pastry scraper in the middle of the bread as a divider. With the tip of your knife, put a small amount of black caviar on half the bread.

2 Put red caviar on the other side.

**Decorate canapés IV,
continued**

3 Using a small measuring spoon, put finely chopped onion in the center.

QUICK BREADS

Shape quick bread in a coffee can

Quick breads, which are leavened by baking powder or baking soda rather than yeast and require no rising, are ideally suited to a coffee can. Brioche dough can also be baked in this way.

1 Remove one end of the coffee can and thoroughly butter the inside.

2 Put the can on kitchen parchment or wax paper and draw a circle around it.

3 Cut out the circle and butter it well.

4 Put it in the bottom of the can with the buttered side up.

5 Spoon in the batter until the can is three-quarters full. Be sure to leave enough room for the dough to rise while it bakes. Bake as you would in any metal pan.

6 The finished quick bread.

MUFFINS

Mix muffins

Muffins prepared this way should be stirred very briefly. Overbeating will produce coarse muffins with air tunnels.

1 Combine milk and melted butter with the beaten eggs.

2 Gently stir the liquids into the combined dry ingredients—flour, baking powder, salt, sugar, and raisin or nuts, if desired.

Mix muffins, continued

3 Mix only to moisten the dry ingredients. The dough should be lumpy.

4 Spoon and scrape the mixture into greased muffin tins. Fill the tins about two-thirds full.

5 The finished muffin has slanted sides and a rounded top.

BISCUITS

Mix and shape biscuits

The only secret to serving light and flaky baking powder biscuits is to handle the dough as little as possible. You do not want to develop the gluten in the flour, which will make the biscuit tough.

1 Add chilled butter and shortening to the sifted dry ingredients.

2 Using a pastry blender or your fingertips, cut the butter and shortening into the flour.

3 Continue until the flour has absorbed the fat and the mixture is crumbly.

4 Make a well in the center and add the cold liquid all at once.

5 Using a wooden spoon, stir slowly to incorporate the dry and liquid ingredients.

6 Then stir more vigorously for about thirty seconds, no more than twenty strokes.

Mix and shape biscuits, continued

7 Turn out the dough onto a lightly floured surface, preferably marble.

8 Knead briefly—three or four times—with the heel of your hand. Don't overknead or you won't have a flaky texture.

9 Roll the dough with a lightly floured rolling pin into a rough oval. The dough can be anywhere from one-quarter to one inch thick, depending on what the biscuits will be used for.

10 Use a floured metal cookie cutter (or a glass) to shape the biscuits.

11 Press down on the cutter—don't twist it. Gather the scraps, roll them out, and cut more rounds.

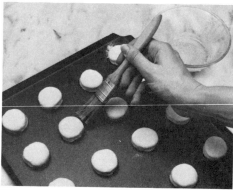

12 Place the biscuits about an inch apart on an ungreased baking sheet. For a brown crust, brush them with milk or melted butter. Bake according to recipe directions.

13 The finished biscuits.

POPOVERS

Mix popovers

Popovers are made with a batter with no yeast or baking powder, yet they puff up from steam. The batter should be beaten vigorously to activate the gluten in the flour.

1 Make a well in the center of the dry ingredients and break the eggs into it.

2 Pour in the milk and melted butter.

Mix popovers, continued

3 Stir with a wooden spoon or wire whisk until well combined and smooth—three or four minutes.

4 Ladle the batter into buttered custard cups or popover pans that have been heated on a baking sheet. Fill them about half full. Bake according to recipe directions.

5 The finished popovers should be removed from the cups and served immediately.

12
PASTRY

PIES, TARTS, QUICHES

Cut in flour and butter

Good bakers should have cold fingertips so that the butter (or shortening) doesn't soften when they mix it with the flour. Have the butter well chilled and cut into small pieces. Have ice water ready to add in small amounts. You can use a pastry blender or food processor, but this is actually a quick and simple process. The same technique is used whether the crust is for a pie, tart, or quiche. If egg yolks are called for, they are often added with the butter.

1 Add pieces of butter and/or shortening all at once to the flour and salt.

2 Lift up small amounts of butter and flour and rub them lightly together between your thumbs and fingertips.

3 Drop it back into the bowl and lift up another batch from underneath. Rub quickly and gently between the fingertips.

4 Continue until all the butter is incorporated with the flour and the mixture looks like coarse bread crumbs. It should take no more than a few minutes.

5 Add a small amount of water and quickly stir with a rubber spatula or a fork.

6 Add a few more drops of water and mix only until all the pastry is dampened. Too much water produces a tough crust; too little makes it crumbly.

7 Gather the dough into a rough ball. Wrap it in wax paper and refrigerate for one-half hour before rolling.

8 If you have made a richer tart crust, called pâte brisée, put the ball of dough on a marble or Formica surface and push it with the heel of your hand to distribute the butter more evenly.

9 Shape into a ball and wrap the dough in wax paper and refrigerate.

10 If the dough is for a two-crust pie, cut the dough into two portions, one slightly larger than the other for the bottom crust. Wrap in wax paper and refrigerate before rolling.

Roll dough

A marble surface is a good investment if you bake a lot because it has a smooth cool surface that keeps the butter in pastry dough from melting. Otherwise, roll the dough on a Formica surface. I prefer to use a long narrow rolling pin because I can control the pressure better than with the ball-bearing kind.

1 Put the ball of dough on a lightly floured surface. Flatten it slightly with a lightly floured rolling pin. Start with your rolling pin in the center of the dough.

2 With light, even pressure, roll the pin away from you to the edge. Don't roll back and forth.

PASTRY 425

Roll dough, continued

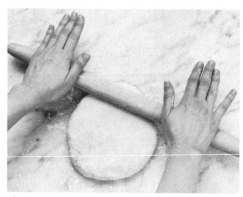

3 Turn the dough a quarter of the way around.

4 Roll again from the center out to the edge.

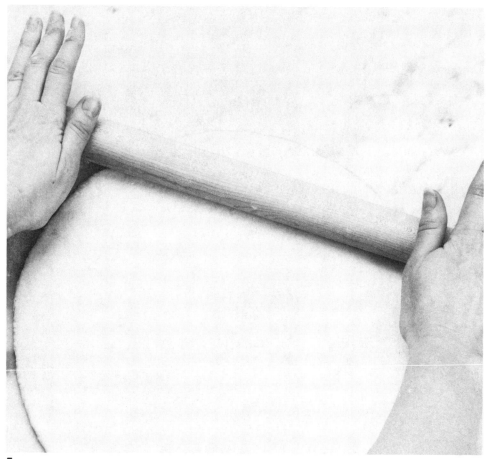

5 Continue to turn and roll the dough from the center until it is about one-eighth inch thick. The rolled circle of dough should be about two inches larger than the pie or tart pan.

Line pie tin

The only trick to lining a pie tin is to be careful not to stretch the pastry. If it is stretched it will shrink in baking. A light-colored metal pie tin produces a light golden crust. Dark metal or glass pans absorb heat and can cause the crust to burn.

1 Loosely roll the dough around the rolling pin.

2 Lift it and unroll it over the pie tin.

3 Gently push the dough into the pie tin with the side of your index finger. At the same time, lift the edge of dough with the other hand and push it over your index finger, forming a one-inch rim.

Line pie tin, continued

4 Cut off excess dough even with the pie tin.

5 Push the rim of dough out so that it hangs over the edge of the tin. Fill and cover with a regular or lattice crust.

Decorate a two-crust pie

1 Roll the top crust around the rolling pin and unroll it over the top of the filled pie.

2 Trim the top crust with a knife or scissors, leaving a one-half-inch overhang.

3 Pull up the rim on the bottom crust and fold it over the top crust, pinching the two together.

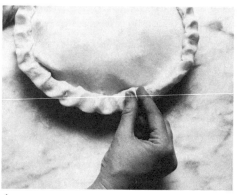

4 Flute the rim by pressing the pastry between the thumb and forefinger all around the edge. This seals the crust and creates a decorative rim.

5 Prick the top all over with a fork to let steam escape and to keep the crust from rising. The pie can be baked at this point, but it is easy and more attractive to decorate it.

6 Roll out scraps of pastry into a rough cricle about one-eighth inch thick. Cut into four triangles.

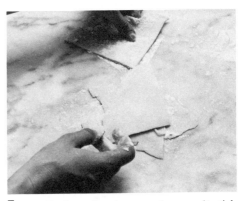

7 Heavily flour the pieces so they won't stick together.

Decorate a two-crust pie, continued

8 Stack the pieces at varying angles.

9 Place the stacked pastry over your thumb.

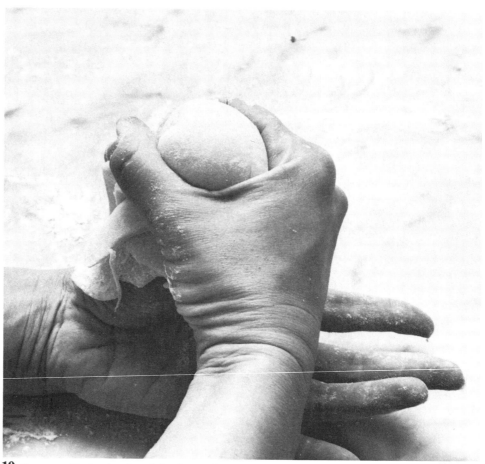

10 Squeeze with the thumb and forefinger of your other hand to create a bulb shape.

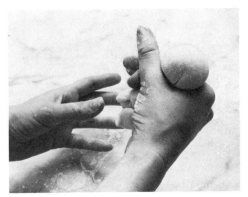

11 Pull the pastry off your thumb.

12 Twist off the bulb. Roll out the rest of the pastry for leaf decorations.

13 With a small sharp knife, make two intersecting cuts about halfway through the bulb.

14 Open out the four outer petals.

15 Use your knife to open out inner petals.

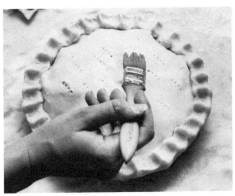

16 Brush the top of the pie crust with egg beaten with water or cream.

Decorate a two-crust pie,
continued

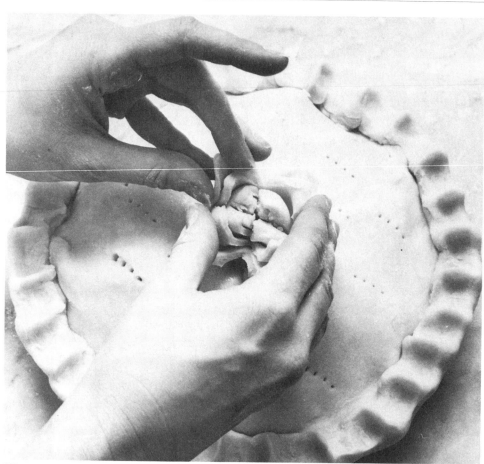

17 Place the flower in the center of the crust.

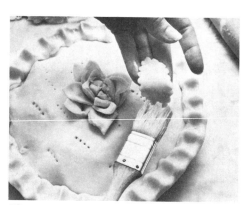

18 Cut out leaves from the pastry scraps and brush them with the egg wash. Use a pastry wheel or a fluted cookie cutter to create a decorative edge.

19 Press the leaves onto the crust and make decorative markings with the tip of your knife.

20 Place the pie on a baking sheet to catch any juices while it bakes. Brush with egg wash and chill for one-half hour before baking.

Top with lattice crust

Pies with bright fruit fillings look attractive with a lattice crust. This is a simple way to form one.

1 Roll out a top crust two inches larger than the top of the pie tin. Using a heavy straight edge as a guide, cut very thin uniform strips.

2 Brush the strips with water and lay them straight across the pie, then diagonally to create a diamond pattern.

Top with lattice crust, continued

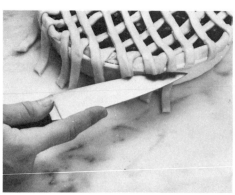

3 Cut off the ends of the strips under the rim of the pie tin.

4 Press the edges into the pie tin. Chill the pie for one-half hour before baking.

Line tart or quiche tin

The best pan for an attractive tart or quiche has straight sides and a removable bottom so that the baked tart can be removed and stand free.

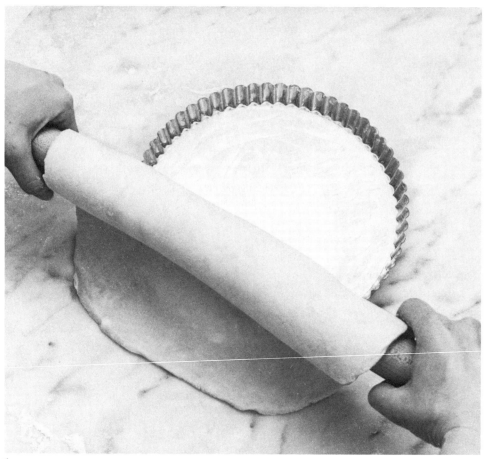

1 Roll the dough onto the rolling pin and unroll it over the tart pan.

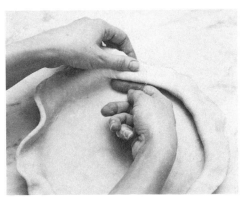

2 Press the dough into the pan with your index finger. At the same time, hold up the edge of dough with the other hand and push it over the index finger to create a one-inch rim.

3 If the pan has a sharp edge, run your rolling pin over the top to cut off excess dough. Otherwise, trim it off with a knife.

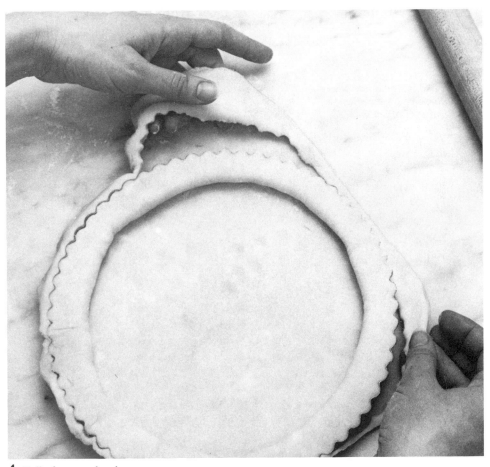

4 Pull of excess dough.

Line tart or quiche tin, continued

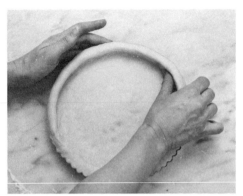

5 Pull up the rim of dough.

6 Push against the rim of dough with the index finger of one hand. Pinch against it with the thumb and forefinger of the other hand to create a fluted edge.

Prebake tart or quiche shell

Many tart and quiche shells are baked for a short time before the filling is added so that the crust will not be soggy. Weighting the shell keeps it from pulling away from the pan.

1 With a fork, prick all over the bottom of the crust.

2 Put wax paper or aluminum foil on the crust.

3 Fill the shell with dried beans or special nuggets sold for this purpose, making sure that they go all around the inside edge. The beans can be reused indefinitely. Bake the crust in a 425-degree oven for fifteen minutes.

4 Lift out the paper with the beans.

5 Brush the bottom of the crust with egg yolk and return it to the oven for two minutes.

Fill tart

Peaches, pears, plums, and many other fruits are used for tarts, with the shell sometimes prebaked. You can spread pastry cream on the bottom, or applesauce for an apple tart. But I prefer it plain, with just a glaze of heated apricot jam on top after the tart is baked.

1 Overlap thin slices of apple all around the outside perimeter of the shell.

2 Put a circle of apple slices in the center. Arrange a few slices upright in the center to simulate a flower. Bake and glaze according to recipe directions.

Cool tart or quiche

Place the cooked tart or quiche on a coffee can to cool. The rim of the tin will drop off and the tart or quiche stands free on the base.

PUFF PASTRY

Roll and fold

Classic puff pastry has hundreds of layers of butter (729 according to Julia Child; I haven't counted) between (730) layers of pastry. These puff up into light and tender patty shells, tart and appetizer cases, napoleons, and crusts for meat or fish. Although it takes about seven hours to prepare puff pastry, most of the time is spent letting the pastry cool and rest in the refrigerator. And it freezes well for future use. The only necessity is a cold surface, preferably marble.

1 Roll out chilled dough (made with all-purpose and cake flour) into a circle about twelve inches in diameter.

2 Soften three sticks of chilled butter by beating them with a rolling pin.

3 Push the butter with the heel of your hand until it is slightly flattened. Do this quickly so it doesn't get warm.

4 Sprinkle one-half cup flour on the butter.

5 Using a pastry scraper, work the flour into the butter until it is smooth.

6 Shape the butter into a block. Chill for fifteen to twenty minutes.

7 Place the block of butter in the center of the rolled out pastry. Lift one edge of pastry over the butter without stretching it.

8 Brush off any flour on the folded-over edge of pastry.

Roll and fold, continued

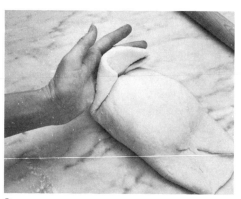

9 Fold over the other edge of pastry and then the side.

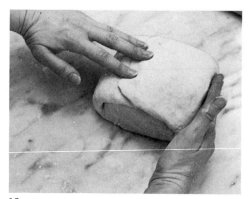

10 Fold over the other side, making a neat package.

11 Turn the package with the seam facing away from you. Tap it with a lightly floured rolling pin and roll it away from you into a rectangle. Use light pressure to spread the butter the length and width of the pastry.

12 Even the sides of the rectangle with the edge of the rolling pin as you go along.

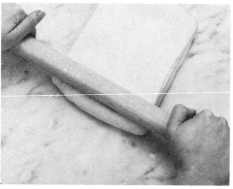

13 When the rectangle is about eight by sixteen inches, press each end lightly with the rolling pin.

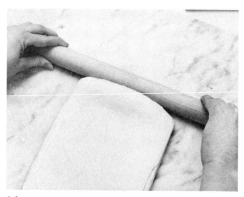

14 Square the ends of the rectangle.

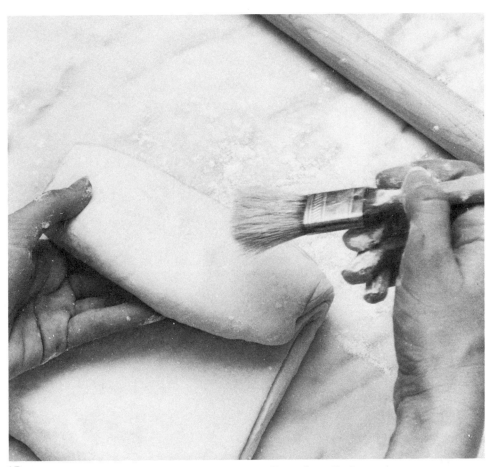

15 Fold one-third of the rectangle toward you. Brush off any flour clinging to the pastry.

16 Fold the near third to cover the first third.

17 Turn the pastry so that the open flap of the rectangle is on your right. Press both short ends with your rolling pin.

Roll and fold, continued

18 Roll the pastry again into a rectangle about eight by sixteen inches.

19 Fold over the far third of pastry and brush off any flour.

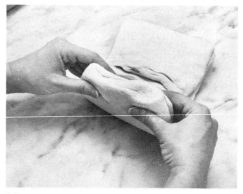

20 Fold the near third over to cover the first third.

21 Turn the pastry so the open flap is on your right. Press two fingers into it to indicate that you have folded the pastry twice.

22 Wrap the pastry in plastic wrap and refrigerate for about an hour to firm the butter and relax the gluten in the flour. Repeat rolling and folding four more times, chilling each time. Then shape for baking.

Shape into patty shells

Patty shells can be small, for individual servings, or large. They make crisp cases for creamed fillings.

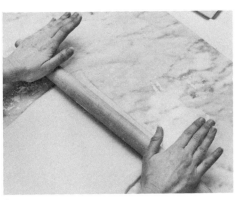

1 Roll out chilled puff pastry into a rectangle one-quarter inch thick.

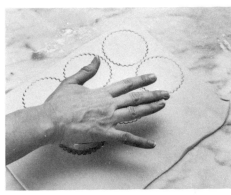

2 Using a fluted or plain cutter about three inches in diameter, press down on the pastry with the palm of your hand. Don't twist the cutter.

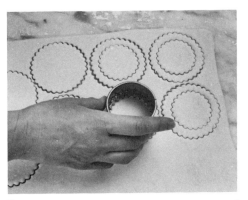

3 Using a two-inch cutter, cut the centers of half of the circles, forming a rim.

4 Carefully lift up the large circles with a pastry scraper or wide spatula.

Shape into patty shells, continued

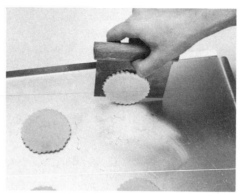

5 Turn them over on a baking sheet lightly sprinkled with water.

6 Prick the rounds with a fork.

7 Brush the perimeter of each round with water.

8 Carefully place a ring of pastry on top of each round. Don't stretch the pastry because it won't rise properly. These rings will form the sides of the shells.

9 Press the back of your knife against the sides of the shell to create a fluted pattern. This seals the rim as well as being decorative.

10 To help insure even rising, push a skewer through the rim and pastry below it in four places.

11 Brush just the tops of the rims with egg beaten with water. Don't let it run down the sides because the pastry won't rise.

12 With the tip of your knife, make a shallow cut around the inside of the rim. When the shell has risen, this center will be cut out for a lid. Refrigerate the shells for an hour before baking.

13 Stack the scraps of pastry. Don't press them into a ball because you will destroy the layering.

14 Roll out the stacked scraps and use to form decorative garnishes (see following instructions).

15 When the patty shells are cooked, cut around the inside of the rim where you previously marked it with your knife.

16 Pull off the lid and set it aside.

Shape into patty shells, continued

17 Pull out any uncooked pastry from the center.

18 The patty shells are ready to be filled.

Form decorative garnishes

Small oval and crescent-shaped pieces of puff pastry, made from scraps, can be used to garnish many entrées, particularly fish dishes. They can be formed and frozen, then baked a few minutes longer than when they are freshly made.

1 Using rolled out pastry scraps (see steps 13 and 14 in the preceding instructions for patty shells), cut out circles with a fluted or plain cutter. Place the cutter across the center of the circle and cut out crescents and ovals.

2 Place the crescents and ovals on a baking sheet brushed with water and brush with egg beaten with water. Bake at 450 degrees for about fifteen minutes.

Shape and cook horns

These puff pastry shells are filled with cheese or seafood for a first course, or are glazed with sugar for a dessert. The cone-shaped metal forms are readily available in shops that sell kitchen equipment.

1 Roll out chilled puff pastry into a rectangle about sixteen inches long and one-eighth inch thick. Using a sharp knife or pastry wheel, cut into strips one inch wide.

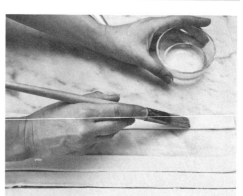

2 Brush each strip with water.

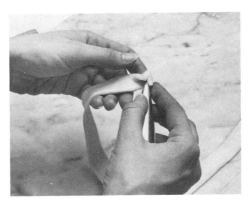

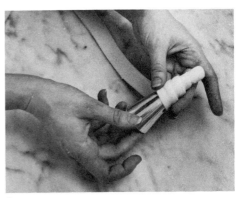

3 Press the end of one strip into the point of a buttered cone.

4 Holding the wide end and turning the cone away from you, wrap the strip around the cone without stretching it. The strip should overlap about one-eighth of an inch.

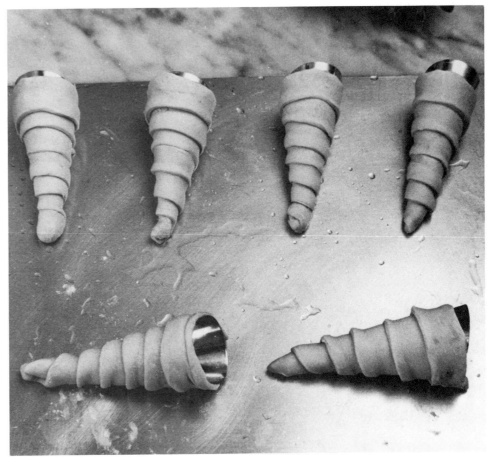

5 Place the cones on a baking sheet brushed with water. Chill, then brush the cones with an egg wash. Bake at 425 degrees for about fifteen minutes.

Shape and cook horns, continued

6 When the horns are cool, they slip off easily.

7 The cooked horns ready for filling.

Cook and decorate napoleons

The pastry is usually not allowed to puff for these crisp and flaky desserts. Napoleons are traditionally iced with fondant and melted chocolate. But they can be sprinkled with confectioners' sugar instead. The only difficulty in making napoleons is in cutting the cooked pastry, which is fragile.

1 Roll out chilled puff pastry to fill a large buttered baking sheet. Prick the pastry all over with a fork. Chill for one hour.

2 Butter the bottom of another baking sheet and place it buttered side down on top of the pastry, which will keep it from rising. Bake at 450 degrees for twenty minutes.

3 Using a gentle sawing motion with a serrated knife, carefully cut the baked pastry into three equal lengths, each about four inches wide.

4 If the pastry seems very fragile, spread warm apricot jam on one length, then spread with pastry cream or whipped cream.

5 Place a layer of pastry over the cream and spread this layer with pastry cream or whipped cream.

6 Fit the third piece of pastry on top and spread with fondant icing. You can also sprinkle the napoleon with powdered sugar.

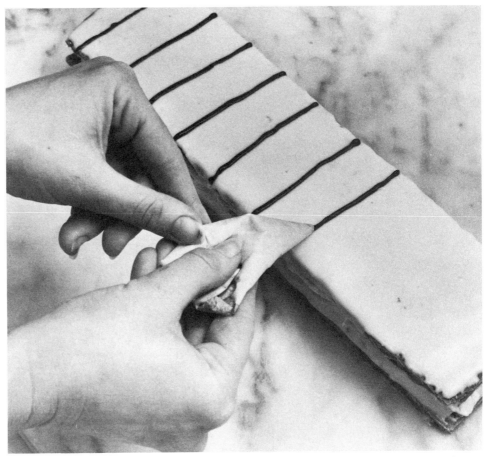

7 Fill a paper cone with melted chocolate and pipe it across the napoleon at one-inch intervals.

**Cook and decorate
napoleons, continued**

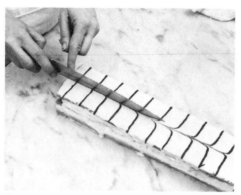 

8 To make the traditional design, run a knife down the center of the napoleon, pulling the chocolate slightly.

9 Turn the napoleon around and run the knife down the napoleon in the opposite direction on either side of the center line.

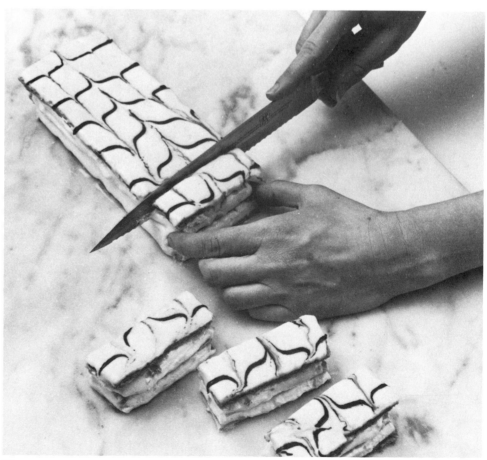

10 Support the pastry with your fingers and cut into serving pieces. Use a light sawing motion because the pastry is fragile and can crack easily.

Shape palm cookies

1 Roll chilled puff pastry into a large rectangle. Sprinkle the work surface and the pastry with granulated sugar, not flour.

2 Roll the sugar into the pastry.

3 Fold in both sides of the pastry to meet in the center.

4 Sprinkle with more sugar.

5 Lengthen the rectangle slightly by rolling away from you.

6 Fold both sides into the center again.

Shape palm cookies, continued

7 Fold in half lengthwise.

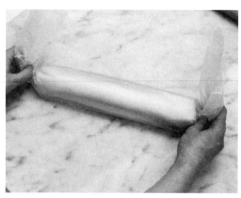

8 Wrap the pastry in wax paper and chill it for an hour.

9 Cut the pastry into one-quarter-inch slices.

10 Moisten a baking sheet and cover with kitchen parchment. Put the cookies on the parchment and turn the corners out.

11 You can also turn the corners in for a more rounded shape. Chill for fifteen minutes before baking.

12 After the cookies have baked in a 425-degree oven for fifteen minutes, turn them over with a spatula.

13 Sprinkle with sugar and bake another ten minutes.

14 The finished palm cookies.

Form and bake fruit tart

Puff pastry can be formed into a variety of shapes for fruit tarts. This one, called a kilometer, is common in French bakeries. The shell is baked and is frequently spread with pastry cream before the fruit is added.

1 Roll chilled puff pastry into a rectangle seventeen inches long and nine inches wide. Cut off a one-inch strip from both sides of the rectangle.

2 Put the rectangle of pastry on a baking sheet brushed with water. Brush the pastry with water down each side.

3 Place the strips on each side of the pastry.

4 Prick the center rectangle of pastry all over with a fork.

Form and bake fruit tart, continued

5 Press the back of the tip of your knife into the sides of the pastry to seal the edges and make a decorative border. Chill for one hour.

6 Brush just the top of the strips with egg beaten with water. Don't let it run down the sides because the pastry won't rise.

7 After the pastry is baked (in a 425-degree oven for about twenty minutes), spread a caramel glaze or warm currant or apricot jam over the bottom. This will keep it from becoming soggy.

8 Place the fruit in neat rows on the tart shell.

9 Brush the fruit with heated currant or apricot jam that has been cooled to lukewarm.

10 The tart is ready to be sliced crosswise into serving pieces.

PÂTE À CHOUX

Mix pastry

This versatile pastry, which takes only a few minutes to make, is used for hors d'oeuvre, cream puffs, éclairs, elaborate towering cakes like gâteau St. Honoré and croquembouche, and the French version of gnocchi. The pastry puffs up from steam, leaving a slightly hollow interior.

1 In a heavy saucepan, melt four tablespoons butter with one cup water and one-quarter teaspoon salt.

2 Bring just to a boil.

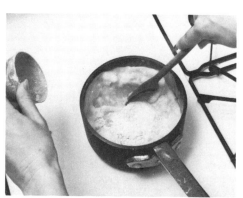

3 Immediately remove the pan from the heat and add one cup flour all at once.

4 Stir vigorously with a wooden spoon.

5 When the flour and liquid are thoroughly combined, return the pan to a very low heat and stir for about five minutes to dry out the pastry.

6 Remove the pan from the heat and let it stand for two minutes.

7 Add four eggs, one at a time, beating vigorously with a wooden spoon after each addition.

8 When the pastry is smooth and creamy, it is ready to be used.

Fill pastry bag

A pastry bag is invaluable for shaping pastry with pâte à choux, as well as for decorating, shaping dumplings, and for stuffing vegetables, pastry shells, and eggs. Use a large washable canvas bag with interchangeable metal tubes of various sizes.

1 Fit a tube inside the pastry bag and twist the bag above the tube.

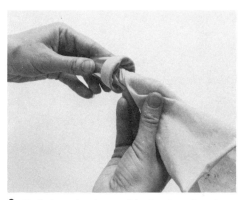

2 Tuck the twisted part of the bag into the tube to prevent the filling from coming out.

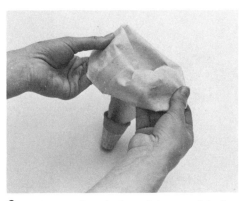

3 Fold about three inches of the top of the bag down.

4 Fill the bag part way with pastry.

Form into various shapes

These are just a few of the things you can make with pâte à choux. I prefer a small version of the éclair, called a salambô, because it's daintier to eat and doesn't look as if it were produced in a commercial bakery. Cream puffs can be small bite-size pieces, or larger ones to be filled with creamed seafood or ice cream. The swans make a decorative dessert.

1 Hold the filled pastry bag parallel to a buttered baking sheet and pipe out cylinders for éclairs.

2 Cut off the ends with a knife.

3 Pipe out rounds of pastry for cream puffs, or profiteroles.

4 Pipe out teardrop shapes for pastry swans. Lift up the bag at the end and cut off the point.

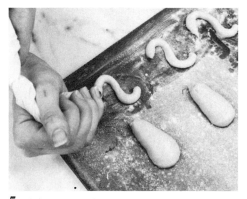

5 Using a number 2 pastry tube, pipe out S-shape necks for the swans.

6 Moisten your finger and smooth the tops of the cream puffs and the ends of the éclairs. Brush all the pastries with egg lightly beaten with water.

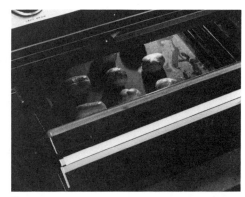

7 Run the back of the tines of a fork over the éclairs. Let sit twenty minutes, then bake in a 400-degree oven for twenty minutes. Remove the swan necks after ten minutes.

8 Turn off the oven and leave the door ajar. Let the pastries dry out in the oven for about an hour before filling.

Fill cream puffs

These small puffs can be filled with cheese or other fillings as an appetizer, or with pastry cream for a dessert.

1 Cut off the top of the shell and pull out any uncooked pastry.

**Fill cream puffs,
continued**

2 Pipe filling into the center.

3 Replace the top of the shell.

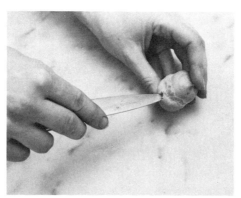

4 You can also poke a small hole in the shell.

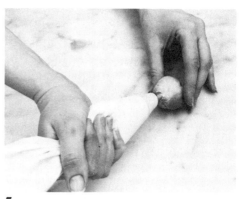

5 And pipe stuffing through the hole.

6 Dip the top of the filled cream puff in caramel syrup or melted chocolate.

7 Or sprinkle with confectioners' sugar.

Fill éclairs

1 Cut off the top of the éclair.

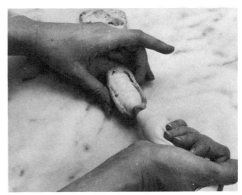

2 Pipe out a small amount of pastry cream down the length of the éclair.

3 Dip the top of the éclair in melted chocolate with butter added to make it shine.

4 The filled éclairs and cream puffs.

Fill and form swan

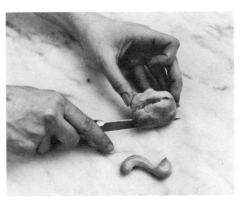

1 Split the body of the swan lengthwise.

2 Cut one piece in two for the wings.

Fill and form swan, continued

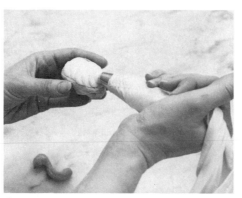

3 Pipe whipped cream into the body cavity.

4 Push the neck and the wings into the whipped cream and sprinkle with confectioners' sugar.

PHYLLO PASTRY

Divide for hors d'oeuvre

Phyllo pastry, paper-thin sheets of stretched flour and water dough, are available frozen in most supermarkets and specialty food shops. Because they are fragile and dry out quickly, work with only two sheets at once. Cover the rest with plastic wrap and a damp cloth. Each leaf is brushed with melted butter to insure that the multiple layers will crisp individually. This is true whether the phyllo pastry is used for hors d'oeuvre, as a wrapping for fish, for strudel, or for that sweet flaky confection called baklava.

1 Lay out and stack as many sheets of phyllo pastry as called for. Cut the pastry into rectangles about three and one-half inches wide.

2 Cut each rectangle into halves.

3 Cover all but two sheets of dough with plastic wrap and a damp towel. Proceed to brush and fill pastry according to the following instructions.

Shape into hors d'oeuvre I

1 Brush two rectangles of phyllo pastry with melted butter.

2 Put one teaspoon of filling (I'm using a feta cheese mixture) on the corner of one sheet, about one inch from the bottom and the side.

3 Lay the second sheet of phyllo on top, buttered side up.

4 Fold the unfilled corner of pastry over the filling, forming a triangle.

Shape into hors d'oeuvre I, continued

5 Lift up the corner and fold the triangle over.

6 Continue to fold in this manner, as if you were folding a flag.

7 Fold any extra pastry under the finished triangle.

8 Brush the triangles with butter and bake on a cookie sheet in a 350-degree oven for fifteen minutes. Or freeze them and bake them frozen for twenty-five minutes.

Shape into hors d'oeuvre II

1 Brush two rectangles of phyllo dough with melted butter.

2 Place one teaspoon of filling (I'm using spinach and feta cheese) about one inch from the bottom in the center of the sheet.

3 Cover with the second sheet of phyllo dough, buttered side up.

4 Press around the filling to get any air out.

5 Fold one long side to the center.

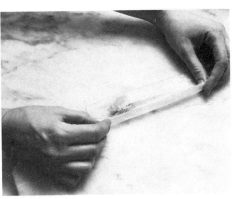

6 Fold the other side to the center.

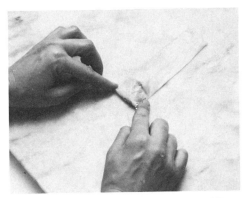

7 Fold the bottom edge of pastry over the filling.

8 Brush the pastry with melted butter.

**Shape into hors d'oeuvre
II, continued**

9 Roll the pastry over itself.

10 Bake the pastries on a cookie sheet in a 350-degree oven for fifteen minutes.

11 The cooked hors d'oeuvre.

Form and bake baklava

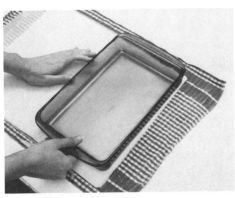

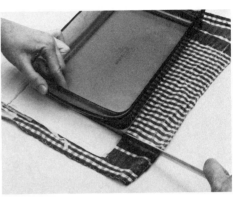

1 Spread as many stacked sheets of phyllo pastry as called for on a damp towel. Place a rectangular baking dish with two-inch sides on top.

2 Cut around the bottom to get pieces of pastry that will fit inside the dish. Repeat cutting around the dish with the rest of the phyllo pastry.

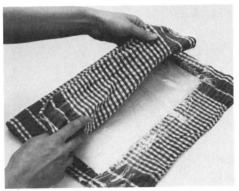

3 Stack the sheets of pastry and cover with plastic wrap and a damp towel.

4 Brush the inside of the baking dish with melted butter.

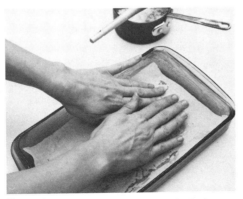

5 Place one sheet of phyllo pastry in the bottom of the pan.

6 Brush the sheet with butter. Place nine more sheets of pastry into the pan, brushing the top of each one with butter as it is added.

Form and bake baklava, continued

7 Sprinkle the pastry with filling (I'm using ground nuts and spices).

8 Cover the nuts with another layer of pastry and brush it with butter. Repeat with another layer of pastry.

9 Continue adding filling and two sheets of pastry, buttering each sheet, until almost to the top of the pan.

10 Put four or five sheets of pastry on the top of the baklava, buttering each sheet as it is added. Pour melted butter over the top.

11 Using a sharp knife, cut through just the top layers of pastry, first lengthwise then diagonally.

12 Sprinkle water over the top to settle the pastry and keep it from curling. Bake the baklava in a 325-degree oven for about one and one-half hours.

13 Remove the baklava from the oven and slowly pour a cooled sugar and honey syrup over it. Let the baklava sit at room temperature for at least four hours.

14 Cut the baklava into serving pieces, following the diamond pattern.

Fill and roll strudel

Although it is not authentic, phyllo pastry produces a light and flaky strudel without the time-consuming element of making traditional strudel dough. Whichever pastry you use, the technique of rolling is the same.

1 Lay one whole sheet of phyllo pastry on a damp kitchen towel and brush the sheet all over with melted butter.

Fill and roll strudel, continued

2 Place the filling across the short side of the pastry, leaving one inch at the bottom and sides.

3 Sprinkle fine cake crumbs over the rest of the pastry if you have used a fruit filling. Use bread crumbs for a seafood or meat filling.

4 Lift up the edge of the towel to roll the edge of pastry over the filling.

5 Start to roll the pastry with your hands.

6 Lift up the towel to continue to roll the pastry and to keep it compact.

7 When it is completely rolled, carefully lift the strudel onto a lightly buttered baking sheet.

8 Tuck the ends of the pastry under.

9 Brush the roll with melted butter. Bake in a 425-degree oven for twenty minutes.

10 Sprinkle the cooked strudel with confectioners' sugar and cut into serving pieces.

13
CAKES
AND COOKIES

CAKES AND COOKIES

Butter and line cake pan

For most cakes, the baking pan should be prepared by buttering it, buttering and flouring it, or buttering and lining it with cooking parchment or wax paper. If you are buttering and flouring the pan, chill it before adding the flour so that it doesn't form a paste that would stick to the cake.

1 Brush the bottom and sides of the cake pan with melted butter.

2 Cut out a piece of cooking parchment or wax paper, using the bottom of the pan as a guide. Put the paper in and brush the top with melted butter.

3 If the pan is to be floured, chill the pan after buttering it and pour in a little flour. Tilt the pan so the flour is evenly distributed over the bottom and sides. Pour out the excess.

Line savarin mold

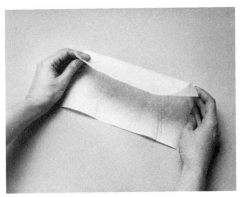

1 Cut out a square of cooking parchment or wax paper slightly larger than the ring mold.

2 Fold the paper in half.

3 Fold in half again to get a square.

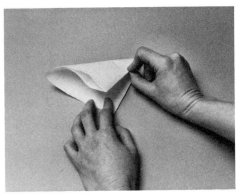

4 Fold one corner over to get a triangle.

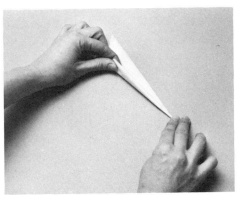

5 Fold the triangle over itself several times to get a long thin triangle.

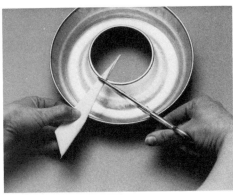

6 Hold the point of the triangle over the center of the mold. Cut the paper at the inside edge of the inner ring.

Line savarin mold, continued

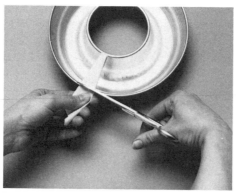

7 Cut it at the inside edge of the perimeter.

8 Open up the paper and fit it inside the mold.

9 You can also use this method for a regular round cake pan. Cut the paper at the inside edge of the perimeter.

10 Open up the paper and fit it inside the pan.

Butter and flour a cookie sheet

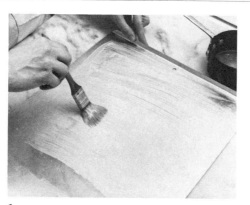

1 Brush the sheet evenly with melted butter.

2 Sift flour lightly onto the sheet.

3 Tip the sheet so the flour coats it evenly.

Sift and measure flour

Measurements must be accurate in baking; be sure to use the right cups for liquid and dry ingredients so you can be precise. Don't shake the flour once it is in the measuring cup to get it level because you will lose the lightness you achieved by sifting it.

1 Spread out a large sheet of wax paper and put the measuring cup on the paper. Sift the flour into the cup.

2 Using a spatula, level the flour with the top of the cup. Pour the flour into a mixing bowl and repeat until you have the number of cups required.

Sieve confectioners' sugar

Confectioners' sugar (also called powdered sugar) should be put through a fine-meshed sieve to get rid of any lumps. Tap the sieve with your hand and the sugar will fall through.

Form paper cone

A paper cone is essential for piping out delicate decorations on cakes, cookies, and canapés. Use kitchen parchment or other heavy paper because the cone must be sturdy.

1 Cut out a large triangle of parchment about sixteen inches by twelve inches by eleven inches. Hold it with the long side facing you.

2 Lift the two corners of the long side of the triangle and cross them over.

3 Slide the two sides against each other, forming a cone with a closed point at the bottom.

4 Turn the cone with the point away from you and bring the three points of the paper together.

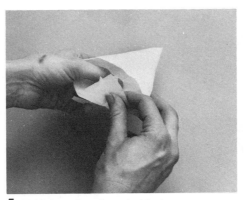

5 Fold the points down inside the cone.

6 Add filling half way to the top of the cone.

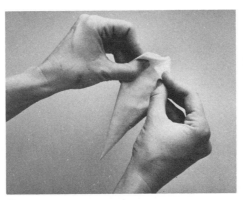

7 Fold in the two sides of the cone.

8 Fold over the top several times. Cut off the tip of the cone so the filling can be piped out in a fine line.

Cook sugar syrup

Sugar syrup is cooked to the soft-ball stage for such things as fondant icing, Italian meringues, and butter creams. It is cooked to the hard-crack stage for many candies and fruit glazes. And there are stages in between that are called for in candy recipes. The most accurate way to determine these stages is to use a candy thermometer. Hold it under warm water before putting it in the boiling liquid.

1 Add one cup sugar to one-half cup water (or according to recipe) in a heavy pan over medium heat.

2 Add a pinch of cream of tartar.

3 As soon as the syrup has slight bubbles, cover the pan and cook for about three minutes. The water will condense and wash down the crystals that form on the sides of the pan.

4 When the syrup is boiling, uncover the pan and lower the flame.

5 Cook wothout stirring until the syrup reaches a temperature of 234 degrees on a candy thermometer. This is the soft-ball stage.

6 If you don't have a thermometer, remove the pan from the stove and test the syrup by dropping a small amount in cold water.

7 At the soft-ball stage, the mixture will hold together and flatten out.

8 If you cook the mixture to a temperature of 300 degrees, which is the hard-crack stage, the syrup will form brittle threads when put into cold water. For a caramel syrup, continue to cook for several minutes until it turns amber.

Form caramel cage

This decorative confection can be used over oeufs à la neige and poached fruits, or as a nest for ice cream and fruits. Cook sugar syrup to the hard crack stage and then caramelize it (see previous instructions), but use two cups of sugar instead of one with the one-half cup water.

1 Place the carmelized syrup in a pan of lukewarm water to stop the cooking and cool it slightly.

Form caramel cage, continued

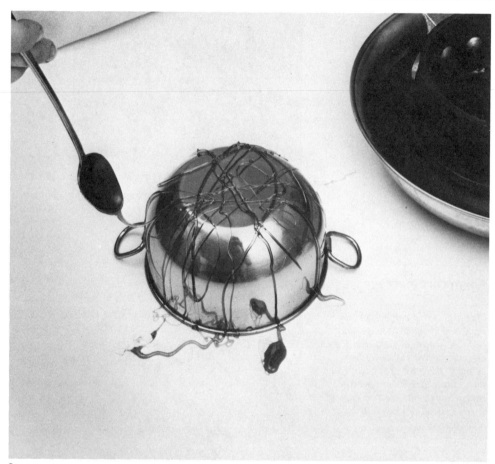

2 When syrup is cool enough to form threads when dropped from a spoon, cross strands of syrup over the outside of a chilled and oiled bowl. Use about one teaspoon of syrup at a time.

3 Make a scallop pattern of syrup around the sides of the bowl.

4 Carefully cut around the bottom of the bowl to detach the cage and make it even.

5 When thoroughly cooled, twist the cage to loosen it and lift it off.

6 The cages can be made a day ahead and stored in a cool dry place, not the refrigerator.

Test cake for doneness

Put a toothpick into the cake just off center. It will come out clean when the cake is done. Also, most cakes will spring back when touched.

Slice into layers

It is easier to slice a cake when it has been allowed to cool for several hours. Use a serrated knife so you don't tear the soft texture of the cake.

1 Put the cake on a flat surface and lightly press the top with the palm of one hand. Hold a long serrated knife with the blade parallel to the surface.

2 Starting one-third of the way down, cut across the cake with a light sawing motion. Your hand can feel where the knife is and move along with it. Turn the cake as you cut.

3 Lift off the top layer with your hands if the cake is firm enough. Turn it over.

4 Or cross two long spatulas under the layer and lift it off.

5 Cut another layer in the same way.

6 Lift it and turn it over on the first layer so they are in the order they came off.

Moisten or glaze before frosting

If you are frosting a cake that is naturally dry or slightly stale, a sugar syrup under the frosting will add moisture to the cake. Glazing with jam is helpful with a cake that has a lot of crumbs. The glaze prevents the crumbs from mixing with the frosting.

1 To moisten a cake, brush each layer with a sugar and water syrup brought just to a boil and cooled to room temperature.

2 Glaze a cake with heated jelly or sieved jam if it has a lot of crumbs.

Frost cake

The trick to a smooth frosting is to have enough frosting between the spatula and the cake. If the edge of the spatula touches the cake itself, you will have crumbs mixed in with the frosting. Support the cake on the bottom so you can lift it to frost the sides.

1 Put the bottom layer or a whole cake on a piece of cardboard cut slightly smaller than the cake. Or use the removable bottom of a cake pan.

2 Put a large mound of frosting in the middle of the cake.

3 Using the tip of a long flexible spatula, push the frosting out from the center in a fan shape. Hold the spatula almost flat on the cake and keep the frosting in front of the tip.

4 Turn the cake and push the frosting out to the edges from the center.

Frost cake, continued

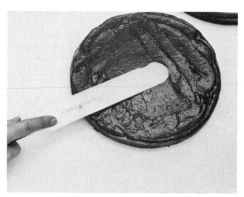

5 Hold the spatula flat and smooth the surface, pushing any excess frosting over the sides.

6 Top with another layer of cake and frost it in the same way, then add the top layer and frost it.

7 Lift the cake on its cardboard base to frost the sides. Hold the base with the flat of your hand, fingers spread out. Pat on frosting around the side of the cake.

8 To smooth the frosting, start with the spatula high on the side.

9 Pull the spatula down to the right.

10 Pull the spatula off the bottom. Continue around the perimeter of the cake.

Glaze cake after frosting

A chocolate glaze adds a lovely smooth and shiny finish to a frosted cake. Refrigerate the cake before you add the glaze so the frosting will be set. The glaze can be made of melted chocolate and honey, corn syrup, or cream. It should be tepid but still liquid.

1 Put the cake on a rack over a pan to catch the drippings. Pour the glaze on the cake all at once.

2 Quickly spread it over the top with a long spatula.

3 Spread it to the edges and down the sides.

4 Lift the rack and shake it to settle the glaze evenly on the cake. Refrigerate and bring to room temperature about one hour before serving.

Decorate with chocolate

This is a simple and attractive way to achieve professional results. Use semisweet chocolate because it is the most flexible to work with; bitter chocolate tends to be brittle.

1 Melt chocolate in the top of a double boiler over simmering water. Stir and watch it carefully because chocolate burns easily.

2 Scrape out onto a large piece of cooking parchment.

Decorate with chocolate, continued

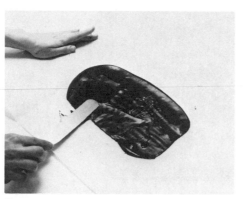

3 Spread the chocolate into a thin, even layer about one-eighth inch thick.

4 Slide the parchment onto a baking sheet and refrigerate the chocolate for at least an hour, or until it is firm.

5 Let the chocolate come to room temperature. Cut out hearts or any desired shape with a metal decorative cutter.

6 Press the cutouts onto the side of the cake.

7 Make a pleasing pattern of cutouts on the top. See color photograph of decorated cake.

Decorate with marzipan I

Marzipan, which is made of almond paste, egg white, confectioners' sugar, and rose water or lemon juice, can be purchased in cans or rolls. It is easy to work with and can be dyed with food coloring appropriate to the design. Add only a small amount at the beginning—you can always add more later if you want a brighter color. Work on a surface that is lightly oiled with sweet almond or vegetable oil.

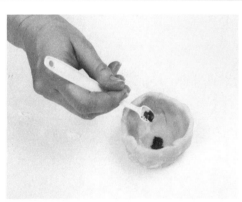

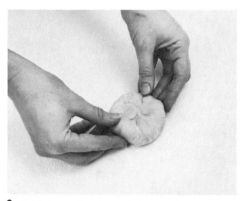

1 Form marzipan into a cup shape three or four inches in diameter. Put a few drops of food coloring in the center.

2 Fold down the edges of the marzipan.

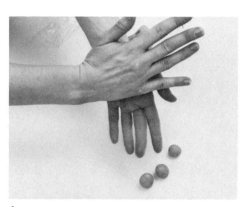

3 Put the marzipan between pieces of plastic wrap and knead until the color is evenly distributed. Don't overknead; a few streaks look more natural.

4 Pull off small pieces of marzipan and roll them between the palms of your hands. For a rose, you will need four small balls and four to six slightly larger ones.

Decorate with marzipan I, continued

5 Press your thumb into each ball to flatten it.

6 Lightly oil a light bulb and roll it three-quarters of the way around the outer edges of the marzipan to thin it. The center, where the petal will be attached, should remain about one-quarter inch thick.

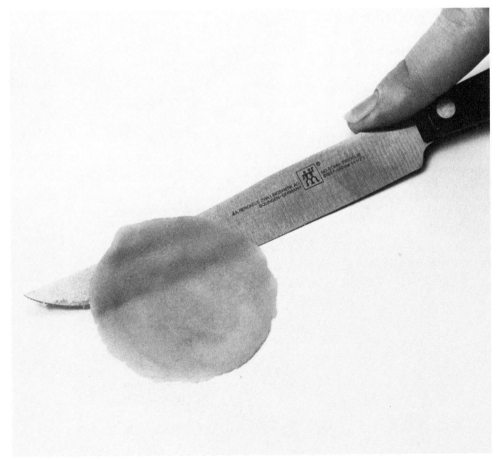

7 Lift one small petal by running a knife under the thicker part.

8 Press the petal against a piece of marzipan rolled into a bell shape.

9 Press another petal tightly around the first, creating a bud. Continue with two more small petals.

10 Press larger petals around the outside of the bud, letting the tops open up.

Decorate with marzipan I, continued

11 With the outside layer of petals, turn the tops down.

12 Roll marzipan that has been dyed green into leaf shapes.

13 Press the leaves onto the bottom of the rose. Use the rose to decorate the center of a cake. See color photograph of finished cake.

Decorate with marzipan II

This is a simple way to decorate a cake if you want to write on the surface.

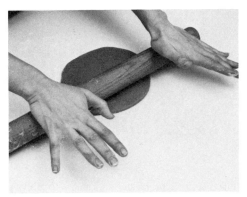

1 Dye the marzipan (see preceding instructions) and roll it out one-quarter inch thick on a surface sprinkled with confectioners' sugar.

2 Use the bottom of the cake pan as a guide to cut out a circle to fit the top of the cake.

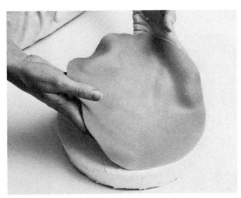

3 Lift the marzipan onto a cake that has been frosted or covered with jam.

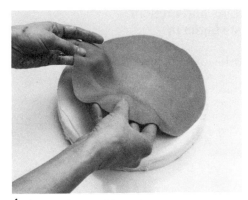

4 Arrange it smoothly on top.

5 Lift the cake and pat ground nuts into the frosting or jam on the sides of the cake. Have the nuts in an open dish so you can reach in and get a handful. Start at the bottom of the cake.

6 Flatten your hand against the side so the nuts go all the way up.

Decorate with marzipan II, continued

7 Brush the marzipan to remove any nuts that fell on it.

8 Fill a paper cone with cooled melted chocolate and pipe out a design, or write Happy Birthday!

Line and unmold springform

Springforms are metal pans that have a removable rim, which makes them ideal for cheesecakes, tortes, and other delicate cakes that would be difficult to remove from a regular cake pan.

1 Butter the bottom of the springform and, if it is for cheesecake, line it with a crumb crust. Press the crumbs over the bottom and sides. Refrigerate briefly before filling.

2 Pour the cheesecake or torte batter into the springform. Cook according to recipe directions.

3 Let the cake cool in the pan after baking. Run a thin-bladed knife around the inside rim to loosen the crust.

4 Set the pan on a large can and very carefully undo the clip on the side of the rim.

5 Let the rim fall to the counter. Lift the cake off the can and put it on a serving platter.

Line and unmold charlotte mold

Dessert molds, which should have slanted sides for ease in unmolding, can be lined with ladyfingers, sponge cake, or cookies. You can soften whatever you are using to line the mold with a light sprinkling of liqueur appropriate to the filling. Don't soak them or they will disintegrate. I'm using a charlotte mold lined with ladyfingers sprinkled with Grand Marnier. The filling is orange Bavarian cream.

1 Using the bottom of the mold as a guide, cut out a circle of cooking parchment.

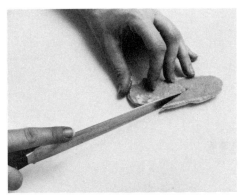

2 Place the parchment on your work surface and cut ladyfingers to fit the circle. Cut in at an angle on either side of the ladyfinger forming a teardrop shape.

Line and unmold charlotte mold, continued

3 When you have a circle of ladyfingers, lift the paper and put it in the bottom of the mold.

4 Place ladyfingers upright around the rim of the mold, as close together as possible so there are few gaps. The curved side of the ladyfingers should be next to the mold.

5 Cut small strips of ladyfingers.

6 Fit the strips between the ladyfingers to fill any gaps.

7 After pouring well-chilled mixture into the mold, trim the ladyfingers with a sharp knife so they are even with the top of the mold.

8 Cover the mold with wax paper and chill it for at least five hours before unmolding.

9 To unmold the dessert, run a thin-bladed knife around the inside rim of the mold.

10 Put a serving plate over the mold.

11 Hold onto the plate and the handles of the mold and invert it.

Line and unmold charlotte mold, continued

12 Turn your hands over and grasp the plate and the handles of the mold. Jerk it up and down quickly.

13 Lift the mold off and remove the paper.

14 Pipe whipped cream between the ladyfingers and on top in any pattern desired.

Fill and roll cake

If you are making a jelly roll, work quickly so the cake doesn't cool before you roll it with the jelly filling. If you are using a cream filling, put the warm cake on a towel sprinkled with confectioners' sugar and roll it up with the towel inside. Let it cool, then unroll, spread with filling, and roll it as for a jelly roll, using the towel instead of wax paper to help you.

1 Remove cooked cake from the oven and cover the pan with a length of wax paper.

2 Invert the cake onto a smooth work surface.

3 Pull off the parchment that lined the pan.

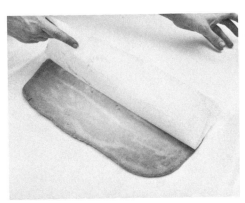

4 Quickly spread a thin layer of filling all over the cake, leaving a one-inch border around the edges.

5 Lift up one end of the wax paper.

6 Roll the cake, lifting the paper as you go along.

Fill and roll cake, continued

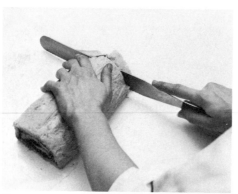

7 Trim off the ends of the jelly roll if they are ragged.

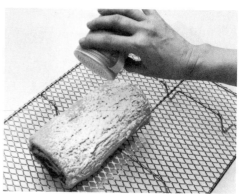

8 Put the cake on a wire rack to cool and sprinkle with confectioners' sugar.

Shape ladyfingers

Ladyfingers are delicious served as cookies, and are used to line molds for many gelatin desserts.

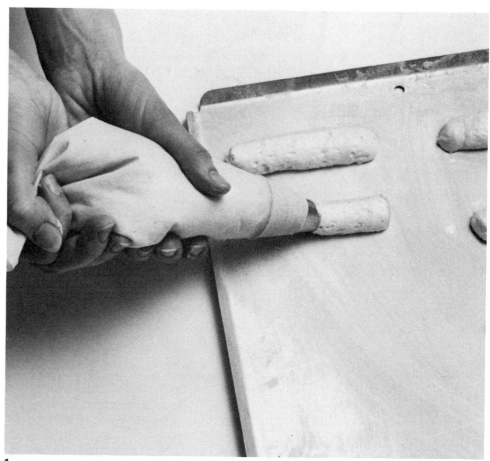

1 Outfit a pastry bag with a plain tube and fill with the dough. Pipe out four-inch lengths onto a buttered and floured cookie sheet.

2 Sprinkle the ladyfingers with confectioners' sugar.

3 Tip the pan and tap it on the bottom to remove excess sugar, which would burn. The ladyfingers won't fall off. Bake according to recipe directions.

Shape and fill jelly cookies

Jelly cookies and the following coutouts are just two examples of cookies that can be shaped with a basic rolled sugar dough.

1 Pull off a small amount of dough and roll it under the palm of your hand.

2 Roll the ball of dough in granulated sugar.

3 Place the balls on a buttered baking sheet about two inches apart.

4 When the cookies have baked five minutes, remove them from the oven and press your thumb into the center of each cookie. Return them to the oven to finish baking.

Shape and fill jelly cookies, continued

5 When the cookies are cool, use a small measuring spoon to fill the centers with jelly.

Shape and decorate cutout cookies

Use confectioners' sugar rather than flour to keep the dough from sticking when rolling it out. Flour will make the cookies tough.

1 Sprinkle confectioners' sugar on a cool surface, preferably marble.

2 Roll the dough out into a large oval about one-quarter inch thick.

3 Press the metal cookie cutters into dough as close together as possible.

4 Lift up the cookies with a spatula and place them on a buttered cookie sheet. Bake as directed.

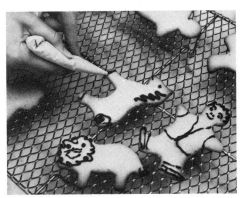

5 Cool the cookies on a rack. Put melted chocolate cooled to lukewarm or a white icing in a paper cone and pipe out in any decoration you choose.

Shape and decorate cutout cookies, continued

6 The decorated cookies.

Shape curled cookies

Warm, thin cookies are easily shaped, but you must work quickly before they cool and become brittle. Cook and shape only one batch at a time.

1 Drop the dough from a teaspoon onto a buttered and floured cookie sheet. Leave three or four inches between each cookie.

2 Flatten the dough with the back of a spoon.

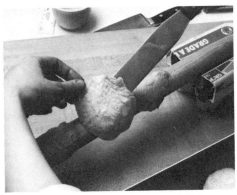

3 Sprinkle with nuts, if desired, and bake according to recipe directions.

4 When the cookies are baked, quickly lift them off with a spatula and put them over a rolling pin or broom handle to cool.

5 You can also roll the warm cookies around the handle of a wooden spoon.

**Shape curled cookies,
continued**

6 The curled cookies.

7 The rolled cookies.

14
FRUITS

APPLES

Core and Peel

I've always peeled round fruits in one piece because as a teen-ager I heard that if you threw the peel over your shoulder, whatever letter it resembled when it fell would be the initial of your future husband. Now that I'm more mature, I do it because it helps me to follow the contour of the fruit.

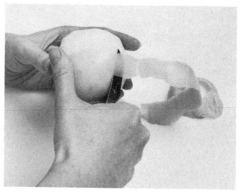

1 Take out the core and seeds with an apple corer or a sharp knife. Push the corer in straight through the stem end, twist, and pull out.

2 Peel around the apple in one piece with a sharp knife.

Slice

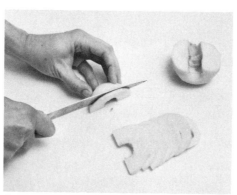

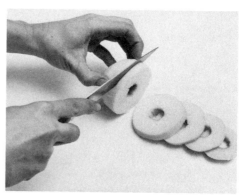

1 For pies and tarts, cut the cored and peeled apple in two lengthwise and put flat side down. Cut into thin slices.

2 For a garnish for meat or for *tarte tatin*, slice the whole apple into rings.

Prepare for baking

If you cut an incision around the apple, it will prevent it from bursting. I also like to peel it down to the incision because it looks more finished and is easier to eat.

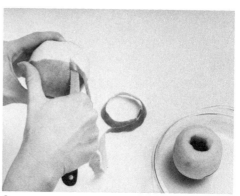

1 Core the apple but be sure not to pierce the bottom. Make an incision in the skin around the middle of the apple.

2 Peel down to the incision. Use a sharp knife rather than a vegetable peeler so that the edge is neat.

3 Rub the peeled part with lemon to prevent discoloring.

4 Fill the center with butter and sugar, or whatever you choose, and bake with a little water in the pan.

Cut into a bird

This is an amusing garnish for a meat or fruit platter and it isn't hard to do. If you rub all the cut pieces with lemon and put the wedges back in so they aren't exposed to the air, the apple will keep its color. But it is best to cut it as close to serving time as possible and fan the wedges out at the last minute.

Cut into a bird, continued

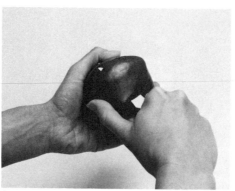

1 Cut a thin slice off one side so the apple will sit firmly.

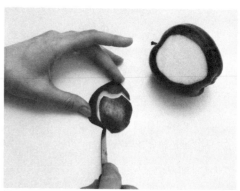

2 Cut out a head for the bird from the thin slice. Rub with lemon juice and set aside.

3 Place the apple cut side down and make a thin wedge-shaped cut on the top, starting near the stem end. This will be the tail of the bird.

4 Remove the wedge.

5 Cut all around the first wedge.

6 Remove another thin piece.

7 Continue with a third wedge.

8 Cut out and remove three similar wedges on either side of the tail to form the wings.

9 Rub the wedges with lemon and lay them back in so they won't discolor.

10 Cut a notch in the blossom end of the apple.

11 Insert the head.

12 When ready to serve, fan out the slices for the tail and wings.

AVOCADO

Slice and peel

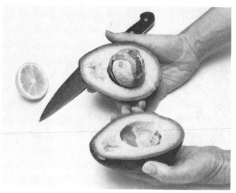

1 Cut the avocado lengthwise around the large seed. Pull the halves apart and rub exposed surfaces with lemon juice to prevent discoloring.

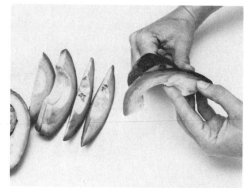

2 Cut one half into wedges and peel each slice. Sprinkle with lemon juice. If you want to save the other half, leave the seed in, which prevents discoloring, wrap with plastic wrap, and refrigerate.

BERRIES

Glaze Strawberries

Make these on a cool dry day when you can leave them at room temperature to dry. Humidity will liquefy the sugar, as will the moisture in a refrigerator.

1 Wipe the berries with a towel. Don't wash them because the berries must be very dry. Rub a marble slab with oil, preferably sweet almond oil.

2 Holding the hull, dip the berry into a sugar syrup that has boiled to the hard-crack stage. The pan of syrup should be in hot water.

3 Rub the berry against the side of the pan to get off the last droplet of syrup. Work quickly because the syrup in the pan will harden.

4 Let the berries dry on the marble. They will keep for about four hours in a cool dry place. Don't refrigerate.

Sieve

1 Place berries in a finely meshed sieve over a bowl and mash with the back of a wooden spoon, pushing the pulp through the sieve.

2 The seedless pulp is ready to be used for sauces or sherbets.

CHERRIES

Pit

A cherry pitter or stoner is a handy gadget if you bake a lot of pies. It is quicker than using a knife and does a neater job.

1 Wash and stem the cherries. Place the cherry in the bowl of the pitter, stem end up.

2 Press down, and the stone is ejected through the hole in the bowl.

CHESTNUTS

Peel

1 With the tip of a sharp pointed knife, make two intersecting cuts in the crown of the chestnut.

2 Put the chestnuts in boiling water to cover, lower heat, and simmer for ten minutes.

Peel, continued

3 Pull off the shell and thin inner peel while the chestnuts are still warm. The skin tends to stick if they are allowed to cool.

4 If necessary, pull off the thin inner peel with a knife.

CITRUS FRUITS

Peel

Use a sharp knife and cut off the peel, including the white part, in one complete piece circling the fruit.

Section

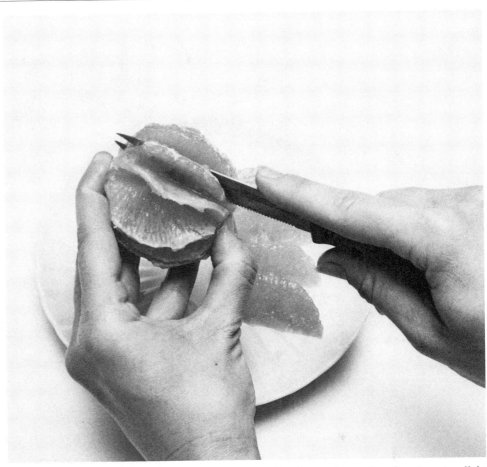

Hold the peeled fruit in one hand and cut down on one side of a membrane, then the other, at a slight angle. Continue around the fruit, removing sections as you go, leaving the membrane attached.

Cut zest

Zest, the thin citrus peel, adds flavor to anything from a martini to the frosting on a cake. There are special gadgets for shaving off the zest, but you can use a knife or a vegetable peeler. The purpose is to get only the oily colored peel, not the bitter white pith underneath.

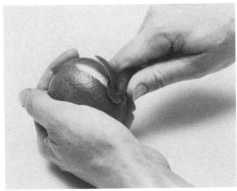

1 With a citrus stripper, pull down on the skin while pushing up on the fruit with your thumb.

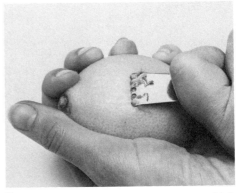

2 To get a finer peel, use a citrus zester, which has small holes with sharp edges that scrape off the peel.

Cut zest, continued

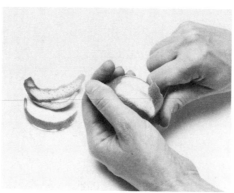

3 You may also use a sharp paring knife or vegetable peeler. Be careful not to cut too deep.

4 The peel, or *zeste* in French, is then cut into julienne, or finely chopped.

Cut garnish I

These are three quick and easy ways to cut decorative garnishes. All are good for lemons and limes; the third technique could also be used for orange slices to decorate a duck or a dessert.

1 Peel a lemon (including the white pith) and cut into thin slices. Take out any seeds with the tip of your knife.

2 Bend each slice in half and dip the fold into finely chopped parsley. This garnish is especially appropriate for fish dishes.

Cut garnish II

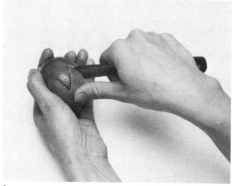

1 Push a thin-bladed sharp knife into the core of a lemon or lime. Make a neat zigzag pattern around the center. Look ahead to your first cut so the points will meet. The width of the blade determines the size of the cut.

2 The two halves will pull apart easily.

3 Remove any seeds with the point of your knife and decorate with parsley.

Cut garnish III

1 Using a citrus stripper, cut thin strips of peel from around the fruit in an even pattern.

2 Slice the fruit and remove any seeds with the tip of your knife.

Cut garnish III, continued

3 Cut to the center of each slice.

4 Twist the cut quarter under and up.

Hollow out for a basket

A citrus basket can be filled with sherbet for individual servings or, as in this case, with radish roses, scallion flowers, and parsley to decorate a buffet table.

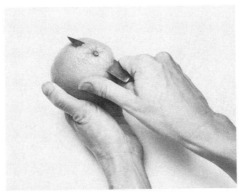

1 Using a sharp paring knife, cut a thin slice from the stem end of the fruit so the basket will sit firmly.

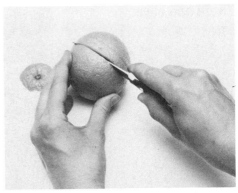

2 Place the fruit on its cut base and slice down halfway through, just off center. Make a parallel cut about one-quarter inch away, on the other side of the center, which will form the handle.

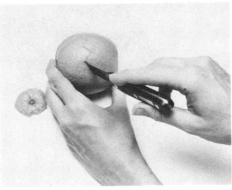

3 Starting at one side of the base of the handle, push the blade of the knife into the core in a zigzag pattern. Be careful not to cut through the handle as you reach the other side.

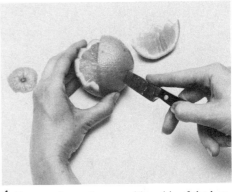

4 Remove the sections on either side of the handle. They pull out easily.

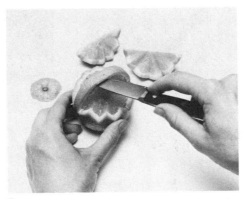

5 Use your knife very gently to scrape out the pulp under the handle.

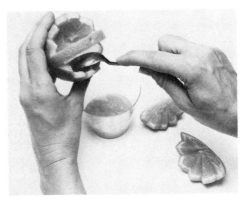

6 Scoop out the pulp in the basket with a grapefruit spoon.

COCONUT

Drain and open

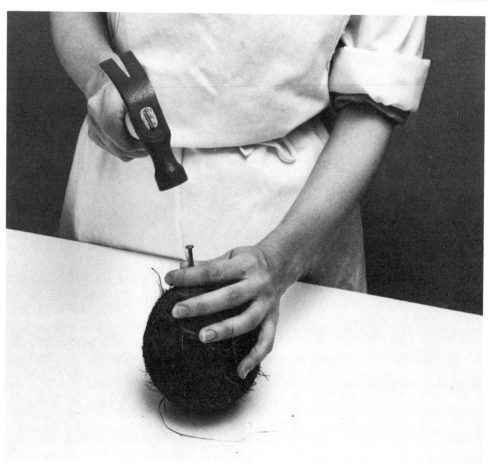

1 Coconuts contain a watery liquid that is sometimes drunk, more often discarded. Pound a nail or ice pick into the three "eyes" on the end of the coconut.

2 Discard the liquid, or strain through a coffee filter or cheesecloth if you want to drink it.

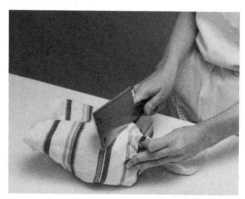

3 Bake the drained coconut in a hot oven for fifteen minutes. When cool, wrap it in a kitchen towel so it won't shatter, and break it open with the back of a cleaver or a hammer.

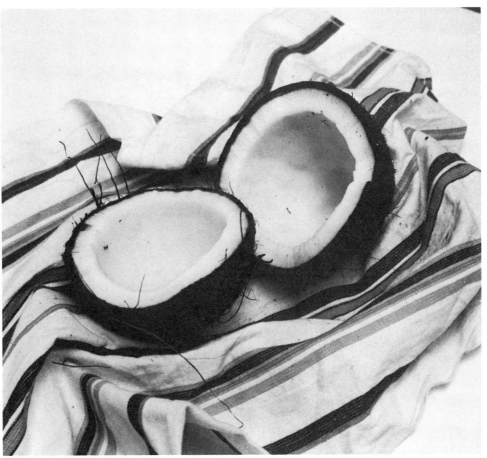

4 It will crack easily.

Remove meat and grate

1 Cut through the white flesh using a sharp knife.

2 Scoop out the meat using a grapefruit spoon or the point of a paring knife.

Remove meat and grate, continued

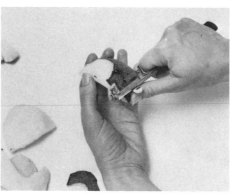

3 Pare off the brown rind on the back of the pieces using a vegetable peeler or a sharp knife.

4 Grate the pieces of coconut on the coarse side of a grater. You may also use a blender or food processor.

Make coconut cream

1 Line a bowl with cheesecloth and put in the grated coconut.

2 Pour about one cup of boiling water over one cup of grated coconut. Cover and let steep for fifteen to twenty minutes.

3 Gather the ends of the cheesecloth and twist them, squeezing out all the liquid. Discard the coconut. The thick liquid is called coconut cream.

GRAPES

Frost

This is a pretty, edible decoration to use on a buffet or, in small bunches, around a roast. The grapes will keep for several hours. Don't refrigerate them because the moisture will melt the sugar.

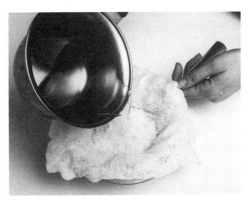

1 Put individual servings or one large bunch of grapes on a rack. Beat egg whites just until frothy.

2 Using a soft pastry brush, paint the grapes with the egg white.

3 Sprinkle with granulated sugar.

4 Put in a cool place to dry.

KIWI

Peel and slice

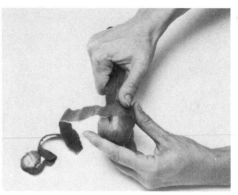

1 This sweet fruit, also known as Chinese gooseberry, is now cultivated in New Zealand. It has a brown skin that should be peeled.

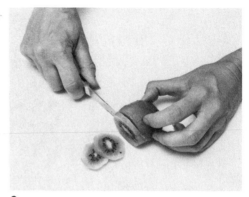

2 When sliced, it has bright green flesh that is pretty with mixed fruits or in a tart.

MANGO

Remove seed

The seed of this kidney-shaped fruit is large and tenacious. If you cut around the narrow side, it makes removal easier. Mangoes lose their flavor quickly once they are cut, so do it just before serving.

1 Cut the fruit lengthwise all around the narrow side to avoid the seed.

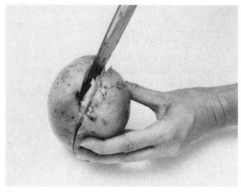

2 Loosen the seed from the flesh with the point of your knife and pull the mango apart.

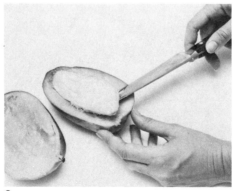

3 Pry the seed out with your knife. If the mango is very juicy, serve it in the shell.

4 You may also cut the halves into thirds and peel each piece by running your knife between the flesh and the shell.

MELON

Cut into serving pieces

This is a simple way to prepare melon for breakfast or an easy dessert.

1 Cut the melon in two through the stem end. Scoop out the seeds with a metal spoon and cut into quarters.

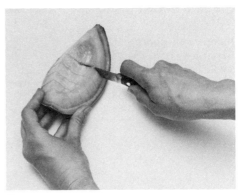

2 Cut the flesh from the rind in one piece and slice the melon across into bite-size pieces.

3 Use the point of your knife to push the pieces in opposite directions, first to one side, then the other. Garnish (I've used lemon and mint) and serve.

Cut into basket I

These are all attractive ways to serve cut-up fruit. The swan and the whale are whimiscal, which I like; the basket is more traditional.

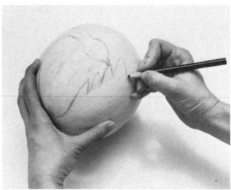

1 Look ahead to the completed swan and draw the pattern on the melon. Be sure to have the beak touch a feather on the wing to give support to the neck, or handle.

2 With a sharp paring knife, cut around the feathers, being careful to leave beak attached.

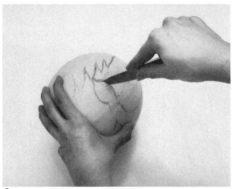

3 Cut around the neck.

4 Cut through the center of one side section, dividing it.

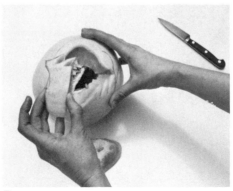

5 Lift out the two sections.

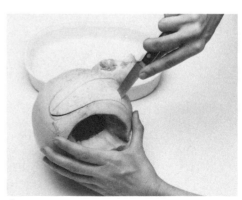

6 Repeat steps 4 and 5 on the other side.

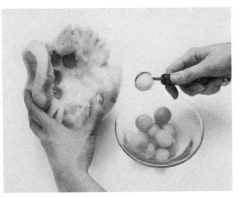

7 Trim the inside of the melon so the feathers aren't too thick.

8 Hollow out melon with a melon-ball cutter and cut balls from the removed sections.

9 Fill with mixed fruit.

Cut into basket II

1 Tie a string around the melon, just below the middle, to give a straight line. Hold a melon-ball cutter on the string and draw halfway around it with a pencil. Keep moving the cutter around the melon following the string.

2 Outline a scalloped handle over the top of the melon by drawing completely around the melon-ball cutter. With a sharp paring knife, cut around all the scalloped edges, but don't remove the pieces. They keep the melon stable.

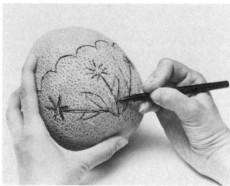

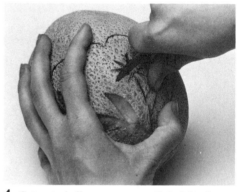

3 Draw a flower pattern on the melon around the bottom of the basket, and make small designs on the scalloped handle.

4 Cut out shallow crescents of rind for leaves and petals.

5 Cut out crescents under the scallops around the middle.

6 Loosen the two large pieces on either side of the handle and remove.

 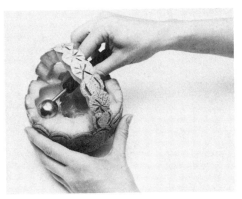

7 Carefully cut out the flesh under the handle.

8 Hollow out the melon, leaving some flesh on the shell. Push down with the melon-ball cutter on the inside edge and twist, giving a scalloped effect.

9 Fill with the melon balls and other fruit.

Cut into basket III

1 Look ahead to the completed whale to determine the pattern; then draw a head, eyes, mouth, and tail on the watermelon. Make the bottom of the tail wide enough to support it.

2 Start cutting around the tail, going all the way into the center. Remove one section and cut halfway around the head and remove that section. Repeat on the other side. Cut out eyes and mouth.

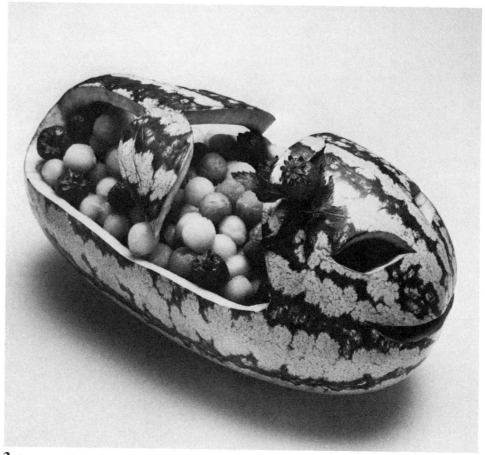

3 Scoop out the melon with a melon-ball cutter and fill with fresh fruit.

PAPAYA

Seed

Cut the fruit into halves lengthwise and scoop out and discard the many black seeds (which look like caviar) using a wooden spoon.

PEARS

Core and Peel

I like to leave pears whole for poaching because they look natural, particularly with the stem left on.

1 Leave the stem attached and core the pear through the blossom end with an apple corer.

2 Peel around in one piece. Drop the whole pears into water and lemon juice to keep them from discoloring.

Core and peel, continued

3 You may also cut the pear in two, removing the stem and core.

PINEAPPLE

Peel and slice

If you peel a pineapple deep enough to take out the "eyes," you will lose valuable flesh. This method prevents that, and the spiral design is a bonus.

1 Grasp the leaves and, using a sharp knife, shave off just enough skin so that you can see the "eyes."

2 The eyes run in a rather uniform diagonal pattern around the pineapple. To remove them, cut in at an angle on either side of the row of eyes and lift out the row.

3 The peeled pineapple with eyes removed has a spiral design.

4 For a decorative way to serve the peeled pineapple, cut off the leaves and set aside. Slice the pineapple and core each slice with a sharp knife, discarding the core.

5 Stack the slices and top with the reserved leaves. If you assemble this ahead, wrap the reshaped pineapple in plastic wrap and refrigerate.

Hollow out a half shell

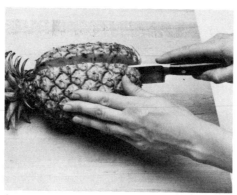

1 Hold the pineapple firmly and cut it into halves lengthwise, cutting through the leaves as well.

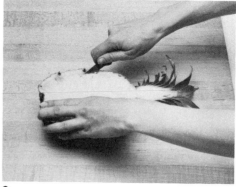

2 With a sharp knife, cut along one side of the core and then around the inside of the shell to loosen a large section of the fruit. Leave about one-half inch of shell. Repeat on the other side of the core.

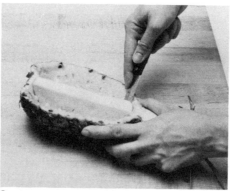

3 Remove the fruit, then cut out the core by running your knife under it from one end to the other. Discard the core.

4 Trim off any ragged leaves with kitchen shears. Fill the shell with cut-up pineapple and other fresh fruit, in this case raspberries and kiwi.

Cut into serving boats

1 Cut the pineapple into halves lengthwise, then cut into quarters, leaving leaves attached. Cut under the flesh of each quarter, leaving at least one-half inch of shell so that the "eyes" remain with the shell.

2 Cut in at an angle on either side of the core, slide the knife under the core, and remove.

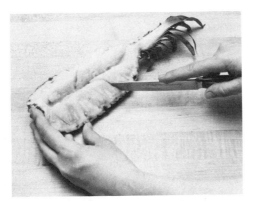

3 Slice the fruit into bite-size pieces.

4 Garnish with raspberries and mint and serve.

Hollow out whole I

This method is used when you want to remove the flesh in one piece so it can be sliced and put back into the shell.

1 Cut off a lid about three-quarters of an inch from the crown.

2 Using a long sharp knife, cut around the flesh about one-half inch in from the shell. Cut almost to the bottom but not through the shell.

3 This is a tricky step. Insert a thin-bladed sharp knife at the bottom. Without making the cut very wide, move the knife from side to side in a sawing motion to loosen the bottom of the pineapple flesh.

4 Lift out the pineapple in one piece. It can then be cored with a long knife and sliced or cut into long fingers.

Hollow out whole I, continued

5 Put the slices or fingers back into the shell and let guests remove them with a long-handled fork.

Hollow out whole II

Use this technique when you want to fill the shell with mixed fruits in their natural juices or in wine.

1 Cut off a lid about three-quarters of an inch from the crown.

2 Using a sharp knife, cut the flesh on an angle to remove a cone shape of pineapple.

3 Remove the cone and set aside. Continue to cut out two or three more cones.

4 After you have cut as many cones as possible, use your knife to clean out the shell, being careful not to pierce it.

5 Cut the pineapple off the core into thin slices. Discard the core.

6 Fill the shell with pineapple and other cut-up fruits. You can add wine or a liqueur and decorate with a raspberry and fresh mint.

POMEGRANATE

Cut for serving or for juice

The only comfortable way to eat the luscious pulp that surrounds pomegranate seeds is to eat the seeds as well. Not only is it inelegant to spit them out, but the seeds are good for you.

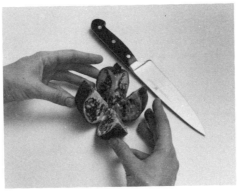

1 Quarter the fruit, without cutting all the way through, and open out for serving.

2 If you want just the juice, use your fingers to scoop out the pulp and seeds; then rub them through a sieve.

RHUBARB

Trim and Peel

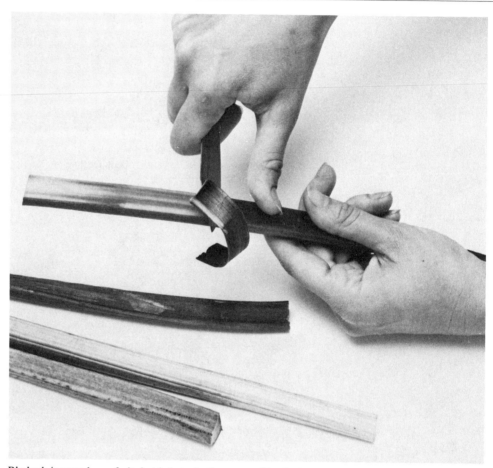

Rhubarb is served as a fruit, but is botanically a vegetable. Its leaves should be discarded because they are bitter and toxic. Hothouse rhubarb usually does not need to be peeled, but the garden variety should have the heavy fibers shaved off.

A

Acorn squash, split and scoop out seeds, 20
Aioli, 342
Al dente, as cooking term, 303
Anchovies, in butter, 356
Apples
    baking, prepare for, 508-509
    core, 508
    cut into bird, 509-511
    peel, 508
    slice, 508
Arborio rice, 315
Artichoke
    bottoms, trim and cook, 24
    stuff, 22-23
    trim, 21-22
Asparagus, peel and trim, 25
Aspic
    clarify stock for, 274-276
    decorate pâté with, 281-282
    in pâté en croûte, 287
    in vegetable pâté, 287-289
Au blanc, as cooking term, 24
Avocado, slice and peel, 512
Aztec mushroom, 47-48

B

Bacon, cook, 129
Bain marie, 279
Baked alaska, 349
Baklava
    bake, 468-469
    form, 467-468
    phyllo pastry for, 462
Ballotine, 194
Bard
    fatback for, 128
    game birds, 208
    meat, 90
Bardes, 90
Baskets
    citrus, 518-519
    melon, 526-530
Basmati rice, 317
Béarnaise sauce, 344
Beat egg whites, 323-324
Beef, 99-110; see also Meat, Roasts, Steak,
        Tenderloin
    Flank steak, 109-110
    Porterhouse, 99-100
    Rib roast, 107-108
    Tenderloin, 101-107
Beets, trim and peel, 25-26
Berries
    glaze, 512
    sieve, 513
Beurre manié, 354
Biscuits, mix and shape, 419-421
Blanch vegetables, 18
Bone
    chicken breast, 176-178
    duck, 186-189
    ham, 130
    leg of lamb, 113-117
    loin of veal, 148-152
Bouquet garni, 18-19
Bouquet of crudités

assemble, 78
    broccoli for, 26-27
    carrot for, 30
    cauliflower for, 30-31
    pepper for, 56
    radish for, 59-61
    scallion for, 62-63
    squash for, 66-67
    turnip for, 74-76
Braciola, 83
Braided loaf, shape, 382-385
Brains, clean and precook, 152-153
Braise vegetables, 17
Bread meat, 85
Bread sticks, shape, 396-398
Breads, 374-422; see also Quick breads, Yeast
        breads, and specific entries
Brioche
    in coffee can, 416
    shape, 403-405
Broccoli
    in bouquet of crudités, 78
    cut into flowerets, 26-27
    trim, 26
Brussels sprouts
    trim, 27
Butter
    clarify, 354
    cream, 355
    cut into curls or balls, 354-355
    mix with flour for thickening, 354
    seasoned, roll and slice, 356-357
Butter cream, sugar syrup for, 480-481
Butterfly
    chop, 87
    fish, 222-223
    flank steak, 109-110
    leg of lamb, 113-117
    shrimp, 266

C

Cabbage
    braise, 17
    core, 28
    stuff
        leaves, 28
        whole, 29
Cakes
    butter and line pan, 474
    cream filling, 499
    croquembouche, 456
    decorate
        with chocolate, 487-489
        with marzipan, 489-494
        paper cone for, 478-479
        pastry bag for, 457
    fill and roll, 499
    frosting, 485-486
        glaze after, 487
        moisten or glaze before, 485
    gâteau St. Honoré, 456
    jelly roll, 499-500
    savarin mold, line, 475-476
    slice into layers, 484
    springform, line and unmold, 494-495
    test for doneness, 483
Canapés
    cylindrical loaf for, 387, 415-416

decorate, 411-416
    pullman loaf for, 386
    slice bread for, 410-411
Candies, sugar syrup for, 480-481
Candy thermometer, 480
Cannelloni
    cut and parboil, 300-301
    fill and roll, 301
Cappelletti, 296
Caramel cage
    form, 481-483
Carpaccio, 83
Carrots
    assemble flower, 30
    in bouquet of crudités, 78
    on pâté, 282
Carve
    ham, 131-133
    leg of lamb, 120-121
    rack of lamb, 113
    rib roast, 107-108
    suckling pig, 142-145
    turkey, 181-182
Caul fat, 91, 285
Cauliflower
    in bouquet of crudités, 78
    re-form after cooking, 31
    trim and cut into flowerets, 30-31
Celery
    in bouquet garni, 18
    braise, 17
    peel, 32
    trim, 32
Celery root, trim and peel, 32
Charlotte mold
    line, 495-496
    unmold, 497-498
Chateaubriand, 105, 107
Cheesecake, springform for, 494
Cheesecloth
    for bouquet garni, 18-19
    for poached fish, 226-228
    form sausage in, 137-138
    stuffed cabbage in, 29
Cherries, pit, 513
Cherry tomatoes
    cut into flowers, 34
    stuff, 33
Chestnuts, peel, 513-514
Chicken; see also Poultry
    breast
        bone, 176-178
        stuff, 178-180
    disjoint, 172-174
        split for broiling, 174-176
Chicken livers, pick over, 155
Chiffonade, 13
Child, Julia, 470
Chili peppers, core and seed, 34
Chinese gooseberry, 523
Chinese pancakes, mix and cook, 366-370
Chinois, 18
Chocolate
    decorate cakes with, 487-489
    decorate cookies with, 502-504
    glaze cake with, 487
    melt, 487

Chop
  fish, 240-241
  garlic, 39-40
  meat, 81
  onions, 50
  shallots, 64
  vegetables (general), 8-9
Chops
  butterfly, 87
  stuff, 127-128
Choron sauce, 344
Citrus fruit
  baskets
    hollow out for, 518-519
    presentation, 40
  garnishes, 516-518
  peel, 514
  section, 515
  zest, cut, 515-516
Citrus stripper
  for citrus garnishes, 517-518
  for decorating cucumbers, 35
  for fluting mushrooms, 49
  for cutting zest, 515
Clams, open, 242-243
Clarify
  butter, 354
  stock, 274-276
Clover rolls, shape, 400
Coconut
  drain, 520
  open, 520-521
  remove meat and grate, 521-522
Coconut cream, 522-523
Coffee cake, 406-407
Conchs, remove meat from shell, 249-250
Consommé, stock for, 274
Cookies
  butter and flour cookie sheet, 476-477
  curled, 505-506
  cutout, 502-504
  in dessert molds, 495
  jelly, 501-502
  ladyfingers, 500-501
  palm, 451-453
  rolled, 504-506
Core
  apples, 508
  cabbage, 8, 28
  chili peppers, 34
  endive, 8
  fennel, 8
  parsnips, 54-55
  pears, 531
Corn, cut off kernels or pulp, 34-35
Crabs
  hard-shell
    prepare for stuffing, 243-245
  soft-shell, prepare for cooking, 245-246
Crayfish, prepare for cooking, 246-247
Cream puffs
  fill, 459-460
  form, 458
Crème anglaise, 345
Crêpes
  cook, 362-363
  fill dessert, 364-366
  mix batter, 361-362

Crescent rolls, shape, 401-403
Croissants, 401
Croquembouche, 456
Croutons, 408-409
Crown roast
  form, 92-93
  paper frills for, 98-99
Crudités
  bouquet, 78
Cucumbers
  decorate, 35
  peel and seed, 36
  slice, 36-37
Curled cookies, shape, 504-506
Custard
  beat egg yolks with sugar for, 326-327
  caramelize mold, 346-347
  cook until it coats spoon, 345
  strain into mold, 347-348
Cut in flour and butter, 424-425
Cutout cookies
  decorate, 503-504
  paper cone for, 478-479
  shape, 502-503

D

Dacquoise, 349
"Daisy" steamer, 14
Dandelion greens, clean and trim, 37
Deep-fried eggs, 332-333
Deglaze, 96
Degrease, 272-273
Demi-glace, 273
Disjoint chicken, 172-174
Dodine
  stuff duck for, 194-197
Doilies; see pancakes, Chinese
Dredge, 84
Duck
  dodine, 194-197
  galantine, 186-193
  Peking, 197-201
Dumplings
  gnocchi, 307, 456
  jao-tze, 311-312
  shape and cook, 304-305
  shiu may, 309-310
  won ton, 307-309
Dust soufflé mold, 339-340
Duxelles, 45

E

Eclairs
  fill, 461
  form, 458
Eel, clean and skin, 248-249
Eggplant
  parboil shell, 17
  remove cooked pulp from, 38
  slice and salt, 38
  stuff, 38-39
Eggs
  bake, 332
  beat whole with fork, 326
  boil, 328-329
  custard, 345-348; see also Custard
  deep fry, 332-333
  fry, 331

hard-boil, 328-329
  hollandaise sauce, 344-345
  mayonnaise, 342-343
  meringue, 349-352; see also Meringue
  mollet, 328-329
  omelets, 335-338; see also Omelets
  oeufs à la neige, see Oeufs à la neige
  peel and slice, 334-335
  poach, 330-331
  scramble, 329
  separate, 322-323
  soft-boil, 328-329
  soufflés, 339-342; see also Soufflés
  test for freshness, 322
  whites
    beat, 323-324
    fold in, 325
  yolks
    add to hot mixture, 326-328
    beat with sugar until ribbon forms, 326-327
    sieve, 335
Endive
  braise, 17
  core, 8

F

Fatback
  for barding, 90
  for larding, 88-90, 128
  line a terrine with, 278-281
Fennel
  core, 8
  trim, 39
Fettucine, 302
Filets mignons, 106, 107
Fillet
  fish, 217-220
  tenderloin, 105-107
  turkey breast, 183-185
Fish, 210-270; see also Flatfish, Roundfish, and
    specific fish
  butterfly, 222-223
  cut
    for serving, 232-233
    into steaks, 239
  decorate cooked, 234-235
  fillet, 217-220
  fillets
    in paper, 237-238
    in puff pastry, 235-237
    roll, 221
    skin, 221
  fins, remove, 210-211
  fresh, recognize, 210
  gut, 213-216
  for mousse, chop, 240-241
  phyllo pastry wrapping for, 494
  poach, whole, 226-228
  for quenelles, chop, 240-241
  scale, 210
  skin, 211-212
  steam, 229-231
  stuff, whole, 223-226
  test for doneness, 231
Flank steak, butterfly and stuff, 109-110
Flatfish
  fillet, 217-218
  gut, 213

remove fins, 210
   skin, 211-212
Flour, sift and measure, 477
Flute mushrooms, 47, 48-49
Fondant icing, sugar syrup for, 480-481
Food mill, 18
Food processor, 18, 81, 240
French bread
   shape, 388-389
   slash and mist, 393-395
French bones, 92, 93, 97, 112, 118
Fried eggs, 331
Frittata, 337-338
Fruit glazes, sugar syrup for, 480-481
Fruit tarts, 437, 453-455
Fruits, 508-538
   apples, 508-511; see also Apples
   avocado, 512
   berries, 512-513
   caramel cage for, 481
   cherries, 513
   citrus, 514-519; see also Citrus fruit
   grapes, 523
   kiwi, 524
   mango, 524
   melons, 525-530
   papaya, 531
   pears, 531-532
   pineapple, 532-537
   pomegranate, 537
   rhubarb, 538

G

Galantine
   bone and stuff duck for, 186-193
Game birds
   bard, 208
   draw, 205-208
   hang, 202
   pluck, 203-205
Garganelli, roll, 304
Garlic
   in butter, 356
   peel and chop, 39-40
Garnishes
   carrots, 30, 282
   cherry tomatoes, 34
   citrus fruit, 516-518
   croutons, 408-409
   horseradish, 40
   lemon, 516-518
   mushrooms, 47-49
   peppers, 56
   puff pastry, 446
   radishes, 59-61
   scallions, 62-63
   squash, 66-67
   tomatoes, 70-73, 136, 282
   turnips, 74-76
Ginger, slice and peel, 40
Glace de viande, 273
Glaze
   berries, 512
   cake, 485, 487
   ham, 131
Gnocchi
   pâte à choux for, 456

shape, 307
Grapes
   frost, 523

H

Ham
   baked
      carve, 131-133
      prepare, 129-130
      score fat and glaze, 131
   re-form boneless, 133-136
Hard-boiled eggs
   cook, 328-329
   peel and slice, 334-335
   sieve yolks, 335
Hard-shell crabs
   prepare for stuffing, 243-245
Herbs
   in bouquet garni, 18-19
   in butter, 356
Hollandaise
   beat yolks and add butter, 344-345
   correct separated, 345
Horns, shape and cook, 446-448
Horseradish
   cut into curls, 40
   peel and grate, 40

I

Ice cream, caramel cage for, 481
Italian meringue, sugar syrup for, 480-481

J

Jao-tze, fill and shape, 311-312
Jellied soup, stock as, 274
Jelly cookies, shape and fill, 501-502
Jelly roll, fill and roll, 499-500
Jerusalem artichokes, slice, 41
Julienne vegetables, 10-11

K

Kale, trim, 41
Kidney, trim, 153
Kilometer, 453
Kiwi
   peel and slice, 524
Knead, 366-368

L

Ladyfingers
   line dessert molds with, 495
   shape, 500-501
Lamb
   crown roast, form, 92-93
   leg
      bone and butterfly, 113-117
      carve, 120-121
      prepare for roasting, 118-119
   rack
      prepare and carve, 111-113
Lamb duck
   form, 121-127
Lard, 88-90, 128
Lardoons, 88
Lasagna, cut and parboil, 300-301
Leeks, trim and clean, 42

Lemon, cut garnishes, 516-518
Lettuce
   braise, 17
   dry, 42
   tear, 43
Liver, trim and slice, 154
Lobster
   cut up
      after boiling, 255-257
      live, 253-255
   determine sex, 251
   split for broiling or baking, 252-253

M

Maltaise sauce, 344
Mango, remove seed, 524
Manicotti
   cut and parboil, 300-301
   fill and roll, 301
Marzipan
   decorate with, 489-494
Mayonnaise
   beat yolks and whisk in oil, 342-343
   correct separated, 343
Meat, 80-157; see also specific kinds of cuts
   bard, 90
   bones
      french, 92-93, 97, 111-112, 118
      paper frills for, 98-99
   bread, 85
   brown cubed, 94
   butterfly chop, 87
   chop, 81
   cube, 80
   cut incisions in fat, 87
   dredge, 84
   grind, 81
   lard, 88-90
   pound, 83
   roasts, see Roasts
   shape meatballs, 82
   shred, 86
   skewer, 80
   slice, 83
   slice across grain, 86
   test for doneness, 95
   variety, 152-157
   wrap in caul fat, 91
Meatballs, shape, 82
Melba toast, 386
Melon
   baskets, cut into, 526-530
   serving pieces, cut into, 525
Meringue
   beat egg whites for, 323-324
   oeufs à la neige; see Oeufs à la neige
   poach, 352
   sugar syrup for, 480-481
   vacherin, 349-351
Mince vegetables, 89
Mousse
   beat egg whites for, 323-324
   chop fish for, 240-241
   fold in egg whites, 325
Muffins, 417-418
Mushrooms
   Aztec, 47-48

clean, 43
extract moisture from, 45
flute, 47, 48-49
garnish, 47-49
sauté, 16
slice, 44
stuff, 46
Mussels
clean, 257-258
cook and trim, 259
Mustard, in butter, 356

N

Napoleons
cook, 448
decorate, 448-450
paper cone for, 478-479
Noodles; *see also* Pasta
cook, 303
cut dough, 303
dry, 302
test for doneness, 303-304

O

Octopus, clean, 260-261
Oeufs à la neige
caramel cage for, 481
poach meringue for, 352
Okra, trim and slice, 49
Omelets
beat eggs for, 326
flat, 337-338
folded, 335-337
Onions
chop, 50
cut into petals, 51
peel small white, 52
scoop out for stuffing, 51
Oursins, 264
Oysters
open, 261-262

P

Pain de mie, 386
Palm cookies, shape, 451-453
Pancakes
Chinese, 366-370
cook, 360-361
crêpes, 361-366
mix, 360
Papaya, seed, 531
Paper cone, form, 478-479
Paper frills, 98-99
Parboil; *see also* Blanch
lasagna, manicotti, cannelloni, 300-301
vegetables, 17
Parsley
dry chopped, 53-54
trim, 53
Parsnips, peel and core, 54-55
Pasta, 292-304
cannelloni, 300-301
cappelletti, 296
dry, 302
fettucine, 302
garganelli, 304
knead

and roll by hand, 293-295
and roll by machine, 295-296
lasagna, 300-301
manicotti, 300-301
mix dough, 292-293
noodles 302
ravioli, 298-299
tagliarini, 302
tagliatelle, 302
test for doneness, 303-304
tortellini, 296-297
torelloni, 299-300
Pastry, 423-471; *see also* Pâte à choux, Phyllo
pastry, Puff pastry, and specific pastries
for lamb duck, 123-127
for pâté, 282
swan, 458, 461-462
Pastry bag, fill, 457
Pâtés
assemble in fatback, 278-279
assemble in pastry, 282-287
decorate with aspic, 281-282
unmold, 289
vegetable, 287-289
weight, 278, 280
Pâte à choux
cream puffs, 458-460
éclairs, 458-460
fill pastry bag with, 457
mix pastry, 456-457
salambô, 458-460
swans, 458, 461-462
Pâte brisée, 425
Pâté en croûte
assemble, 282-285
cook, 285-287
Patty shells, 443-446
Pears
core and peel, 531-532
poach, 531-532
Peas; *see* Snow peas and Sugar snaps
Peasant bread
shape, 392-393
slash and mist, 393-395
Peel
apples, 508
asparagus, 25
beets, 26
celery, 32
celery root, 32
citrus fruit, 514
cucumbers, 36
garlic, 39-40
ginger, 40
horseradish, 40
kiwi, 524
onions, 52
parsnips, 54
pears, 531-532
peppers, 55
pineapple, 532-533
pumpkin, 58
rhubarb, 538
rutabaga, 61
shallots, 64
tomatoes, 68
vegetables, general, 8
Peking duck, 197-201

Peppers; *see also* Chili peppers
cut into flowers, 56
peel, 55
remove seeds and fibers, 55
Phyllo pastry
for baklava, 467-469
hors d'oeuvre, 462-466
for strudel, 469-471
Pies
cut in flour and butter, 424-425
decorate two-crust, 428-433
lattice crust, 433-434
line tin, 427-428
roll dough, 425-426
Pilaf, cook, 317-318
Pineapple
hollow out
half shell, 534
whole, 535-537
peel, 532-533
serving boats, cut into, 534-535
slice, 533
Pita, shape, 399-400
Poach
eggs, 330-331
meringue, 352
pear, 531-532
Pomegranate, cut for serving, 537
Popovers, mix, 421-422
Pork, 127-145; *see also* Bacon, Ham, Sausages,
Suckling pig
fatback, 128
chop, 87-127-128
crown roast
form, 92-93
Porterhouse steak, 99-100
Potatoes
baked, scoop out and refill, 57
balls, 56
cubed, 56
french fries, 56
matchstick, 56
shoestring, 56
Poultry, 160-208; *see also* Chicken, Duck, Game
birds, Turkey
arrange on spit, 169
brown whole bird, 170
clean and season cavity, 160
shred, 171
stuff
cavity, 164-166
under skin, 162-164
test for doneness, 171
truss, 166-169
wings, cut off, 161
wishbone, remove, 161-162
Pound
chicken breast, 180
meat, 83
peppercorns into steak, 100-101
Proof yeast, 376
Profiteroles; *see* Cream puffs
Puff Pastry
decorative garnishes, 446
fish fillets in, 235-237
fruit tarts, 453-455
horns, 446-448
napoleons, 448-450
palm cookies, 451-453

patty shells, 443-446
roll and fold, 438-443
Pullman loaf
  for canapés, 410
  for croutons, 408-409
  shape, 386
Pumpkin, prepare and peel, 58
Purée vegetables, 18

Q

Quenelles
  chop fish for, 240-241
  shape and poach, 241, 242
Quiches
  cool, 438
  cut in flour and butter, 424-425
  line tin, 434-436
  prebake shell, 436-437
  roll dough, 425-426
Quick breads
  coffee cake, 406-407
  shape in coffee can, 416-417

R

Rack of lamb
  paper frills for, 98-99
  prepare and carve, 111-113
Radishes, cut into flowers, 59-61
Ravioli, fill and cut, 298-299
Reduce stock, 273
Refresh vegetables, 18
Rémoulade sauce, 342
Rhubarb, trim and peel, 538
Rib roast, carve, 107-108
Rice
  arborio, 315
  basmati, 317
  boil, 314-315
  pilaf, 317-318
  in ring mold, 318-319
  risotto, 315-317
  steam, 312-313
Ring mold; see also Savarin mold
  line, 475-476
  form rice in, 318-319
  unmold, 319
Risotto, cook, 315-317
Roasts
  brown, 94
  crown, 92-93
  leg of lamb, 118-119
  loin of veal, 148-152
  rib, 107-108
  sirloin, 105, 107
  tenderloin, 101-104
  test for doneness, 95
Rolled cookies, shape, 504-506
Rolls
  clover, 400
  crescent, 401-403
Rouladen, 83
Roundfish
  fillet, 219-220
  gut, 214-216
  remove fins, 211
Rutabaga, peel and cube, 61

S

Sabayon, 326

Salambô; see Éclairs
Sandwiches
  cylindrical loaf for, 387
  pullman loaf for, 386
Sauces
  aioli, 342
  béarnaise, 344
  choron, 344
  crème anglaise, 345
  hollandaise, 344-345
  maltaise, 344
  mayonnaise, 342-343
  rémoulade, 342
  sabayon, 326
  seasoned butter in, 356
  sieved berries for, 513
  tartar, 342
Sausages
  form in cheesecloth, 137-138
  prepare casings for, 136
  stuff by machine, 137
Sauté vegetables, 16
Savarin mold, line, 475-476
Scallions
  cut into flowers, 62-63
  greens
    in bouquet of crudités, 78
    for pâté, 62, 282
    to tie stuffed cabbage, 28
  trim, 62
Scaloppine, 83, 183
Scallops, open, 262-263
Scrambled eggs
  beat, 326
  cook, 329
Seasoned butters, 356-357
Sea urchin, open, 264-265
Seed
  chili peppers, 34
  cucumbers, 36
  papaya, 563
  peppers, 55
  tomatoes, 69
Separate eggs, 322-323
Shallots, peel and chop, 64
Shellfish
  in butter, 356
  clams, 242-243
  conchs, 249-250
  crayfish, 246-247
  hard-shell crabs, 243-245
  lobster, 251-257
  mussels, 257-259
  oysters, 261-262
  sea urchin, 264-265
  scallops, 262-263
  shrimp, 265-266
  soft-shell crabs, 245-246
Shiu may, fill and shape, 309-310
Shred vegetables, 13-14
Shrimp
  butterfly, 266
  peel and devein, 265-266
Sieve
  confectioners' sugar, 488
  egg yolks, 335
  berries, 513
Sirloin roast, 105, 107
Skewer meat, 80

Slice
  cucumbers, 36, 37
  meat, 83, 86
  mushrooms, 44
  vegetables, general, 9-10
Snails
  remove cooked, 267
  stuff shells, 266-267
Snip vegetables, 13
Snow peas, string, 64
Soft-shell crabs, prepare for cooking, 245-246
Soufflés
  dust mold, 339-340
  beat egg whites for, 323-324
  fill mold, 340-341
  fold in egg whites, 325
  frozen, 340
  test for doneness, 341-342
  tie collar, 340
Spaghetti squash
  prepare and scoop out cooked pulp, 65
Spätzle, shape and cook, 306
Spinach
  drain, 66
  trim, 65
Spit, arrange poultry on, 169
Sponge cake, in dessert molds, 495
Springform, line and unmold, 494-495
Squash; see also Acorn squash, Spaghetti squash, and Zucchini
  cut into flowers, 66-67
Squid
  clean, 267-268
  stuff, 269
Steak
  cut incisions in fat, 87
  flank, 109-110
  porterhouse, 99-100
  pound peppercorns into, 100-101
  tenderloin, 101-103
Steak tartare, 106
Steam
  fish, 229-231
  rice, 312-313
  vegetables, 14
Stir-fry
  shred poultry for, 171
  slice meat for, 86
  vegetables, 15-16
Stock
  for aspic, 274
  clarify, 274-276
  for consommé, 274
  degrease, 272-273
  for jellied soup, 274
  reduce, 273
  skim, 272
Strawberries, glaze, 512
String peas, 64
Strudel
  fill and roll, 469-471
  phyllo pastry for, 462
Stuff
  artichokes, 22-23
  cabbage, 28, 29
  cherry tomatoes, 33
  chicken breasts, 178-180
  eggplant, 38-39

fish, 223-226
flank steak, 109-110
mushrooms, 46
onions, 51
peppers, 55
potatoes, 57
poultry, 162-166
sausages, 137
suckling pig, 138-140
tomatoes, 73
zucchini, 77
Suckling pig
carve, 142-145
roast, 141-142
stuff, 138-140
Sugar, sieve confectioners', 478
Sugar snaps, string, 64
Sugar syrup, cook, 480-481
Swans
apple, 509-511
melon, 526-527
pastry, 458, 461-462
Sweetbreads, trim and weight, 155-156
Swiss chard, 67

T

Tagliarini, 302
Tagliatelle, 302
Tartar sauce, 342
Tarts
cool, 438
cut in flour and butter, 424-425
fill, 436
line tin, 434-436
prebake shell, 436-437
roll dough, 425-426
Tatin, 508
Tenderloin
cut into steaks, 105-107
shape for roasts, 103-104
trim, 101-103
Terrines, line with fatback, 128, 278
Tomatoes; *see also* Cherry tomatoes
form roses, 70-73
on boneless ham, 136
on pâté, 282
hollow out for stuffing, 73
peel, 68
seed, 69
Tongue, peel, trim, and slice, 156-157
Tortellini, shape, 296-297
Tortelloni, fill and cut, 299-300
Tortes, springform for, 494
Tortillas
cook, 372
shape, 370-371
Tournedos, 105-107
Trout, tie, 270
Truites au bleu, 270
Truss
with needle, 166-167
with string only, 167-169
Turkey
breast, fillet, 183-185
carve, 181-182
as veal scaloppine, 183
Turnips, cut into flowers, 74-76

U

Unmold
Charlotte mold, 497-498
ring mold, 319
springform, 495
vegetable pâté, 289

V

Vacherin, shape and decorate, 349-351
Variety meats
brains, 152-153
kidneys, 153
liver, 154
chicken livers, 155
sweetbreads, 155-156
tongue, 156-157
Veal, 145-152
breast,
cut pocket and stuff, 145-147
chops, butterfly, 87
crown roast, form, 92-93
loin, bone and roll, 148-152
scaloppine, 83
turkey as, 183
Vegetables, 8-78; *see also* specific kinds
blanch, 18
braise, 17
bouquet of crudités, 78
chop, 8-9
core, 8
cut into ovals, 12
cut on bias, 12
julienne, 10-11
parboil, 17
peel, 8
purée, 18
refresh, 18
sauté, 16
shred, 13-14
slice, 9-10
snip, 13
steam, 14
stir-fry, 15-16
Vegetable pâté, assemble and unmold, 287-289

W

Watermelon, whale, 530
Weight pâté, 278-281
Wishbone, remove, 161-162
Wok
as fish steamer, 230
in stir-frying, 15-16
Won ton, fill and shape, 307-309

Y

Yeast breads
bread sticks, 396-398
brioche; *see* Brioche
clover rolls, 400
coffee cake, 406-407
crescent rolls, 401-403
croutons, 408-409
knead, 376-378
loaf, shape, 380-382
braided, 382-385
cylindrical sandwich, 387

French, 388-391, 393-395
long, 388-391, 393-395
peasant, 392-393, 393-395
pullman, 386
mist, 393-395
mix dough, 374-376
pita, 399-400
proof yeast, 374
punch down, 379-380
rise, 378-379
slash and mist, 393-395
test for doneness, 396

Z

Zabaglione, 326
Zest, cut, 415-416
Zucchini, scoop out and stuff, 77